国家级一流本科专业建设配套教材

英语词汇学通论

AN INTRODUCTION TO ENGLISH LEXICOLOGY

杨连瑞 陈颖 李旭奎

主编

清华大学出版社

北京

内 容 简 介

本书以现代语言学理论为基础，以英语词汇为研究对象，共12章，内容涉及英语词汇的构成、发展变化、形态结构、构成方式及语义关系、词义的发展变化、词的搭配与习语、美式英语与英式英语的词汇区别以及英语词汇学习策略等。每章末设有活泼多样的练习题，以深化读者对理论知识的理解与应用。书后另附美式英语与英式英语词汇对照表，供读者参考使用。

本书适合普通高校英语专业学生和具有一定英语基础、对英语词汇学感兴趣的读者使用。

图书在版编目（CIP）数据

英语词汇学通论/杨连瑞，陈颖，李旭奎主编.—北京：清华大学出版社，2023.2（2024.7重印）
国家级一流本科专业建设配套教材

ISBN 978-7-302-61642-9

I.①英… II.①杨…②陈…③李… III.①英语—词汇—高等学校—教材 IV.①H313

中国版本图书馆CIP数据核字（2022）第145440号

责任编辑：许玲玉
封面设计：李伯骥
责任校对：王凤芝
责任印制：刘海龙

出版发行：清华大学出版社
　　　网　　　址：https://www.tup.com.cn, https://www.wqxuetang.com
　　　地　　　址：北京清华大学学研大厦A座　　　邮　　编：100084
　　　社 总 机：010-83470000　　　邮　　购：010-62786544
　　　投稿与读者服务：010-62776969, c-service@tup.tsinghua.edu.cn
　　　质量反馈：010-62772015, zhiliang@tup.tsinghua.edu.cn
印 装 者：三河市东方印刷有限公司
经　　销：全国新华书店
开　　本：185mm×260mm　　　印　　张：18　　　字　　数：375千字
版　　次：2023 年 2 月第 1 版　　　印　　次：2024 年 7 月第 3 次印刷
定　　价：75.00元

产品编号：096343-01

前　言

　　英语词汇学是高校英语专业一门语言学基础专业理论课程，它运用现代语言学的有关理论，研究英语语言中的词汇问题。学习本课程可以使英语专业学生系统掌握英语词汇知识，深入了解英语词汇的现状及其历史演变过程，并能对现代英语词汇发展中出现的各种词汇现象做出理论分析和解释，提高对英语词语的理解、阐释和综合运用能力。由此，英语词汇学不是一般意义上的"学词汇"，尽管它对英语词汇的学习很有帮助。我们需要明确，像英语词汇学这类语言学课程的开设和教学也是高校培养创新型外语专业人才的应有之意，具有重要的理论价值和实践意义。

　　本书是在 2010 年出版的《新编英语词汇学》基础上修订而成，融合了词汇学研究的最新成果和英语词汇的最新发展与应用。在参考国内外词汇研究著作优点的基础上，以现代语言学理论为指导，以英语词汇为研究对象，内容涉及英语词汇的构成、发展变化、形态结构、构成方式、词的意义及语义关系、词义的发展变化、多词表达、习语、英式英语与美式英语的词汇区别及词汇学习相关研究等。全书引用的例证多选自经典文学作品或国内外知名报刊文章，力求较为全面地反映现代英语词汇使用的特点和发展趋势。

　　整体而言，本书主要特色如下：

　　教学内容系统性与前沿性并重：本书从词汇形态、词汇意义、词汇使用、词汇学习四个维度构建脉络清晰的知识结构体系，同时坚持研究成果进教材，及时反映英语词汇研究的前沿动态与趋势。例如，多词表达是词汇研究的热点，本书专门介绍了多词表达的基本概念及其在词汇学习中的重要作用。

　　理论知识与丰富实例自然融合：本书精选学习素材，将高度抽象的词汇学概念和理论自然融入丰富多样的语言实例中，生动具体地阐释词汇学的相关理论，增强学生对核心概念的理解，提升学习效果。

　　词汇知识与研究能力培养兼顾：本书在帮助学生系统掌握完整的英语词汇知识、深入了解英语词汇的现状及其历史演变过程之外，还设有层层递进、活泼多样的单元练习题，以引导学生观察英语词汇发展中的各种词汇现象并进行理论分析与解释，激发学生的研究兴趣，提高其发现问题、分析问题和解决问题的能力。

国内专家与国际学者联合打造：本书三位主编长期深耕国内英语词汇研究与教学，发表了一系列高水平科研与教学成果；国际二语词汇习得与加工领域的学者 Anna Siyanova 博士参与编写部分章节，并协助审核全书书稿。国内、国际专家携手合作，为本书奠定了较好的专业基础，提供了前沿研究视角。

需要说明的是，编者在国内讲授英语专业本科生英语词汇学课程二十余载，在教学和编写讲义的过程中，参考了大量国内外相关文献；由于边教学边编写，时间跨度大，书中部分观点和例句来源未能一一标明出处，在此谨对相关作者表示谢忱。

本书系中国海洋大学国家级一流本科专业英语专业建设成果之一。

本书根据高等院校英语专业英语词汇学教学要求编写而成，主要用作高等院校英语专业教材，同时对广大英语教师和相关研究者及英语词汇学爱好者亦有一定的参考价值。

囿于编者水平，本书疏漏之处在所难免，敬请广大读者批评指正。

编者

2022 年 12 月

Contents

Chapter 1

Introduction

1.1 What Is Lexicology?

Lexicology, a branch of linguistics, inquires into the origins and meanings of words. The term "lexicology" comes from Greek morphemes *lexi* and *logos*; the former means "word or phrase", while the latter "a department of knowledge". In a word, it is the science of the word. English lexicology aims at investigating and studying the morphological structures of English words and word equivalents, their semantic structures, relations, historical development, formation and usages. Generally speaking, the term "vocabulary" refers to all the words of a given language, while the term "word" refers to the fundamental unit of a given language, with sound and meaning, capable of performing a given syntactic function.

English Lexicology is a theoretically-oriented course. It is chiefly concerned with the basic theories of words in general and of English words in particular. However, it is a practical course as well, for in the discussion, we shall inevitably deal with copious stocks of words and idioms, and study a great many usage examples. A great deal of practice is therefore a must.

1.2 English Lexicology and Its Relation to Other Disciplines

English lexicology itself is a sub-branch of linguistics and can be further classified into academic disciplines such as morphology, semantics, etymology, stylistics, and lexicography. Each of them has already been established as a discipline in its own right.

To begin with, morphology is the branch of grammar, which studies the structure or forms of words, primarily through the use of morpheme construction—one of the major concerns of lexicology. We shall discuss the inflections of words and word formation and examine how morphemes are combined to form words and how words are combined to form sentences.

Traditionally, morphology is used for the study of the origins and history of the form and meaning of words. Modern English, for example, is derived from the languages of early Germanic tribes with a fairly small vocabulary. We shall study how this small vocabulary has grown into a large modern English vocabulary and explain the changes that have taken place in the forms and meanings of words. In addition, morphological structure is the study of meanings of different linguistic levels: lexis, syntax, utterance, discourse, etc. But lexicology will also focus on the lexical level. The types of meaning and sense relations such as polysemy, homonymy, synonymy, antonymy, hyponymy, and semantic field all fall under the scope of semantic study and constitute an important part of lexicology.

Semantics is the study of the meanings of words and other parts of language including phrases, sentences, and larger units of discourse. It studies the nature, structure, development and changes of word meaning. Polysemy, homonymy, synonymy, antonymy, metaphor, metonymy and other rhetorical devices are all within the scope of semantics.

Etymology studies the meanings, origins, and history of individual words and their development. Historical lexicology studies from a historical point of view the development of vocabulary as a whole on the basis of etymology.

Stylistics is the study of style. It is concerned with the user's choices of linguistic elements in a particular context for special effects. Among the areas of study (e.g., lexis, phonology, syntax, and graphology), we shall concentrate on lexis, exploring the stylistic values of words.

Lexicography shares with lexicology the same concerns: the forms, meanings, origins, and usages of words, but they have a pragmatic difference. A lexicographer's task is to record the language as it is used so as to present a genuine picture of words to the reader, thereby providing authoritative reference. In contrast, a lexicologist's task is to acquire the knowledge and information of lexis so as to increase lexical awareness and capacity of language use.

Even though English lexicology covers a great many academic areas, our task remains one and the same: to study English words in different aspects and from different angles.

1.3 Methods of Word Study

There are generally two approaches to the study of words, namely the synchronic method and the diachronic method. From a synchronic point of view, words can be studied at a point in time, disregarding whatever changes might be taking place. For example, the word *wife* now means "a married woman, especially in relation to her husband". This is the current meaning. It has an obsolete meaning (woman), which is only preserved in *midwife*, *housewife*, etc. However, if we were to take a diachronic perspective, we would consider the word historically, looking into its origin and changes in both its form and meaning. In this light, the word *wife* evolved from the Old English form *wif*, meaning "woman", but in the course of development it became specialized to today's modern meaning "a married woman". In our linguistic inquiry into the English vocabulary, though our focus is on the synchronic description of words, we need the diachronic approach as a supplement, precisely because a knowledge of the historical development of the vocabulary can immensely aid our understanding of language study.

Aims and Significance of the Course

Language study involves the study of speech sounds, grammar, and vocabulary. Among them, vocabulary has proved particularly important and certainly the most difficult. In the discussion of the relationship between words and structure, the lexicologist McCarthy (1990: 12) asserts that:

> *No matter how well the student learns grammar, no matter how successfully he masters the sounds of a L2, without words to express a wide range of meanings, communication in that language cannot happen in any meaningful way. The role of vocabulary in communication calls for continuing vocabulary learning.*

Since English Lexicology deals with English vocabulary, this course will definitely be beneficial. Thus, a good knowledge of the morphological structures of English words and the rules of word formation will help learners develop their personal vocabulary and consciously increase their word power. The information about the historical development and the principles of classification will give them a deeper understanding of word meaning and will enable them to organize, classify, and store words more effectively. The understanding of the semantic structures of words and the types of meaning and their sense relations will gradually raise learners' awareness of meaning and usages, and will enable them to use words more accurately and appropriately. A working knowledge of dictionaries will not only improve learners' skills of using reference books but also raise their problem-solving ability and efficiency of individual study. In a word, the study of lexicology will ultimately improve learners' receptive and productive skills in both language processing and language production.

Exercises

I. Briefly answer the following questions.

1. What is lexicology?

2. What is the nature and scope of English lexicology?

3. What subjects is English lexicology associated with? And to what extent?

4. Why should a student of English study English Lexicology?

II. Complete the following statements with a suitable word for each blank.

1. Lexicology is a branch of linguistics, inquiring into the origins and _____ of words. English lexicology is both a theoretically-oriented course and a(n) _____ course. On the one hand, it is chiefly concerned with the basic _____ of words in general and of English words in particular. On the other hand, we have to deal with copious stocks of words and idioms with _____ examples, which is of great importance to language learning.

2. English lexicology investigates and studies the _____ structures of English words and word equivalents, their semantic structures, relations, historical development, _____ and usages.

3. English lexicology is associated with morphology, _____, etymology, stylistics, and lexicography. _____ comes to work when the inflections of words and word formation are discussed, and the combination of morphemes to form words and words to form sentences is examined in the study of English lexicology; semantics when English lexicology deals with polysemy, homonyms, synonyms, _____, hyponymy, and semantic field of words; _____ when English lexicology deals with the origins and historical changes of English words in their forms and meanings; _____ when English lexicology deals with the styles or the stylistic values of words; _____ when English lexicology deals with the compiling of a dictionary to provide authoritative reference to readers.

Chapter 2

Basic Concepts of Words and Vocabulary

2.1 Definition of a Word

What is a word? The definition of a word has engaged the attention of philosophers and linguists for ages. The ancient Greek philosopher Aristotle defined a word as "the smallest significant unit of speech"—a definition traditionally accepted for centuries. But modern linguists have maintained that the smallest meaningful unit of speech is not a word, but a morpheme. A word may consist of one or more than one morpheme, e.g., *antiestablishment*, which contains three morphemes (*anti-*, *establish*, *-ment*).

The American linguist L. Bloomfield defines a word as "a minimum free form" in his *Language* published in 1933. He distinguishes between two types of linguistic forms: free forms and bound forms. A free form is one that can occur as a separate word, while a bound form is one that cannot exist on its own as a separate word. Take *antiestablishment* for example. It contains a free form or morpheme *establish* and two bound forms or morphemes *anti-* and *-ment*. The former (*establish*) can be used independently as a word, while the latter (*anti-* and *-ment*) cannot appear in isolation, but must be attached to the free form or morpheme *establish*.

The French linguist A. Meillet (1921/1982: 30) gives his definition as follows: "A word is defined by the association of a particular sense with a particular set of sounds that has a particular grammatical use" (cited from Haspelmath, 2011: 35). This definition shows a unity of meaning and sound with special emphasis on the word function in the grammatical structure.

Given the above two definitions by Bloomfield and Meillet, we may define a word as an independent lexical unit and a minimum free form, with a unity of sound and meaning (both lexical and grammatical), capable of performing a given grammatical function. A word may act as a complete utterance, as in exclamations "Liar!", "Help!", and in replies such as "Tom" in answer to the question "What is his name?" or "Five." to the question "How old is he?". But more frequently, a word is used as a part of a sentence (subject, predicate verb, object).

Words may also be defined in phonological and orthographical terms. Phonologically, a spoken word is a phoneme or combination of phonemes, marked by a given position of stress. Orthographically, a written word is a printed symbol, with a space on either side of it but none within it, with the exception of compounds either hyphenated or written open like *air-blower* and *air base*.

Words can be simple and complex, yet all must comply with these criteria. *Man* and *fine* are simple, but they each have sound, meaning, and syntactic function, and each can be used alone in a sentence. Naturally, they are words. However, there are words which can be complex, such as *mis·for·tune*, a polysyllabic word that can function as a subject, object, or predicate in a sentence. Though *misfortune* can be further divided into *mis* and *fortune*, *mis* cannot stand alone as a word. In contrast, *blackmail* can be separated into *black* and *mail*, and both can work as independent units in a sentence, the meaning of each, however, is by no means the combination of the two. *Black* is a color, opposite to *white*, and *mail* denotes "something sent by post", yet when they are put together, the combined form means "compel, compulsion, to make payment or action in return for concealment of discreditable secrets, etc." Hence *blackmail* is a different word.

2.2 Sound and Meaning

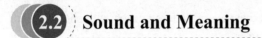

A word is a symbol that stands for something else in the world. Each of the world's cultures has certain sounds representing certain persons, things, places, properties, processes, and activities outside the language system. This symbolic connection is almost always arbitrary, and there is no logical relationship between the sound which stands for a thing or an idea, and the actual thing or idea itself. A dog is called a *dog* not because the sound and the three letters that make up the word automatically suggest the animal in question. It is only symbolic. The relationship between them is conventional because people of the same speech community have agreed to refer to the animal with this cluster of sounds. In different languages, the same concept can be represented by different sounds. On the one hand, *woman* becomes *Frau* in German, *femme* in French, and *funü* in Chinese. On the other hand, the same sound /miːt/ is used to mean *meet*, *meat*, or *mete*. *Knight* and *night*, for example, denote entirely different things, yet have the same sound.

2.3 Sound and Form

In the days of Old English, the speech of the time was represented very much more faithfully in writing than it is today. With the development of the language, however, more and more differences have occurred between the two. The reason for this is that the English alphabet was adopted from the Romans, which does not have a separate letter to represent each sound in the language, so some letters must do double duty or work together in combination.

Similarly, pronunciation has changed more rapidly than spelling over the years, and in some cases, the two have come to represent distinct characteristics. During the last five hundred years, though the sounds of speech have changed considerably, there have been no corresponding changes in spelling.

Sound changes aside, and some of the differences were created by the early scribes. In the early days, the spelling differences did not matter very much as people were not so used to seeing words in print, and the spelling was not fixed as it is today. As a result, not everyone was sure how some English words should be spelled. Sometimes, people deliberately changed the spelling of words either to make a line even or to make recognition easier. Before the printing press was brought to England, everything was written by hand. Those scribes, who made a living by writing for other people often worked in haste to meet the needs of the King, Church, and merchants. One problem was that several letters written with short vertical strokes such as *i, u, v, m, w,* and *n* looked all alike. Consequently, their handwriting caused misunderstanding. To solve the problem in part, they changed the letter *u* to *o* when it came before *m, n,* or *v*. This is how *sum, cum, wuman, wunder, munk* came to be written as *some, come, woman, wonder, monk*. At some point, too, the scribes seemed to have decided that no English word should end in *n* or *v*. Thus, in time, an *e* was added to such words as *live, have, due,* and *true* but not pronounced.

Finally comes the borrowing, which is an important channel for enriching the English vocabulary. When English borrowed words from other languages, it borrowed spelling as well. The early borrowings were assimilated and the later ones, however, do not conform to the rules of English pronunciation and spelling, e.g., *stimulus* (Latin), *denouement* (French), *fiesta* (Spanish), *eureka* (Greek), *kimono* (Japanese), and *mahjong* (Chinese).

The written form of English is, therefore, an imperfect representation of the spoken form. In spite of the differences, at least 80% of the English words adhere to consistent spelling patterns. And even those spellings that appear to be irregular may have more regularity and usefulness than we may realize. In words such as *hymn, condemn,* and *bomb*, for example, the last letter is always silent. But when these words are extended into longer ones, the silent letters become audible: *hymnal, condemnation,* and *bombard*. This is a general rule.

2.4 Vocabulary

The term "vocabulary" is used in different senses. For many people, the word "vocabulary" is primarily associated with the collection of words known by an individual or by a large group of people; one either has a large or a small vocabulary. It can stand for all the words used in a particular historical period, e.g., Old English vocabulary, Middle English vocabulary, and Modern English vocabulary. We also use it to refer to all the words of a given dialect, a given book, or a given discipline ("the vocabulary of science"). The following are two recent examples of the use of vocabulary:

- But the shifts in the language of London amount to more than the borrowing of vocabulary or changes in pronunciation: There are structural changes, too. (*The New Yorker*, February 6, 2022)
- Perhaps no other writer enriched the popular imagination of intelligence work as much as le Carré, who gave the public a colorful vocabulary with which to talk about it. (*The New York Review of Books*, February 10, 2022)

2.5 Classification of Words

The English vocabulary consists of words of all kinds. They can be classified by different criteria and for different purposes. Words may fall into the basic word stock and non-basic vocabulary by use frequency, into content words and functional words by notion, and into native words and borrowed words by origin.

2.5.1 Basic Word Stock and Non-Basic Vocabulary

The basic word stock is the foundation of the vocabulary accumulated over centuries and forms the common core of the language. Though words of the basic word stock constitute a small percentage of the English vocabulary, it is the most important part of it. These words have distinct characteristics.

(1) All national character. Words of the basic word stock denote the most common things and phenomena of the world around us, which are indispensable to all the people who speak the language. They include words relating to categories such as:

Natural phenomena: *rain, snow, fire, water, sun, moon, spring, summer, wind, hill…*;

Human body and relations: *head, foot, hand, face, father, mother, brother, sister, son, daughter…*;

Names of plants and animals: *oak, pine, grass, pear, apple, tree, horse, cow, sheep, cat, dog, chicken…*;

Action, size, domain, and state: *come, go, eat, hear, beat, carry, good, evil, old, young, hot, cold, heavy, white, black…*;

Numerals, pronouns, prepositions, and conjunctions: *one, ten, hundred, I, you, your, who, in, out, under, and, but, till, as…*

Any speaker of English, irrespective of class origin, education, profession, geographical region, culture, etc. cannot avoid using these words.

(2) Stability. Words of the basic word stock have been in use for centuries, e.g., *man, fire, mountain, water, sun, moon.* As they denote the most common things necessary to life, they are likely to remain unchanged. Stability, however, is only relative as the basic word stock has been undergoing some changes. Words like *arrow, bow, chariot,* and *knight* have now moved out of the word stock whereas such words as *electricity, machine, car, plane, computer, radio,* and *television,* which denote new things in today's modern way of life, have entered the stock. But this change is slow. There are many more words joining in than dropping out.

(3) Productivity. Words of the basic word stock are mostly root words or monosyllabic words. They can each be used alone, and at the same time can form new words with other roots and affixes. For example, *dog* is the father of *doglike, doghood, dog cart, dog-cheap, dog-ear, dog-fall, dogfight, doghole, dog-paddle,* and *dogsleep.*

(4) Polysemy. Words belonging to the basic word stock often possess more than one meaning because most of them have undergone semantic changes in the course of use and have become polysemous. One example will suffice for illustration. In *Longman Dictionary of Contemporary English* published in 1978, the verb *take* may mean "move or carry from one place to another; to remove or use without permission or by mistake; to seize or capture; to get for oneself; to get hold of (something) with the hands; to be willing to accept; to bear or endure; to need (a stated amount of time); to perform the actions connected with; to test or measure; to write down; to have the intended effect or to work successfully."

(5) Collocability. Many words of the basic word stock exhibit quite a number of set expressions, idiomatic usages, proverbial sayings, and the like. Instances are numerous. Take *heart* for example: *a change of heart, after one's heart, a heart of gold, at heart, break one's heart, cross one's heart, cry one's heart out, eat one's heart out, have one's heart in one's mouth, heart and hand, heart and soul, one's heart sinks within one, take something to heart, wear one's heart upon one's sleeve, with all one's heart* and so on.

Of course, not all the words of the basic word stock have these characteristics. Pronouns and numerals, for instance, enjoy nationwide use and stability, but are semantically monosemous and have limited productivity and collocability. Therefore, "all national character" is the most important of all features that may differentiate words of common use from all others.

Words, void of the stated characteristics, do not belong to the common core of the language. They include the following:

(1) Terminology consists of technical terms used in particular disciplines and academic areas as in medicine: *photo-scanning, hepatitis, indigestion, penicillin*; in music: *symphony, orchestra, sonata, concerto*, etc.

(2) Jargon refers to the specialized vocabularies by which members of particular arts, sciences, trades, and professions communicate among themselves such as in business: *bottom line* for "inescapable implication, unavoidable result, ultimate version"; *ballpark figures* for "estimate"; in horse-racing: *hold him back* for "prevent a horse from winning", *hold him in* for "force a horse to run behind at the beginning of a race so as to reserve speed for the finish". Generally speaking, people outside the circle have difficulty understanding such words.

(3) Slang belongs to the sub-standard language, a category that seems to stand between the standard general words including informal ones available to everyone, and in-group words like cant (shoptalk of any sub-group), jargon, and argot, all of which are associated with, or most available to, specific groups of the population. Certain words are labeled "slang" not because of their appearance or pronunciation but because of their usage. *Dough* and *bread*, for instance, are standard when they are used as food terms but slang in the sense of "money". Such words as *beaver* (girl), *bear* (police), *catch* (talk to), *holler* (call), *roger* (understand), and *X-rays* (radar) are all slang words. The concept "head" can be referred to by *nut, dome, upper, bean, block*, and so on; in the same way, the meaning of "drunk" can be expressed in as many terms as over three hundred such as *elevated, merry, jolly, comfortable, boiled, grassy, tight, knocked out, blue-eyed, fried, paralyzed, pickled, stiff, stunned*. These examples indicate that much of the slang is created by changing or extending the meaning of existing words, though some slang words are new coinages altogether. Slang enjoys popular use because it is colorful, blunt, expressive, and impressive.

(4) Argot generally refers to the jargon of criminals. Its use is confined to the sub-cultural groups, and outsiders can hardly understand it, e.g., *can-opener* (all-purpose key), *dip* (pick-pocket), *persuader* (dagger).

(5) Dialectal words are words used only by speakers of the dialect in question. For example, *beauty* (Australian English = excellent, great), *chook* (Australian English = chicken), *auld* (Scottish English = old), *coo* (Scottish English = cow), *hog* (Irish English = swamp).

(6) Archaisms are words or forms that were once in common use but are now restricted only to specialized or limited use. They are found mainly in older poems, legal documents,

and religious writing or speech. Here are some examples: *thou* (you), *ye* (plural you), *thee* (objective you), *wilt* (will), *brethren* (brother), *quoth* (said), *hereof* (of this, concerning this), *therefrom* (from that or there).

(7) Neologisms are newly-created words or expressions, or words that have taken on new meanings. Here are some examples from *12,000 Words: A Supplement to Webster's Third New International Dictionary* published in 1986: *microelectronics* = the branch of electronics dealing with integrated circuits, *futurology* = a study that deals with future possibilities based on current trends, *AIDS* = acquired immune deficiency syndrome, *E-mail* = electronic mail, the sending of messages via computer systems.

2.5.2 Content Words and Functional Words

As already seen, words can be grouped into content words and functional words. Content words denote clear notions and thus are known as notional words. They include nouns, verbs, adjectives, adverbs, and numerals, which denote objects, phenomena, actions, qualities, states, degrees, quantities, etc. *Earth, cloud, run, walk, bright, dark, never, frequently, five,* and *December* are all content words. In contrast, functional words do not have notions of their own, which explains why they are also called empty words. Since their chief function is to express the relation between notions, the relation between words as well as between sentences, thus they are also known as form words. Prepositions, conjunctions, auxiliaries, and articles belong to this category. Examples are *on, of, upon, and, but, do (does, did), be (am, are, were, is), a, the,* and others. Content words, which constitute the main body of the English vocabulary, are numerous, and the number is ever-growing, whereas functional words, which make up a very small number of the vocabulary, remain stable. Unlike content words, functional words do far more work of expression in English on average than content words.

2.5.3 Native Words and Borrowed Words

As far as the origin of the words is concerned, English words can be classified into native words and borrowed words. Native words are words brought to Britain in the 5th century by the Germanic tribes of the Angles, the Saxons, and the Jutes. These native words are also known as Anglo-Saxon words. Words of Anglo-Saxon origin are small in number, roughly 50,000 to 60,000, but they form the mainstream of the basic word stock and stand at the core of the language. Therefore, what is true of the basic word stock is also true of native words. In contrast to borrowed words, native words have two other features which are distinctly different from the characteristics of the basic word stock mentioned above:

(1) Neutral in style. Since native words denote the most common things in human

society, they are used by all people, in all places, on all occasions, and at all times. Therefore, they are not stylistically specific.

(2) Frequent in use. Native words are most frequently used in everyday speech and in writing. The proportion of their use in relation to borrowings is perhaps just the opposite of their number. The percentage of native words in use is as high as 90%.

Words taken over from foreign languages are known as borrowed words, loan words, or borrowings in simple terms. The English language borrows heavily and has adopted words from all the other major languages of the world. It is estimated that English borrowings constitute about 80% of the modern English vocabulary. The English language is equally noted for the remarkable complexity and heterogeneity of its vocabulary because of its extensive borrowings.

Exercises

I. Briefly answer the following questions.

1. What is vocabulary?

2. Can you illustrate the relationship between sound and meaning with examples?

II. Complete the following statements by supplying an appropriate term for each blank.

1. A phonetically-defined word is a(n) _____ or combination of _____ marked by a given position of stress.

2. There is no _____ relationship between sound and meaning as the connection between them is _____ and conventional.

3. Archaisms are words no longer in _____ use or _____ in use.

4. Content words are changing all the time whereas functional words are _____. Functional words enjoy a(n) _____ frequency in use than content words.

5. A word whose meaning was borrowed from another language is called _____.

Chapter 3

The Developing English Vocabulary

3.1 The Indo-European Language Family

It is assumed that the world has approximately 3,000 languages (some put it as high as 5,000 languages, which can be grouped into roughly 300 language families on the basis of similarities in their basic word stock and grammar. The Indo-European language family is one of them. It is made up of most of the languages of Europe, the Near East, and India.

The surviving languages show various degrees of similarity to one another. The similarity bears a more or less direct relationship to their geographical distribution. They accordingly fall into eight principal groups which can be grouped into an Eastern set (Balto-Slavic, Indo-Iranian, Armenian, Albanian) and a Western set (Celtic, Italic, Hellenic, Germanic).

In the Eastern set, Armenian and Albanian are the only modern languages here. The Balto-Slavic comprises such modern languages as Prussian, Lithuanian, Polish, Czech, Bulgarian, Slovenian, and Russian. In the Indo-Iranian we have Persian. Bengali, Hindi, and Romany are the last three, all of which are derived from the dead language Sanskrit.

In the Western set, Greek is the modern language derived from Hellenic. In the Celtic, we find Scottish, Irish, Welsh, Breton, etc. The five Romance languages, namely, Portuguese, Spanish, French, Italian, and Romanian, all belong to the Italic through an intermediate language called Latin. The Germanic family consists of the four Northern European languages: Norwegian, Icelandic, Danish, and Swedish, generally known as Scandinavian languages. Then there is German, Dutch, Flemish, and English.

All these languages have influences on English to a greater or lesser extent because each has lent words to the English vocabulary. Some of them have played a considerable role in the course of the development of English vocabulary.

3.2 A Historical Overview of the English Vocabulary

English is a West Germanic language with its origin in England; it is most closely related to German and Dutch. The history of the English language has traditionally been divided into three main periods: Old English (450 CE–1100 CE), Middle English (1100 CE–1500 CE), and Modern English (since 1500 CE). Despite linguists and scholars vigorously contesting these labels, and arguing about when or how each period begins precisely, we can observe a distinct change in the language during these three periods.

3.2.1 The Period of Old English (450 CE–1100 CE)

Before about 450 CE there was no English language in Britain. Britain was then inhabited by the Celts, who had dwelt there for centuries. They spoke a language which was an ancestor of modern Welsh and the Gaelic of Ireland and Scotland. In 55 BCE Julius Caesar led the first Roman invasion of the island. By the end of the first century CE, the conquest was complete, and a Roman colony, which stretched as far north as what is now Lowland Scotland, was established. This Roman occupation of Britain lasted roughly 400 years and came to an end in 409 CE when Roman legions withdrew to defend the capital against attacks by the barbarian Goths.

With the Romans gone, the Celts had only a short breathing space. Three Germanic tribes—the Angles, the Saxons, and the Jutes—began to press across the English Channel starting about 450 CE. During the next two centuries, the Celts were driven into the mountains of Wales and Scotland. These three tribes had similar languages and cultures, and eventually fused into one people. The language they spoke was Anglo-Saxon or Old English.

Thus, the history of the English language began with the conquest and settlement of the British Isles by the Anglo-Saxon people about the middle of the 5th century CE. The next 650 years (450 CE–1100 CE) are known as the Old English or Anglo-Saxon period of the English language. The vocabulary of Old English was predominantly Anglo-Saxon words, with a small mixture of Old Norse words as a result of the Scandinavian or the Danish conquest of England in the 9th century. Most noticeable additions from the Danish are words containing the /sk/ sound, e.g., *skull*, *skulk*, *sky*, *scant*, *skill*, *skin*, *scrape*, *bask*, and *skirt*. English also received three personal pronouns from Danish, *they*, *their*, and *them*, which replaced the native forms. According to Isaac Taylor, more than six hundred towns in the east of England have names ending in *-by*, from the Danish word for "town". Place names in *-beck*, *-dale*, *-thorp*, *-thwaite*, and *-toft* are likewise of Scandinavian origin. Similarly, English names like *Johnson*, *Jackson*, *Stevenson*, *Thompson*, and *Harrison* contain the Scandinavian ending *-son*.

Some Latin words had been acquired from traders in Europe even before the migration to England—*bargain*, *cheap*, *cup*, *dish*, *kettle*, *inch*, *pound*, *wall*, *wine*, and the like. The English language continued to borrow words from Latin during the Old English period, especially after the introduction of Christianity to Britain in 597 CE. It is only natural that most of the Latin words borrowed at that time were related to religion. Words such as *abbot*, *altar*, *angel*, *apostle*, *bishop*, *candle*, *disciple*, *hymn*, *martyr*, *nun*, *pope*, *priest*, *shrine*, and *temple* are notable examples as the objects and concepts indicated by these words had been unknown to the English people.

3.2.2　The Period of Middle English (1100 CE–1500 CE)

The conquest of England by the Norman French in 1066 CE marked the end of the Old English period and the beginning of the Middle English period. The name "Norman" means north-France from Norway and Sweden. The Normans settled in the province of Normandy on the coast across the English Channel. They quickly adopted the language and culture of the French who lived there. By 1066 CE the Normans had become thoroughly French, and William, Duke of Normandy, was using the pretext of a distant blood relationship to lay claim to the vacant throne of England after Edward the Confessor died childless in January of 1066 CE. When Harold, Earl of Wessex, was given the throne, William the Conqueror invaded England, defeated Harold's army, and killed him at the Battle of Hastings on October 14, 1066 CE, and made England a Norman state.

The conquerors became masters of the country for a long time and had a deep impact on the English language. Since the French-speaking Normans were the ruling class, French was used for all state affairs and for most social and cultural matters. Written English went underground for almost 200 years. Most literature written in England during this time was written in either French or Latin.

But it would be erroneous to assume that all the English people began to speak French. French was spoken by the upper classes, while the lower classes still spoke English. Consequently, England became a bilingual country at that time. This fact accounts for a great influx of French words in the English vocabulary. It is estimated that about 40% of the modern English vocabulary is derived from French. Indeed, thousands of French borrowed words found their way into English in the years between the 11th and 16th centuries. The French borrowed words were found in every section of the vocabulary, such as:

Law: *attorney, defendant, judge, judgment, juro*r, *justice, plaintiff, plea, prison, punishment*...;

Government: *administration*, authority, council, *court, crown, empire, government, parliament, scepter, sovereig*n, *state*...;

Military affairs: *arms, army, conquer, enemy, defense, peace, soldier, troop, navy, retreat, siege, war*...;

Religion: *abbes*s, *baptism, clergy, communion, confession, devotion, divine, faith, lesson, prayer, religion, sermon, vicar*...;

Clothing: *coat, costume, dress, garment, gown, robe*...;

Food: *bacon, beef, biscuit, cream, lemon, mutton, pork, sugar*...;

Art and literature: *art, beauty, color, figure, image, design, learning, painting, sculpture, story, tragedy...*;

Science and medicine: *anatomy, ointment, medicine, pain, plague, pulse, remedy, stomach, surgeon...*

It is worth noting here that the borrowings from French, though the most numerous and influential, were not the only ones: A thin trickle of Celtic continued and Latin words kept coming in small numbers. It is also during this period that the bulk of the Scandinavian influence came on the English language.

The period of Middle English experienced the general leveling of inflectional endings, the loss of "grammatical gender" in favor of "natural gender", and the increasing use of normal word order. In grammar, English changed from a highly inflected language to a basically analytical language. The vocabulary changes were as drastic as those in grammar. Many English words disappeared altogether only to be replaced by French and Latin words. The very core of the vocabulary, however, remained English.

3.2.3 The Period of Modern English (After 1500 CE)

The English language from 1500 CE to the present is called Modern English. In the Early Modern English period (1500 CE–1700 CE), the vocabulary had increased tremendously, chiefly because of the Renaissance, an intellectual and cultural movement which began in Italy in the 15th century and swept over England and Europe in the 16th and 17th centuries. During this period, the study of the Latin and Greek classics was stressed and the result was the wholesale borrowing from Latin and Greek. The Latin loan words were mostly connected with science and abstract ideas (e.g., *area, chemist, education, emancipate, expectation, exist, function, irony, scientific, theory...*). Greek borrowings were mostly literary, technical, and scientific words (e.g., *anonymous, astrology, astronomy, arithmetic, comedy, criterion, drama, geometry, lexicon, physics, system, tragedy...*). Some Greek words entered either through Latin or French. In addition, Greek prefixes like *anti-, anthropo-, auto-, chrono-, geo-, hemi-, hetero-, hydro-, litho-, phono-, photo-,* and *physio-*, and suffixes like *-gram, -graph, -meter, -phobia, -phone,* and *-scope* have now become the main source of neo-classical compounds.

The Renaissance also brought new words into English directly from French, Spanish, and Italian. French loans continued to enrich the English vocabulary from the end of the Middle English period down to this era. The French words are connected chiefly with arts, food, and fashion, politics and science: *machine, moustache, pilot, promenade, rendezvous, vase,* and *volley* were borrowed in the 16th century; *ballet, champagne, detail, group, parole, rapport,* and *soud* were borrowed in the 17th century; *brochure, critique, liqueur, picnic, police,* and *regime* were borrowed in the 18th century; *chauffeur, fiancee, menu, prestige, renaissance, resume*, and *restaurant* were borrowed in recent centuries.

From Italian, borrowings were particularly dominant in the fields of art and music, for example, *allegro, andante, concert, concerto, duet, libretto, opera, oratorio, piano, sonata, soprano, tenor, trio*, and *violin*; and also in the field of architecture, for example, *balcony, dome, grotto*, and *piazza*.

From Spanish came *banana, canyon, cargo, cigar, cocoa, embargo, guerrilla, hurricane, mosquito, potato, vanilla*, and so on.

English also adopted words from other European languages. German contributed *hamburger, hinterland, kindergarten, nickle, quartz, sauerkraut, wanderlust*, and *zinc;* from Dutch came many nautical terms such as *deck, dock, freight, keel, orlop, skipper, sloop*, and *yacht*; from Portuguese, *buffalo, cobra, fetish, joss, junk, pagoda, port*, and *veranda*; from Russian, *ruble, sputnik, stepper, troika, tsar*, and *vodka*.

As a result of exploration, colonization, and trade, many words came in from non-European languages. Some examples are: *alcohol, alcove, amber, cotton, gazelle, giraffe, magazine, mosque, minaret, sultan*, and *syrup* from Arabic; *azure, bazaar, caravan, divan, jasmine, khaki, pajama*, and *shawl* from Persian; *amen, manna, sabbath, Sabra, Satan*, and *seraph* from Hebrew; *bangle, bungalow, coolie, cot, loot, pundit, rajah*, and *thug* from Hindi; *bohea* (武夷茶), *cheongsam* (旗袍), *chopsuey* (炒杂碎), *kowtow* (磕头), *litchi* (荔枝), *loquat* (枇杷), *pekoe* (白毫茶), *sampan* (舢板), *tea* (茶), and *yamen* (衙门) from Chinese; *hibachi, karate, kimono, rickshaw, samurai*, and *tycoon* from Japanese. In fact, English has borrowed words from almost every known language in the course of its historical development.

As summed up in *The Encyclopedia Americana* (Smith, 1980: 423), "The English language has vast debts. In any dictionary, some 80% of the entries are borrowed. The majority are likely to come from Latin, and of those more than half will come through French. A considerable number will derive directly or indirectly from Greek. A substantial contribution will come from Scandinavian languages, and a small percentage from Portuguese, Italian, Spanish, and Dutch. Scattered words will be from various sources around the globe."

All this has made the English vocabulary extremely rich and heterogeneous. The Anglo-Saxon vocabulary of about 50,000 words has increased to more than a million words and the end is still not in sight. As a consequence of the widespread borrowing of words, the English language possesses a wealth of synonyms and idioms, which will be dealt with in subsequent chapters.

3.3 Growth of Present-Day English Vocabulary

It is a known fact that new words sweep in at a rate much faster than at any other historical period of time. New words are being invented or introduced every day to express new things and new changes in society, both material and intellectual. Meanwhile, they are coined and used to arouse public attention and interest. In time they gain acceptance and become part of the English vocabulary.

3.3.1 The Rapid Development of Science and Technology

Science and technology are the most important source of new words. The 20th century witnessed tremendous new advances in all fields of science and technology, and this led to the creation of tens of thousands of new words in the English language.

The exploration of the moon and space has given us words for novel experiences: *moonflight*, *moonfall*, *mooncraft*, *moonwalk*, *earthrise*, *lunar rover*, *space shuttle*, *space walk*, *spacemen*, *spaceport*, and *space sickness*.

The discovery of the mechanism of protein synthesis has provided many new terms concerned with genetics, such as *genetic code*, *messenger RNA* (a ribonucleic acid which carries genetic messages from the DNA in the nucleus of a cell to the ribosomes in the cytoplasm). Medicine too is a major contributor to new terms, such as *AIDs*, *open-heart surgery*, *heart-man*, *transsexual operation*, and *test-tube baby*.

As physicists pry deeper and deeper into the atomic nucleus, they have discovered more sub-atomic particles: *kaon*, *lambda*, *muon*, and *pion*. They believed that in the hypothetical world of antimatter, there exist antiparticles such as *antiquark*, *antiproton*, *antineutron*, and *antineutrino*. Computer science is another field that adds to the growing English vocabulary: *software*, *hardware*, *input*, *output*, *database*, *programming*, *Fortran* (an algebraic and logical language for programming a computer), and *BASIC* (Beginner's All-purpose Symbolic Instruction Code). Improvement in microtechnique has contributed new terms like *microform*, *microtext*, *micro-film*, *microdot*, and *micro-publishing*.

Modern science and technology have not only provided us with machinery to lighten our work and raise efficiency, but also made possible the invention of destructive weapons such as *cruise missiles*, *clean bombs*, and *nuclear bombs*. Nuclear weapons cause *chain reaction*, *radioactivity*, *fall-out*, *overkill*, and *megadeath*.

3.3.2　Political, Economic, and Cultural Changes in Society

Science and technology are not the only source of new words. The recent decades have seen considerable political and social ferment, and this ferment has left its mark on the language. Besides *hippies* and *flowers*, we have *yippies*, *groupies* (teenage girls who are fans of rock n'roll singing groups), and *teenyboppers* (girls or boys in the early teens who follow the current fashions and fads in clothing, music, etc.).

In 1960, four black students of the Greensboro Agriculture and Technical College in North Carolina went to a Woolworth's store for a cup of coffee. The waiter refused to serve them simply because they were black. When the students insisted on being served, they were taken away. This event gave rise to the term "sit-in", and a list of words with the combining form *-in* such as *kneel-in, swim-in, bed-in, die-in, work-in, lock-in, pray-in, fish-in*, and *lie-in*.

Black culture itself has given many new words. A new academic subject, black studies, has been added to the curriculum of many American schools. And other neologisms concerned with black people include *Black Nationalists*, *the Black Panthers*, *the Black Power*, *soul brother*, *soul sister*, *soul music*, and *soul food*.

The Women's Liberation Movement in the US has brought a great impact on the language. Words with the element *man* are regarded especially by feminists as "sexist words" or words connoting male chauvinism. Consequently, neologisms such as *chairperson, congressperson, spokesperson, mailperson, salesperson, newspeople*, and *camera operator* are invented. Some people even go so far as to prefer *person-eating* animals to *man-eating* animals. We wonder whether we may one day read *personcott, person-of-war, ottoi*, and *highthing* instead of the well-accepted *boycott, man-of-war, ottoman*, and *highboy*. New social habits and new living conditions necessitate the introduction of new words. Now we are already familiar with *pressure cooker, microwave oven, air-conditioner, vacuum cleaner*, and *spin-drier*. Sometimes we do not cook at our kitchenette but go to a *supermarket* to buy ready-mixed cakes or instant food.

Education is another source of new vocabulary, giving us *open classroom* (a classroom in which open discussions and individualized activities replaced the traditional subject-centered studies), *open enrollment* (a policy of unrestricted admission to a college or university that permits poor or unprepared students to matriculate), and *computer-assisted instruction* (CAI), *grade point average, underachiever, overachiever*, and so on.

New entertainment has brought into being such new expressions as *sitcoms* (situation comedies), *soap opera, simulcast* (simultaneous transmission), *guerrilla* or *street theater* (drama or mime, usually performed in an informal setting outdoors as on streets or in parks), *acid rock*, *hard rock*, *folk rock* and *call-in* (of a radio program). Sports continued its steady production of vocabulary with new sports such as *skateboarding*, *surfriding*, *body surf*, *roller-hockey*, *skydiving* (the sport of jumping from an airplane and executing various tumbles and dives before pulling the rip cord of a parachute), and *snowmobiling* (the sport of riding a snowmobile).

The history of a people is most reflected in the words they use. During the five decades of 1940–1990, additions to the English vocabulary mirror the experiences of English speakers during the period.

The first half of the 1940s were dominated by World War II: *airlift*, *beachhead*, *big lie*, *brown out* (*black out* had preceded by nearly a decade), *crash landing*, *debrief*, *declassify*, *genocide*, *guided missile*, *lend-lease*, *nerve gas*, *paratroops*, *quisling*, *radar*, and *top secret* all bear witness to the martial preoccupations of the time. A number of new words began as military terms but have survived in more general senses as they moved into the civilian vocabulary: *blockbuster*, *dry run*, *escalate*, *gremlin*, *rundown*, *sitting duck*, *snorkel*, and *task force*. The second half of the 1940s continued to coin military terms, but the *hot war* was succeeded by the *cold war* in the atomic age: *atom bomb*, *bug* (wire tap), *doublethink*, *fall out*, *hydrogen bomb*, *nuclear-powered*, *retrorocket*, *space ship*, and *space station*.

Other new words in the decade of the 1940s attest to social and cultural forces of more peaceable but no less explosive force: *acronym*, *apartheid*, *automation*, *babysit*, *bit* (binary digit), *bobby-socks*, *carpool*, *catbird seat*, *circuitry*, *cookout*, *DDT*, *deep freeze*, *discount house*, *fanzine*, *fax* (although neither the word nor the thing was to enter popular consciousness for another forty years), *flying saucer*, *freeze-dry*, *gizmo*, *gobbledygook*, *hot rod*, *jetliner*, *latchkey child*, *mambo*, *petrochemical*, *rumble*, *teenager's fight*, *starlet*, *tape recorder*, *theater in the round*, *tollway*, *VIP*, *wind shear*, and *xerography* (the highly successful brand name Xerox appeared in the following decade and was not used as a verb until the 1960s).

In the springtime of the 1940s, young men's and women's fancies lightly turned to thoughts of *beefcake*, *bikinis*, *call girls*, *falsies*, and *see-through (blouses)*.

The 1950s continued and intensified concern with space: *blastoff*, *cosmonaut*, *countdown*, *moonshot*, *space medicine*, *spaceport*, and *sputnik*. The last term popularized the suffix *-nik*, which had earlier enjoyed a limited use in Yiddish-derived words; the first of the newly popular forms was *beatnik*. International politics and the military were still productive: *brainwashing*, *brushfire war*, *common market*, *H-bomb*, *hotline*, *Dremlinology*, *McCarthyism*, *neutron bomb*, *nuke* (nuclear submarine, the innocent use of the word as a verb to mean "cook in a microwave oven" was still far in the future), and *overkill*. *Desegregation* became a major social concern in the US. Other aspects of society continued to innovate: *agribusiness*, *automate*, *brainstorming*, *bubble chamber*, *discotheque* (shortened to disco during the following decade), *do-it-yourself* (frequently abbreviated to DIY in Britain), *egghead*, *hard sell* and *soft sell*, *high-rise*, *LSD*, *metermaid*, *moonlighting*, *Ms*, *name-dropping*, *panelist*, *paramedic*, *parenting*, *Parkinson's Law* (one form of which holds that work expands to fill the time available for its completion), *pass-fail* (grading system in American higher education), *real-time* (on a computer), *roll bar*, *sci-fi*, *scuba*, *senior citizen*, *shopping mall*, *slumlord*, *sonic boom*, *teleconference*, *teleprompter*, and *telethon*.

The 1960s saw affirmative *action*, *black nationalist*, *reverse discrimination*, and *tokenism* in the US. Britain worried about the *brain drain* and looked to the new *postcodes* or *postal codes* to speed the Royal Mail, a function performed for the US Post Office by the *ZIP code*. The fad for Euro-words began with forms like *Eurobond*, *Eurocrat*, and *Eurodolla*, and was to intensify during the following decades. New social concerns embraced *biodegradable substances*, *bionics*, *brain death*, *cryobiology*, *cryosurgery*, *cryonics* (the practice of freezing the bodies of those who died of disease or degeneration with the hope of thawing and reviving them when medical science had advanced to a state of cure), *cybernation*, *genetic engineering*, *microelectronics*, *plea-bargaining*, and *under-achievers*. Entertainment and leisure activities included *bikeways*, *cable television*, *pop art*, *theater of the absurd*, and *theme parks*. In a less permissive age than our own, censors bleeped offensive words on TV. The culinary arts expanded to *fast food* and *microwave oven*. Politics saw *executive privilege* and *hardliners*. Counter-productive masters were put on the *back burner* (*front burner* did not become fashionable until the 1970s). Transportation saw *the carpool*, *jet lag*, and *jet ports*, while the space program continued with *soft landings*, *space shuttles*, and *spacewalks*.

In the 1970s, international politics involved *the boat people*, *petrodollars*, and *shuttle diplomacy*. The US politics was obsessed with *Watergate*, which quickly became a common noun for any political scandal with an attempt at a cover-up, and had such derived forms as *Waterbugger*, *Waterbungler*, *Waterfallout*, *Watergaffe*, *Watergateana*, *Watergateite*, *Watergateman*, *Watergater*, *Watergatese*, *Watergatish*, *Watergatism*, *Watergative*, *Watergatology*, *Watergimmick*, and *Watergoof*. The second half of the word became a prolific suffix denoting "a scandal" that is still highly productive; sample forms are *Cartergate*, *Cattlegate*, *Dallasgate*, *Hollywoodgate*, *Koreagate*, *Laborgate*, *Lancegate*, *Mediagate*, *Motorgate*, *Scrantongate*, *Volgagate*, and *Winegate*. *Turf* became a general term for "sphere of influence, customary activity". Other voguish words of the decade were *bottom line*, *condo*, *corn row* (a style of hairdressing popular among blacks), *designated hitter* (a baseball term that later radiated to other forms such as *designated driver* [person who abstains from alcohol in order to drive others after a party]), *downsize, empty nester, flextime, Heimlich maneuver* (succeeding the 1960s British "Kiss of Life"). The combining element *eco-* was used to form words like *ecocatastrophe* and *ecofreak*, which reflected consciousness-raising about the environment, the latter also resulting in *gas guzzler* and *gasohol* during the oil crisis.

The 1980s witnessed the rise to popular consciousness of *Argy* (Argentinian), during the Falkland Islands Crisis, but *perestroika* and *glasnost* came out of Russia. A decline in the birthrate produced *baby bust* and *baby buster*. On the other hand, *stock market trading* in London underwent a *Big Bang* (the term had also been used since the 1950s for a cosmological theory), but a sudden fall in the market was known as *Black Monday* or, *Bloody Monday*, in Britain. Merchandising adopted the technique of *cold calling* (random telephone dialing of prospective customers). *Home shopping* became possible through *telemarketing* on a *shopping network*. British consumers in old-fashioned shops paid for their purchases at a *cash point* or *till point*. *Channeling*, a form of mediumship, was a fashionable activity among New Agers, who celebrated a harmonic convergence and many of whose British analogs were *whole-foodies*. Those who preferred passive entertainment sought refuge as *couch potatoes, cocooning* in front of the TV set on which they watched *informercials*. The popularity of Britcoms was measured by a *clapometer*. *Page-three girls* were the British cheesecake for the 1980s. The *silent majority*, a much older term adopted as a label by religious fundamentalists in the US who were also politically reactionary, promoted *creation science* or *scientific creationism* as a euphemism for scriptural literalism in opposition to evolution. Identifiable by their *Filofax* (a fashionable brand of the personal organizer), *yuppies* (young urban professionals) came onto the scene in force and spawned a vast number of similar terms, many ephemeral, including the *bluppie* (black urban professional), *dink* (double income, no kids), *guppy* (gay urban professional), *mimstud* (middle-aged male stick-in-the-mud), *sampy* (sexually active, multiple-partnered youth), *whoopie* (well-off older person), and *yumpie* (young upwardly mobile person). *Yuppies* favored *power breakfasts* and *lunches*, as well as *power neckties, suits, colors, games*, and *writing*. Businesses parted from employees with *golden handshakes* or *golden parachutes* or retained them with *golden handcuffs*. The streets of cities were blocked by *gridlocks* (which quickly developed metaphorical uses for what was earlier called a *bottleneck*, which the clever found a way to wire around). *Hub-and-spoke airports* became a pattern for transportation as *near-collision* more accurately replaced the older *near miss*. A *black spot* in Britain was a place on a road where accidents were likely to occur. The Reagan administration in the US was plagued by *kiss-and-tell books* written by those who were in the loop. Politicians of all varieties did their best to put a favorable spin on stories affecting them through the use of *spin doctors* who specialized in *spin control*. *Necklacing* was a nice-sounding term for a nasty act of terrorism: the igniting of a gasoline-soaked tire placed around the neck of a victim favored in some of the developing countries of the world.

After the September 11 Attacks in the US, many new terms about terrorism were invented: *plane* (noun→verb, to use planes as missiles), *theo-terrorism* (terrorism resulting from religious extremism), *talibanize* (the takeover of a government by Islamic fundamentalists), *ground zero* (the rubble left behind where the twin towers once stood), *debris surge* (massive clouds of dust, glass shards, and papers that swept through lower Manhattan in New York), etc.

Wars, political scandals, international relations, terrorism, Euro-unification, economic shocks and revolutions, falling walls and rising curtains, technological developments, medicine, space exploration, scientific theory, the New Age, family structure, social stratification and integration, the women's movement, an aging population, lifestyles, ethnic identity, pop culture, sports, drugs, sexual mores, merchandising, communications, transportation, entertainment, the green revolution, and ecology, these are some of the areas that have been lexically active during the past half century. They are also the areas that most strikingly set the end of the century apart from its beginning. If clothes make the man, words make the culture. In such words as these, we read the values, concerns, and preoccupations of our time.

3.3.3　The Formation of New Vocabulary

In the Modern English period, especially after World War II, though borrowing still plays an important role in English vocabulary expansion, the English language relies more on the use of its own existing materials to form new words, for example, coin a new word by word-formation rules or form a new word by adding new meanings to an existing word.

One common method of forming new words is compounding, combining two or more existing words to form a new one. Typical examples are such words as *pressure cooker*, *microwave oven*, and *vacuum cleaner* mentioned above. Another word-formation method is derivation, adding a prefix, suffix, or combining form to a word base: *antimatter*, *minibus*, and *sit-in*. Another method often resorted to is conversion, turning a word from one word class straight into another word class. For example, *to author* means "to be the author of", and *to pressure* means "to put pressure, either political or mental, upon somebody".

Sometimes two old words are blended to form a new term, e.g., *botel* (boat hotel), *lidar* (light radar), *comsat* (communication satellite), etc. Like blending, another method called "clipping" also plays its part in the creation of such new words as *disco* (discotheque), *narc* (narcotics agent), and *copter* (helicopter). Another type of shortening is "acronymy", using the first letters of words to form a proper name or a technical term, e.g., *OPEC* (Organization of Petroleum Exporting Countries), *AIDS* or *Aids* (acquired immunodeficiency syndrome) and *laser* (lightwave amplification by stimulated emission of radiation).

A process somewhat similar to clipping is known as back-formation. A back-formation is formed by the deletion of a supposed affix from an already existing word. *Laser*, for example, although it is an acronymic formation, looks like an agent noun formed from a verb. The apparent agent suffix is removed and the verb *lase* is formed. Similarly, *commute* is back-formed from *commutation*, *free-associate* from *free-association*, and *soft-land* from *soft-landing*.

Compared with the process of word formation, the process of adding new meanings to existing words is much simpler. Quite a few English words and phrases have taken on new meanings to fit new situations in the course of time, especially in the past few decades. *Environment*, for example, comes to mean "a work of environmental art". And the phrase *second banana* should not be taken literally but means "one who plays a secondary part". Even the simple words *cold* and *hot* have changed their meanings in the phrases *cold war* and *hot war*.

Many new English words are derived neither from the process of word formation nor from the process of adding new meanings to already existing words. They are borrowed from other languages. For much of its history, English has been a great borrower, building its vocabulary by culling new and useful terms from languages all over the world.

The English vocabulary keeps constantly growing. Its constant growth can be illustrated by the fact that after the publication of *Webster's Third New International Dictionary* in 1961, Merriam-Webster editors soon added an eight-page Addenda Section to the dictionary in 1966, increased it to sixteen pages in 1971, to thirty-two in 1976, to forty-eight in 1981, and to fifty-six in 1986. Moreover, the rate of its growth is ever-accelerating. Therefore, some knowledge of the growth of the English vocabulary is beneficial to students of English.

3.4　Modes of Vocabulary Development

On the basis of the discussion so far in this chapter, we can conclude that modern English vocabulary develops through three channels: creation, semantic change, and borrowing.

Creation refers to the formation of new words by using the existing materials, namely roots, affixes, and other elements. In modern times, this is the most important way of vocabulary expansion.

Semantic change means an old form takes on a new meaning to meet the new need. This does not increase the number of word forms but creates many more new usages of the words, thus enriching the vocabulary.

Borrowing has played a vital role in the development of vocabulary, particularly in earlier times. Though still at work now, it can hardly compare with what it did in the past. It can be said that with the change of the world situation and the development of the economy, the role of each foreign contributor will change accordingly.

Exercises

I. Briefly answer the following questions.

1. What are the main foreign elements making up the English vocabulary during the Old English period?

2. How did the Norman Conquest influence the Middle English language?

3. What impact did the Renaissance have on Early Modern English?

4. What are the causes of the rapid growth of the present-day English vocabulary?

5. Can you describe the main methods of word formation whereby new words are created?

II. Decide whether the following statements are true or false.

1. Modern English developed from Old English spoken by three Germanic tribes—the Angles, the Saxons, and the Jutes.

2. The English spoken by William Shakespeare and his contemporaries was Middle English.

3. In the Indo-European language family, English is a language in the Germanic group of the Western set.

4. The Middle English period witnessed the influx of a great number of French words in

the English language.

5. Before about 450 CE, the English language in Britain was spoken by the Celts.

6. The vocabulary of Old English were Anglo-Saxon words.

7. The conquest of England by the Norman French in 1066 CE marked the end of the Old English period and the beginning of the Middle English period.

8. In the Middle English Period, English was spoken by the upper classes while the lower classes spoke French.

9. During the Renaissance Movement, the two languages that made the greatest contributions to the English vocabulary expansion were Latin and Greek.

10. The expansion of the English vocabulary mirrors the experiences of English speakers.

III. Match the groups of words in Column A with the languages from which they are borrowed in Column B.

A	B
skull, skulk, sky, scant, skill, skin, scrape, bask, skirt	Chinese
bohea, cheongsam, chopsuey, kowtow, litchi, loquat	Italian
judge, administration, peace, soldier, baptism, costume	Danish
ruble, sputnik, stepper, troika, tsar, vodka	French
allegro, andante, concert, concerto, duet, libretto, opera	Russian
hamburger, hinterland, kindergarten, nickle, quartz	German
area, chemist, education, emancipate, expectation, exist	Latin
banana, canyon, cargo, cigar, cocoa, embargo, guerrilla	Spanish

Chapter 4

Morphological Structure of Words

4.1 The Concept of Morpheme

The term "morpheme" is derived from the Greek *morphe* (= form) + *-eme*, which denotes the smallest unit or the minimum distinctive feature. The morpheme is the smallest meaningful linguistic unit of language, not divisible or analyzable into smaller forms. For example, when we analyze the word *internationalization* into its smallest meaningful linguistic units, we can identify five minimum meaningful components: *inter-*, *nation*, *-al*, *-ize*, and *-tion*. These five meaningful components which cannot be semantically further analyzed are called morphemes.

A morpheme is also a two-facet language unit, which possesses both sound and meaning. In this case, a morpheme is like a word. But unlike a word, it cannot be uttered alone unless the morpheme is just a word. It appears only as a constituent part of a word, although a word may consist of a single morpheme.

Words are composed of morphemes. Some words are formed by one morpheme, such as *book*, *red*, and *take*, and others contain two or more morphemes, such as *bookshop*, *reddish*, and *take-home*. A morpheme is not identical to a syllable. It may be represented by one syllable, like *book*, *red*, and *take* mentioned above, or by two or more syllables, as in *zebra*, *hippopotamus*, *rhinoceros*.

The same morpheme may adopt variant forms as conditioned by position or adjoining sounds. For example, a prefix like *im-* occurs before words with the initial letters *p*, *b*, or *m* (e.g., *impractical, imbalance, immortal*); its variant forms are *ir-* before words with the initial letter *r* (e.g., *irrational, irregular*), *il-* before words with the initial letter *l* (e.g., *illegal, illegible*); *in-* before words beginning with all the other consonants and vowels (e.g., *insecure, incoherent, inactive, inexperienced*). In the above list, *im-*, *ir-*, and *il-* are called allomorphs of the morpheme *in-*. Allomorphs also occur among suffixes. For example, the allomorphs *-ion*, *-tion*, *-sion*, and *-ation* are the positional variants of the same suffix. They do not differ in meaning and function but show a slight difference in sound depending on the final phoneme of the verb to which they are attached; for instance, verbs ending with the sound /t/ usually take *-ion* (*act-action*); verbs ending in *-d*, *-de*, or *-mit* take *-sion* (*expand-expansion*; *decide-decision*; *omit-omission*); verbs ending in *-ify* and *-ize/-ise* take *-ation* (*justify-justification*; *modernize-modernization*); verbs ending with other consonants take *-tion* (*absorb-absorption*).

4.1.1 Types of Morphemes

1. Free morphemes and bound morphemes

Morphemes may be classified into free morphemes and bound morphemes. A free morpheme is one that can stand alone as a separate word. A free morpheme is a simple word, e.g., *book*, *famous*, and *produce*. Free morphemes display a strong ability to combine with another morpheme, free or bound, to form a compound or a derivative. Two free morphemes constitute a compound, as in *book-shop*, *world-famous*, *mass-produce*. They are a compound noun, compound adjective, and compound verb respectively. All free morphemes contain their own lexical meaning and can be used alone. Thus, they are also called content morphemes or lexical morphemes.

A bound morpheme cannot appear in isolation. It cannot stand alone. It must appear with at least one other free or bound morpheme. All English affixes are bound morphemes. Bound morphemes can be further divided into derivative bound morphemes and inflectional bound morphemes.

Derivative bound morphemes are added to stems (linguistic forms to which affixes can be added) to form derivative words, for example:

stem		derivative affix		word
• *book*	+	*-let*	→	*booklet*
• *famous*	+	*in-*	→	*infamous*
• *produce*	+	*-er*	→	*producer*

Inflectional bound morphemes are those that are added to stems to indicate grammatical categories or grammatical relations, the following are some examples:

- Comparative degree or superlative degree

-er: wise	+	*-er*	→	*wiser*
-est: wise	+	*-est*	→	*wisest*

- Plurality

-s: book	+	*-s*	→	*books*

- Third-person singular number

-s: investigate	+	-s	→	investigates

- Possessive case

-'s: student	+	*-'s*	→	*student's*

- Past tense

-ed: work	+	*-ed*	→	*worked*

Inflectional bound morphemes possess only grammatical meanings. The noun plural ending *-s* and the verb ending *-ed,* for instance, have no other meaning except the grammatical notions of plurality and past tense, so they are also called "grammatical morphemes".

A word can be formed by a single free morpheme such as *water* and *friend*, or by two free morphemes such as *blackboard*, or by a free morpheme combined with one or more bound morphemes such as *watery* and *nationalization*, or by bound morphemes such as *prediction* and *antecedent*.

2. Lexical morphemes and grammatical morphemes

Morphemes, whether free or bound, can also be divided into lexical morphemes and grammatical morphemes according to whether they carry primarily lexical or grammatical meanings. Lexical morphemes have primarily lexical meanings, e.g., *computer*, *car*, *-ize*, and *en-*, while grammatical morphemes carry mainly grammatical meanings. Morphemes such as *the*, *of*, *by*, *-ing*, and *-s* are grammatical morphemes.

It can be seen from the examples that lexical and grammatical morphemes can be either free or bound. It is also clear that function words and inflectional morphemes are grammatical morphemes, whereas content words and derivational morphemes are lexical morphemes.

4.1.2　Roots, Stems, and Bases

According to Bauer (1983: 20), "A root is a form which is not further analyzable, either in terms of derivational or inflectional morphology. It is that part of a word form that remains when all the inflectional and derivational affixes have been removed." This means that a root cannot be broken into further meaningful units. For example, in the word *untimely*, the root is *time*, to which the suffix *-ly*, and then the prefix *un-* are added. Another example is *friendships*, whose root is *friend* when the affix *-ship* and the plural form *-s* are removed. In compound words such as *textbook*, there are two roots, *text* and *book*.

Some roots must carry a prefix, a suffix, or a combining form to appear as a word. In this case, they are bound roots. For example, the root *-scribe,* which means "write", cannot stand alone as a word. It must appear with such prefixes as *pre-*, *sub-*, and *trans-* to become individual words.

Roots are the core of English words. You will have a great chance to correctly guess the meaning of an unknown word if you know the meaning of its root.

As defined by Bauer (1983: 20), "A stem is of concern only when dealing with inflectional morphology… Inflectional (but not derivational) affixes are added to it: It is the part of the word form which remains when all inflectional affixes have been removed." In the above example, *studies*, the stem is also *study*, because *-s*, an inflectional affix, has been added to it.

A base is any form to which affixes of any kind can be added. This means that any root or stem can be termed as a base. A base, however, differs from a root in that the former is a derivationally or inflectionally analyzable form to which affixes of any kind can be added, while the latter is a form that is not further analyzable. For example, in the word *untimely*, the base is *timely*, to which the prefix *un-* is added, but the root is *time* because *time* permits no further analysis. However, in the word *timely*, the base is *time* because the suffix *-ly* has been added to it; the root remains unchanged, i.e., the root is *time*. In the word *studies*, the stem and the root coincide.

A base is also different from a stem because both derivational and inflectional affixes can be added to a base, whereas only inflectional affixes can be attached to a stem. For example, in the word *untimely*, *timely* is the base to which the prefix *un-* is added, but it cannot be considered as a stem because it does not permit the addition of inflectional affixes.

To sum up, a root is minimal in that it cannot be further analyzed into meaningful units; it can be free or bound morphemes. A stem is a form to which inflectional affixes can be added. A based is any form to which affixes, either derivational or inflectional, can be attached.

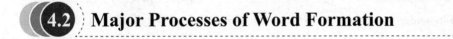 4.2 Major Processes of Word Formation

As one of the main branches of lexicology, word formation studies the internal structures of words, in this case, the English words, and the processes through which new words are created. Derivation, conversion, and compounding are the three major processes of word formation. Other word-formation processes include clipping, blending, acronymy, back-formation, words from proper names, neoclassical formation, reduplication, and analogy. All these word-formation processes have played an important role in the making of English words.

Since World War Ⅱ, the majority of the new English vocabulary have been created by these word-formation types, as shown below (Zhang, 1992):

- Derivation or affixation (about 17.5% of total new vocabulary)
  Prefixation: *deescalate, antihero, reboot*
  Suffixation: *hawkish, globalize*
- Conversion (about 10.5%): *bottle (v.), bargain (n.), can (v.)* in *canned food*
- Compounding or composition (about 27%): *raindrop, snow-white, dry-clean, web*

page, online shopping

- Clipping (about 2%): *phone, flute, lab, app*
- Blending (about 6%): *brunch, airtel, webinar*
- Acronymy (about 9%): *UN, COVID, IM (Instant Messaging), NPC (National People's Congress), IT (information technology), WWW (world wide web), CEO (chief executive officer)*
- Back-formation (about 1%): *gangle, vacuum-clean, televise*
- Words from proper names (about 2%): *Uncle Tom, xerox*
- Neoclassical formations (about 4%): *psychedelic, neurolinguistics*
- Reduplication (about 1%): *walkie-talkie, go-go*
- Others (about 20%): *pizzazz, gazump*

Words formed by the three major processes of derivation, conversion, and compounding constitute 55% of the new vocabulary, and words formed by the minor processes account for 25% of the new vocabulary. The remaining 20% is from other processes such as coinage and borrowing, e.g., *pizzazz, discotheque, ombudsman*.

4.2.1 Derivation

Derivation, also called affixation, indicates a word-formation process whereby a new word is derived by adding a prefix or suffix to a word base. Below is a detailed account of the types and meanings of prefixes and suffixes.

1. Prefixation

The process by which a new word is formed by adding a prefix or combining form to a word base is called prefixation. Prefixes are classified into the following ten groups according to their meaning:

- Negative prefixes (*a-, dis-, in-, non-, un-: amoral, disloyal, inexact, non-smoker, unhappy*)
- Reversative or privative prefixes (*de-, dis-, un-: decentralize, disconnect, unwrap*)
- Pejorative prefixes (*mal-, mis-, pseudo-: maltreat, mislead, pseudoscience*)
- Prefixes of degree or size (*arch-, co-, hyper-, mini-, out-, over-, sub-, super-, sur-, ultra-, under-: arch-enemy, co-education, hypermarket, minibus, outgrow, over-population, substandard, superman, surtax, ultra-modem, under-development*)
- Prefixes of orientation and attitude (*anti-, contra-, counter-, pro-: antislavery, contraflow, counteract, pro-student*)
- Locative prefixes (*fore-, inter-, sub-, super-, trans-: foreleg, international, subway,*

superstructure, transatlantic)

- Prefixes of time and order (*ex-, fore-, post-, pre-, re-: ex-president, foresee, post-election, pre-school, rebuild*)

- Number prefixes (*bi-, di-, poly-, multi-, semi-, demi-, tri-, uni-, mono-: bicycle, dioxide, polysemy, multiform, semicircle, demigod, triangle, unicycle, monologue*)

- Miscellaneous neo-classical prefixes (*auto-, extra-, neo-, paleo-, pan-, proto-, tele-, vice-: autobus, extra-large, neorealism, paleoanthropology, pan-American, prototype, television, vice-chairman*)[1]

- Conversion prefixes (*a-, be-, en-, em-: alive, becalm, enslave, empower*)

Derivation is a word-formation process as old as the English language itself. Some of the old English prefixes such as *ed-* and *ge-* have disappeared in the course of time, while others are still used in making new words. A few of these, however, have acquired a new meaning that is not at all implied in their earlier use. Moreover, some of the prefixes have become much more productive than before. Below is a discussion of the prefixes *anti-, non-, super-,* and *un-*, which have not only developed their new meanings but also become more productive in recent years.

anti-: The changing political aspect of modern society has given rise to many terms beginning with *anti-*, such as *antiauthoritarian, antiestablishment, antiracism* and *antifeminist*. Besides being frequently used in politics, the prefix is also used in such technical terms as *anticancer, anticonvulsant, antiflammatory, antiabortion, antiballistic* and *antidepressant*.

In present-day English, the prefix *anti-* has developed two new meanings: *anti-* generally means "against, opposite or opposing, and contrary". In medicine, *anti-* often connotes "counteracting or effective against" as in *antibacterial, anti-infective*, and *antiviral*. Sometimes medical terms containing *anti-* take on new meanings as has occurred in *antibiotic* and *antibody*. As a prefix, *anti-* may be shortened to *ant-* as in *antacid*.

non-: *Non*, in its original sense of "not", continues to beget new words such as *nonaddict, noncandidate, nondairy, nondiscrimination, nondrinker, nonfictioneer, non-involved, nonmusician, nonproductive* and *non-U* (not upper-class).

Non- has also developed two new meanings given below:

(1) Lack or absence of a natural or typical quality associated with the referent, as in *nonbook* (a book which has little literary merit or factual information and which is often a

---

1 Some linguists regard them as combining forms rather than prefixes as they were originally full words in Latin or Greek. Combining forms can be added to an affix as well as to the base to form a new word.

compilation, as of pictures or press clippings), *nonperson* (a person regarded as not existent or having no social or legal status), *nonfriend* (a false friend), *nonstory* (story without news value).

(2) Unlike the conventional form or characteristic, as in *nonhero* (a hero whose unconventional characteristics are opposite to those of a traditional hero, another word for *anti-hero*), and *non-novel* (novel not written in the traditional way).

super-: This old prefix came into fashion after Bernard Shaw's *Man and Superman* was published in 1903. It has begotten many technical terms and advertising jargons with the meaning "above, beyond, or superior in quality or size" such as *superalloy, superplastic, supercity, supermart, superstate, supertrain, superweapon, supersoft, superdigestible, supermom*, and *supersell*.

un-: This prefix often expresses a reversative or negative action or process with the sense of "the opposite of" or "not" as in *uninformative* (not providing information), *unnational* (not belonging to or characteristic of an individual nation), and *untie* (to loosen or unfasten anything tied).[2]

un- has developed a new meaning in the word *unbook* (book which is not bought to be used, but to be given as a present), *unpeople* (people lacking semblance of humanity or individuality) and *unperson* (a political or other public figures who have lost his importance or influence and has been relegated to an inferior or inconsequential status).

Both *un-* and *in-* (*im-, il-, ir-*) are negative prefixes. There is often a teasing uncertainty or incertitude about whether the negative form of a word should be made with *un-* or *in-*. Based on H. W. Fowler's *A Dictionary of Modern English Usage* (1965) are the following three principles guiding their usage:

(1) *Un-* is a native prefix, so it is attached to native words; *in-* is Latin and goes with loan words. But many exceptions occur.

(2) Words with *-ed* ending take only *un-*; *undigested* but *indigestible, unanimated* but *inanimate, uncompleted* but *incomplete, undetermined* but *indeterminate, unlettered* but *illiterate, unlimited* but *illimitable, unredeemed* but *irredeemable*.

(3) Words with *-ing* ending take *un-* too, such as *unceasing* but *incessant, undiscriminating* but *indiscriminate*.

Both *un-* and *in-* (*im-, il-, ir-*) belong to the same type of negative prefixes, but their

---

2　The use of *un-* does not always express a negative or reversative meaning. *Uneasy* means "worried" rather than "not easy"; *loosen* and *unloosen* have the same meaning "to make or become less tight".

meanings differ in the following pairs:

- *unmoral* (neither moral nor immoral)

  immoral (morally bad)

- *unartistic* (not concerned with art)

  inartistic (lacking an artistic sense or appreciation)

- *unreligious* (not concerned with religion)

  irreligious (not religious, showing disregard for or hostility to religion)

2. Suffixation

The process through which words are formed by adding a suffix or combining form to the base is called suffixation. Unlike prefixes, most suffixes do not add new meanings to the base, but only change the original word class or part of speech.[3] So it is convenient to group the suffixes by the word classes they form into noun suffixes, adjective suffixes, verb suffixes, and adverb suffixes.

1) Noun suffixes

(1) Noun → noun suffixes. Suffixes denoting occupation: *-ster, -eer, -er, -ian* as in *gangster, songster, engineer, pamphleteer, glover*, and *musician*.

Suffixes denoting diminutive and feminine meaning: *-let, -ette, -eteria, -ess, -ling, -y, -ie* as in *booklet, leaflet, cigarette, kitchenette, grocerteria, luncheteria, actress, hostess, duckling, princeling, daddy*, and *auntie*.

Suffixes denoting status or domain: *-hood, -ship, -dom, -ocracy, -ery* as in *boyhood, brotherhood, friendship, membership, kingdom, officialdom, democracy, autocracy*, and *slavery*.

Other denominal noun suffixes include *-ing, -ful*, and *-ite*, as in *bathing, matting, cupful, handful, Israelite*, and *laborite*.

(2) Adjective → noun suffixes. De-adjectival noun suffixes include *-ity, -ist, -ism, -ness* as in *rapidity, regularity, loyalist, idealism, kindness*, and *falseness*.

(3) Verb → noun suffixes. De-verbal noun suffixes include *-ant, -ee, -er, -or, -age, -al, -ation, -ing, -ment*, as in *inhabitant, payee, driver, actor, postage, refusal, starvation, opening*, and *movement*.

---

3   Exceptions include *cigarette, friendship, Londoner* and *booklet*.

2) Adjective suffixes

(1) Noun → adjective suffixes. De-nominal adjective suffixes include *-ed*, *-ful*, *-ish*, *-less*, *-like*, *-ly* and *-y* as well as *-al*, *-esque*, *-ic*, *-ous*, *-some*, *-worthy*, *-arian* as in *walled*, *delightful*, *childish*, *careless*, *statesmanlike*, *manly*, *hairy*, *musical*, *picturesque*, *atomic*, *grievous*, *burdensome*, *praiseworthy*, and *authoritarian*.

(2) Verb → adjective suffixes. De-verbal adjective suffixes are *-able* and *-ive*, as in *changeable*, *drinkable*, *attractive and productive*.

3) Verb suffixes

Only a few verb suffixes occur with great frequency in English, and only *-ize* is highly productive. All are concerned with forming transitive verbs of basically causative meaning. Verbs may be derived from nouns or adjectives by adding suffixes such as *-ize*, *-en*, *-ify*, *-fy* as in *hospitalize*, *publicize*, *modernize*, *legalize*, *widen*, *amplify*, and *identify*.

4) Adverb suffixes

The commonest of adverb suffixes is *-ly*, which can be very generally added to an adjective to turn into an adverb. Examples are *nicely* and *happily*. Other adverb suffixes include *-ward(s)*, *-wise*, *-fold*, as in *backward(s)*, *clockwise*, and *twofold*.

Below is a brief description of some productive suffixes *-ee*, *-ese*, *-in*, *-ish*, *-nik* and the combining form *-in*.

-ee: This old noun suffix shows the fairly characteristic passive meaning in words such as *advisee*, *appointee*, *awardee*, *detainee*, *expellee*, *interviewee* and *murderee*. But in spite of the strong passive idea evoked by the suffix, it is still capable of being used in a non-passive sense. Words with the sense of active agent include *absentee*, *escapee*, *refugee* and *resignee*. *Cursee* means either the person who curses or the person who is cursed.

-ese: The suffix refers to a language, literary style, etc.: *academese*, *Amencanese*, *anchormanese*, *bureau gotfese*, *journalese*, *newspaperese*. The suffix is often added to a proper name of a person or a place to express a specific style or feature associated with the person or place, as in *Johnsonese*, *Carlylese*, *Kiplingese*, *Manhattanese*, *Madison Avenuese*, and *Pentagonese*.

-in: This is a combining form of the adverb *in*, being added to a verb to form a noun with the sense of "public demonstration, protest or group activities". It was introduced during the 1960s by the American civil rights movement. In January 1960, four black young men entered a restaurant which served only whites and refused to leave as a protest against racial

discrimination (as mentioned in 3.3.2). This event created the word *sit-in*, meaning "an act of social protest or demonstration by a group of people". Ever since then, many words with *-in* have mushroomed: *be-in* as "an informal gathering, usually in a park or other public places, for the purpose of being together and doing whatever one likes" (Lo, 1980), *bed-in* as "an act of sleeping at public places as a form of protest" (*ibid*), *die-in* as "a form of demonstration in which the protesters threaten with death" (*ibid*), *kneel-in* as "an act of entering the church of whites for prayer", *lie-in* as "a lying down of a group of people in a public place to disrupt traffic, etc. as a form of protest or demonstration" (*ibid*), *lock-in* as "a protest demonstration in which a group locks itself within a building, office, etc." (*ibid*). Other examples are *kiss-in*, *love-in*, *sleep-in*, *ride-in*, *smoke-in*, *sing-in*, *swim-in*, *teach-in*, and *work-in*, all denoting an act of public demonstration or social gathering.

-ish: This suffix was first used to form adjectives from national names, as in English, *British*, *Swedish*, and *Turkish*; and then it came to mean "having the nature of", as in *selfish*, and *snobbish*. This second group of adjectives is often pejorative. Then *-ish* developed the peculiar sense of "somewhat" when affixed to adjectives. At first, it was used in this sense with words of color like *bluish*, *greenish,* and *reddish*; then it was affixed to adjectives other than color terms such as *poorish* and *youngish*, and in recent colloquial English, it has come to be added to numerals as well to indicate an approximate time or age. *Sixish* equals "at about six o'clock" in "See you sixish". Likewise, *fortyish* means "about forty years of age". "Perhaps the fashion for this suffix is to be ascribed to an unconscious fear of appearing too precise or dogmatic in expression, or to a careful refusal to say more than is warranted by the facts." (Foster, 1981: 191)

-nik: The suffix *-nik* came into fashion after the Soviet Union had launched its artificial satellite "Sputnik" in 1957. According to *The Random House College Dictionary*, the current meaning of this suffix refers to "usually derogatorily, persons who support or are connected or associated with a particular political cause or group, cultural attitude, or the like." Sample words are *beatnik* (a member of the Beat Generation that came of age after World War Ⅱ, especially in the late 1950s), *peacenik* (an active opponent of war), *neatnik* (a person who is fastidious about neatness), *no-goodnik* (a person who is a good-for-nothing).

English has many pairs of words with the same root but different suffixes. In most cases, different suffixes possess different meanings, e.g., *informant* (a person who gives information, especially someone who gives details of his language, social customs, etc. to someone who is studying it) and *informer* (a person who informs against another, especially to the police), *childish* means "(derogatory) having a manner unsuitable for grown-ups" while *childlike* means "(often appreciative) of or typical of a child, especially having a natural guiltless lovable quality", *economic* means "of economics, connected with commerce and industry", whereas *economical* means "not wasteful, careful in the spending of money, time, etc. and in the use of goods".

It is a thorny point to distinguish between adjective endings *-ic* and *-ical*. Adjectives usually ending in *-ic* are as follows: *academic, artistic, athletic, automatic, eccentric, energetic, epic, exotic, heroic, optimistic, pacific, patriotic, periodic, pessimistic, photographic, plastic, romantic, scholastic,* and *syntactic.*

Adjectives usually ending in *-ical* are as follows: *biographical, biological, chemical, critical, cynical, grammatical, hypocritical, logical, mechanical, physical, practical, psychological, rhetorical, statistical, technical, theatrical,* and *typical.*

Adjectives that can either end in *-ic* or *-ical* are as follows: *alphabetical, electrical, emphatical, fanatical, fantastical, geographical, hysterical, idiomatical, magical, poetical,* and *theoretical.*

4.2.2　Conversion

Conversion is the word-formation process in which a word of one grammatical form is used as a word of another grammatical form without any changes to spelling or pronunciation. For example, the noun *e-mail* appeared in English before the verb: "A decade ago I would have sent you an e-mail (noun) whereas now I can either send you an email (noun) or simply e-mail (verb) you." The original noun *e-mail* experienced conversion, thus resulting in the new verb *e-mail.*

Modern English displays great flexibility in word formation; a word from one part of speech can be converted or shifted into another part of speech with no formal difference. This is brought about by the loss of inflections, which makes two words of different parts of speech, e.g., a noun and a verb, identical in form. Many scholars, therefore, suggest that conversion can be referred to as zero derivation or null derivation with the assumption that the formal change between words results in the addition of an invisible morpheme. However, some linguists argue for a clear distinction between the word-formation processes of derivation and conversion.

Before the Modern English period, Old English and Middle English showed word inflections to different degrees. Take the word *hope* for illustration. As a noun, it had the form of *hopa* in late Old English and belonged to the class of weak masculine nouns. The corresponding verb also belonged to a weak class, with its form *hogian* in Old English. Towards Middle English, the nominal *hopa* became *hope*, and the verbal *hopian* became *hopien* or *hopen*. These were the forms employed by Chaucer in his *Canterbury Tales*. The subsequent centuries witnessed a further reduction of the inflected forms, and the noun and the verb became identical. Shakespeare and other Elizabethan writers used *hope* as both a noun and a verb. Changes of this sort are important because they create the possibility of shifting a word from one class to another class without the pasting or cutting of troublesome affixes, as is done in the majority of other Indo-European languages.

1. Conversion to verb

Today the most productive form of conversion in English is from nouns to verbs. Here are some examples of recent appearances:

- Now media leaders are really taking bold steps to *position* their companies for growth and long-term success. (*The Hollywood Reporter*, February 25, 2022)
- Don't *microwave* plastic food-storage bags or plastic bags from the grocery store, even if the package is marked as safe for microwaving. (*Washington Post*, March 5, 2021)
- It's not about being Chamberlain or Churchill; Zelensky's dilemma is real and no one will *pressure* him to compromise or fight. (*National Review*, March 15, 2022)

This noun-to-verb conversion may be subdivided into the following groups, based on *A Comprehensive Grammar of the English Language* (Quirk et al., 1985).

(1) To put in/on N: The nouns are usually locative nouns indicating a place, a container, or a specified location; for instance, *to position* means "to put somebody or something in a given position". Other examples are *bottle* (to put into a bottle), *can* (to put into a can), *corner* (to put into a difficult position), and *shelve* (to put books, etc. on the shelves).

(2) To give N or to provide with N: *shelter* as in "The tree sheltered the cows." (The tree gave shelter to the cows.), *coat* (to give a coat to), *commission* (to give a commission to), *mask* (to give a mask to), and *plaster* (to give a plaster to).

(3) To deprive of N: *core* (to remove the core from), *peel* (to take the peel off fruit, vegetables, etc.), *skin* (to take the skin off), and *weed* (to cut off weeds).

(4) To do with N: *brake* as in "The driver suddenly braked the car." means "to stop by means of a brake". Other examples: *knife* (to cut or stab with a knife), *finger* (to touch with the fingers), and *nail* (to fasten something with a nail).

(5) To be or act as N: *father* (to act as a father), *nurse* (to act as a nurse), *pilot* (to act as a pilot), and *parrot* (to repeat words like a parrot).

(6) To make or change into N: *cash* (to change into cash), *cripple* (to make somebody a

cripple), *group* (to make into a group).

(7) To send or go by N: *bicycle* (to go by bicycle), *boat* (to travel into a boat), *mail* (to send by mail), *telegraph* (to send news, etc. by telegraph).

Two types of noun-to-verb conversion must be distinguished: permanent conversion and temporary conversion. The italic verbs of the foregoing examples may all be regarded as belonging to the first type, with some of them in an informal style. Many verbs of this type are scientific and technical terms, e.g., *auto* (= drive an auto), *taxi* (= drive a taxi), *message* (= send [as] a message, *dock* [of space vehicles] join together in outer space).

Conversion of the second type—temporary conversion—are nonce words, and are usually employed for certain stylistic purposes. The following are two examples.

- A: My dear fellow. I…
  B: Don't *my dear fellow* me. (*The Zoo Story*, 1962)
- A: "Now, listen, kid." said Sylvester.
  B: Don't *kid* me (= Don't call me kid). ("The Jockey", 1941)

Not infrequently, a new noun-converted verb has a meaning different from the original noun. In any American university automat, one can see such a notice: "Bus Trays to Dishroom!" The verb *bus* here does not mean "to transport". The notice says that anyone who eats here should send his trays to the dishroom. The verb *service* acquires the meaning of "to repair or put (a vehicle, machine, etc.) in good condition".

Verbs converted from adjectives fall into two groups:

(1) Intransitive verbs meaning "to be or become the quality denoted by the adjective", such as *dry* (to become dry), *pale* (to turn pale), *sour* (to go sour), *slim* (to become slim).

(2) Transitive verbs meaning "to cause somebody or something to be or become the quality denoted by the adjective", such as *calm* (to make calm), *dirty* (to make dirty), *tame* (to make tame), and *warm* (to make warm).

Verbs can be converted not only from nouns and adjectives but from almost any other part of speech, though less commonly. For example:

- Decker suggested they buy a thousand calves the next spring because the war would *up* the price of beef. (*Legends of the Fall*, 1994) (adverb into verb)
- We all *ooh* and *ahh* over the (at least in my memory) huge lights and decorations that illuminate every house and the snow that blankets each lawn along our drive. (*Better Homes & Gardens*, November 29, 2021) (interjection into verb)

- Don't "but" me! (Woody Allen, *Death Knocks*, 1975) (conjunction into verb)

2. Conversion to noun

The free interchange between different parts of speech demonstrates itself in many ways. Conversion from verbs into nouns is now very common. Here is a brief sketch of the tendency:

- After losing to Colorado State in the conference tournament and finishing seventh overall in the Mountain West, Odom and the Aggies may have had some doubts about receiving a postseason *invite*. (*The Salt Lake Tribune*, March 15, 2022)
- No other book in so few pages gives us such a piercing *feel*. (*The Atlantic*, March 11, 2022)
- She replied, "you've got another *think* coming." (*Reader's Digest*, Vol. 3, 1983)
- "What happened to your eyes?" Jan asked Macimer.
  "I don't think that'll help. I think you need a *transplant*." (*Reader's Digest*, Vol. 3, 1983)

A list of some quite recent verb-converted nouns collected from up-to-date dictionaries runs as follows: *buy* (something bought), *clutch* (critical situation; emergency), *drag* (slang, a dull or boring person, situation or experience), *give* (compromise; flexibility), *pull* (special advantage), *steal* (slang, a bargain).

The deverbal nouns may be used:

(1) To denote the state of mind or sensation: *desire, dismay, doubt, love, smell, taste, want*

(2) To denote an event or activity: *attempt, fall, hit, laugh, release, search, swim*

(3) As object of the given verb: *answer, bet, catch, find*

(4) As subject of the given verb: *bore* (somebody who or something that bores/is boring), *cheat, coach*

(5) As instrument of the given verb: *cover* (something with which to cover things), *paper, wrap, wrench*

(6) As manner of the given verb: *walk* (manner of walking), *throw, lie*

(7) As place of the given verb: *divide* (a period marking the divide, especially watershed), *retreat, rise, turn*

It should be pointed out that some deverbal nouns, just like some denominal verbs already discussed, acquire a new meaning of their own. For example, both *meet* and *meeting* refer to a gathering of people, but *meet* indicates particularly "a gathering of people for sports events". The noun *exhibit* also differs from *exhibition* in that an exhibit is only one of the things found at an exhibition.

On occasion, some stylistic differentiation exists between two words. For example, *invite*, when used as a noun, is a colloquial expression, e.g., "I've got a dinner invite from Mr. Smith." But when you send someone an invitation to dinner, you must use *invitation* instead of *invite*. The noun *invite* strikes many ears as casual or even slangy and is not appropriate to the occasion.

Nouns can be converted not only from verbs but from almost any other part of speech as well, though less commonly. For example:

- The manager has a fit of the *blues*. (adjective into noun)
- You should know all the *ins* and *outs* by now. (adverb into noun)
- Would you like a *with* or a *without*? (preposition into noun)
- Is Joan's new baby a *he*? (pronoun into noun)
- This book is a *must* for students of English. (auxiliary verb into noun)
- His talk contains too many *ifs* and *buts*. (conjunction into noun)

This kind of conversion without formal distinction is often accused of causing ambiguity (e.g., Her eyes like angels watch them still), but in the majority of cases it is certain that no ambiguity arises. The context and the syntactic structures will usually rule out the possibility of ambiguity. No doubt conversion contributes to the economy of the English language, and this partly accounts for the rapid growth of words converted.

4.2.3 Compounding

Compounding or composition is a word-formation process consisting of joining two or more bases to form a new word. As one of the oldest methods of word formation, it has been productive in every period of the English language. English now makes more use of compounding than at any previous time in its history. The percentage of new words coined by compounding is estimated to be 27 % of the total new vocabulary after World War Ⅱ.

A compound is a lexical unit consisting of more than one base and functioning both grammatically and semantically as a single word. However, there is no one formal criterion that can be used for a general definition of compounds in English. The relative criteria of a compound word suggested by linguists are as follows:

1. Orthographic criterion

solid: *motorcycle, bottleneck*

hyphenated: *baby-sitter, sun-bathing*

open: *living room, walking stick*

Besides, some compounds may link their components by a vowel (*handicraft, speedometer*), by a preposition (*brother-in-law, man of war*), or by *-'s* (*New Year's Eve, Women's Day*). But the bulk of compounds are formed in the first three ways.

Spelling varies in many words and some compounds may even occur in three different forms, "solid", "hyphenated" and "open". For example:

year book	*year-book*	*yearbook*
girl friend	*girl-friend*	*girlfriend*
flower pot	*flower-pot*	*flowerpot*

The general tendency nowadays is for compounds to be written solid as they become established; otherwise, they are written open. The ready examples are time adverbs *today, tonight* and *tomorrow*, which were formally written as *to-day, to-night,* and *to-morrow* in *The Oxford English Dictionary* when it was published in 1909.

2. Phonological criterion

Many compounds have a so-called compound accent, i.e., a single stress on the first component, as *'keyhole* and *'doorway*; or the main stress on the first component and a secondary stress on the second component, as *'dark ˌroom, 'hot ˌhouse* and *'black ˌbird*.

A compound accent is different from a free phrase accent, which has a secondary stress on the first word and then the main stress on the second word, as in a *dark 'room,* a *hot 'house,* and a *black 'bird*. Usually, compounds differ from structurally similar free phrases in meaning. A *'dark room* is a room in which photographs can be developed while a *dark 'room* simply means a room which is dark; a *'hot house* indicates a warm building where flowers and delicate plants can grow, whereas a *hot 'house* merely denotes a house that is hot; a *'black bird* is a species of European and American birds, including a European singing bird with a yellow beak, whereas a *black 'bird* is just a bird that has very dark feathers. From these examples, we can see that a compound expresses a single idea that is not identical in meaning to the sum of the meanings of the words in a free phrase.

However, the phonological criterion does not always work. As we know, well-established compounds may be accented as phrases as in *head'master, cottage'cheese,* and *mountain'ash*.

Compounds of the participial adjective-noun kind, like *minced 'meat, inverted 'comma*, and *split in'finitive* always have phrase accents.

3. Semantic criterion

According to Jespersen (2014), the orthographic and phonological criteria are not satisfactory as they have defects and many exceptions. He defines a compound as a unit forming a single idea. But this is still a rather vague criterion. What does this single idea represent? Does it refer to the sum of the combined meanings of components of a compound or to the single meaning not expressed by the combination? In actual usage, either of the above two types of compounds exists. For example, *night school* is a school that opens at night; but *nighthawk* or *nightbird* denotes a person with the habit of staying up and doing things at night. So, it is better to say that the meaning of a compound may be closely related to but cannot always be directly inferred from the meanings of its component parts.

Compounds are classified according to their parts of speech into noun compounds, adjective compounds, and verb compounds.

1) Noun compounds

Noun compounds are sub-classified into the following types according to the syntactic relation of the component parts.

(1) Subject and verb: The subject may be either before or after the verb; when the verb stands before the subject, the former may adopt the *-ing* form. For example:

bus stop	*daybreak*
layboy	*search party*
helping hand	*cleaning lady*

(2) Verb and object: The object may stand either before or after the verb; the verb may adopt the *-ing* form when being placed after the object. There is a productive subtype of "object + agential noun in *-er/-or*". For example:

bookreview	*haircut*
bookkeeping	*sightseeing*
songwriter	*radio-operator*

(3) Verb and adverbial: The noun adverbial may express place, instrument, time, and other meanings. For example:

writing desk (writing at a desk)

sewing machine (sewing with a machine)

sun-bathing (bathing in the sun)

sleep walking (walking in one's sleep)

smallpox vaccination (vaccinating against smallpox)

(4) Subject and object. For example:

coal fire (coal lights the fire)

oil well (well produces oil)

security officer (officer who looks after security)

(5) Subject and complement. For example:

killer shark (The shark is a killer)

woman writer (The writer is a woman)

catfish (The fish is like a cat)

frogman (The man is like a frog)

(6) Restrictive relation (the first element restricts the meaning of the second). For example:

window curtain (a curtain for the window)

lunch time (time for lunch)

night school (a school at night)

raindrop (a drop of rain)

website (a site on the web)

(The last three types listed above are verbless compounds.)

Compound nouns can also be formed from phrasal verbs, e.g., *breakdown*, *take-off*, *building-up*, and *hold-up*. But these may also be regarded as examples of conversion.

2) Adjective compounds

Adjective compounds are also sub-classified according to the syntactic relation of the constituents.

(1) Subject and verb: The verb is in the form of a *-ed* participle. Examples are *man-made* satellite which means "man makes the satellite", and *mother-dominated* family means "mother dominates the family". Other examples include *frost-bitten, hen-pecked, ice-bound, noon-struck, moss-grown, moth-eaten, poverty-stricken, rat-infested, rocket-assisted, self-appointed, self-taught, sun-baked, tailor-made*, and *windswept*.

(2) Verb and object: The verb is in the form of *-ing* participle, e.g., *English-speaking*

(countries) means "countries that speak English"; *heart-breaking* (news) means "news that breaks the heart". Other examples are *breath-taking, death-defying, eye-catching, fact-finding, freedom-loving, hair-raising, life-giving, painstaking, record-breaking, self-sacrificing, time-consuming,* and *time-serving*.

(3) Verb and adverbial: The verb is in the form of *-ing* participle or *-ed* participle; e.g., *daydreaming* (to dream during the day), *fist-fighting* (to fight with fists), *spoon-fed* (to be fed with a spoon), and *heartfelt* (to be felt by heart).

(4) Verbless compounds: *carsick* (sick due to traveling in a car), *duty-free* (free from duty), *deaf-mute* (both deaf and mute), *bitter-sweet* (sweet but bitter), *user-friendly* (friendly to users), and *camera-shy* (shy before the camera).

Adjective compounds may also be formed from:

(1) Bare infinitive or an adjective/adverb + an infinitive. For example:

- Then a wicked, *just-dare-me* smile crosses his face. (*Reader's Digest*, May, 1983)
- Others are convinced that the *lock-'em-up* approach is meaningless. (*Newsweek*, September 13, 1982)
- an *easy-to-follow* text
- a *soon-to-be-completed* internal airport (*Newsweek*, April 11, 1983)

(2) Clauses. Premodifying clauses contain two types: the hyphenated and the unhyphenated. For example:

- Reagan's packaging was as careful as his *I'm-not-war-monger* prose. (*Newsweek*, September l, 1980)
- …in the current "*Smoking-Is-Dangerous-To-Your-Health*" era. (*The New York Times*, January 4, 1981)
- …his off-the-cuff, "*if you've seen one redwood you've seen them all*" remarks (*Newsweek*, March 7, 1983)

A premodifying clause is itself an imperative or a complex sentence. For example:

- This brusque, *let's-get-on-with-it* transition caters to Shaw's penchant for rapid movement. (*Linguistics and Literary Style*)
- Then *I-have-a-granddaughter-who-writes-too* conversational gambit has the additional effect. (*Newsweek*, March 21, 1983)

The placing of attributive complexes such as infinitive phrases and clauses before the headword is a significant sign that the English language is developing into a more highly analytic language. In this particular aspect, English is approaching the syntactic sequence of Chinese, which invariably places an attribute, whether a noun, an adjective, a phrase, or a clause, before the headword. The following sentences, if interpreted into Chinese, would be similar to the Chinese counterparts in word order. For example:

- …*his I-don't-care-whether-you're-listening* manner
- The media's traditional *bad-news-is-good-news* policy (*Newsweek*, February 14, 1983)

3) Verb compounds

Verb compounds may arise in two ways: by back-formation from a noun or adjective compounds, and by conversion from noun compounds. Verb compounds are likely to be written solid or hyphenated; they appear as two separate components much less often than noun compounds. As far as accent is concerned, derived verb compounds follow the pattern of their source constructions.

(1) Verb compounds are formed by back-formation, which is a reversal of derivation, for example, *to globe-trot* is formed by deleting *-ing* and *-er* from *globe-trotting* and *globe-trotter*. Similar examples are *to brainwash, to ghost-write, to sleep-walk*. It often cannot be decided with certainty whether the form with *-er* or the form with *-ing* provides the starting point for a back-formed verb compound. *Brainwashing* seems the most likely source for the first of the three examples, *ghost-writer* for the second; the *-er* and the *-ing* endings for *to sleep-walk* seem equally probable sources.

Further examples of compound verbs formed by the deletion of an *-er* or *-ing* ending are:

to air-condition	*to baby-sit*	*to book-keep*
to browbeat	*to caretake*	*to gatecrash*
to gift-wrap	*to housekeep*	*to mass-produce*
to proof-read	*to sightsee*	*to spring-clean*
to stage-manage	*to tape-record*	*to window-shop*

(2) Verb compounds formed by conversion. In this case, the verb compounds are converted from noun compounds. For example:

to blue-pencil	*to cold-shoulder*	*to honeymoon*
to machine-gun	*to nickname*	*to outline*
to shipwreck	*to snowball*	

There are two types of syntactic relations in verb compounds formed by back-formation:

object + verb: *sightsee* (to see sights), *brainwash* (to wash one's brain)

adverbial + verb: *day-dream* (to dream during the day), *tape-record* (to record on magnetic tape)

English compounds have the following two characteristics.

(1) Indivisibility: This refers to the impossibility of inserting another element between the components of a compound. This is especially true with noun compounds and verb compounds. As to adjective compounds made up of an infinitive or a clause, the tie between the elements is not so tight. In some cases, it is possible to add a modifier or replace a word in one place or another. For example, one can say *a very-easy / difficult-to-read text*. This is due to the nonce character of adjective compounds of the type.

(2) Brevity and vividness: Compounds are often used because of their brevity and vividness. For example, *a night school* is more concise than "a school which opens at night". A paraphrase of "a *buy-what-you-need* kind of Christmas" would read as "a kind of Christmas when you should or could buy what you need", by adding the relative adverb, the subject, and the modal verb. It is their brevity and also their vividness and impressiveness brought about by their unusual syntactic position that have formed a striking feature of journalistic writing. Moreover, attributive complexes of adjective compounds cater to the journalistic need to save space. Consequently, their use is on the increase at present.

4.3 Minor Processes of Word Formation

Besides the three major processes of word formation (derivation, conversion, and compounding), English also employs some minor word-formation processes. Here are some minor ones.

4.3.1 Clipping

This term refers to the subtraction of one or more syllables from a word, which is also available in its full form. The clipped form is normally felt to be informal. Clippings may be put into four types:

1. Front clippings

The deletion occurs at the beginning of a word: *phone* (telephone), *plane* (aeroplane), *bus* (omnibus), *copter* (helicopter), *varsity* (university), *chute* (parachute), *quake* (earthquake), and *cab* (taxicab).

2. Back clippings

The deletion may occur at the end of a word. This is the most common type of clipping. Examples: *ad* (advertisement), *exam* (examination), *lit* (literature), *gym* (gymnasium), *lab* (laboratory), *photo* (photograph), *taxi* (taxicab), *memo* (memorandum), *dorm* (dormitory), and *corona* (coronavirus).

3. Front and back clippings

It is not a common type of clipping. The deletion occurs at both ends of a word: *flu* (influenza), *fridge* (refrigerator), *script* (prescription), and *tec* (detective).

4. Phrase clippings

This involves the shortening of an adjective-noun phrase into a word, and usually, a part of the adjective is retained. Examples are *lube* (lubricating oil), *op* (optical art), *pop* (popular music), *pub* (public house), *prefab* (prefabricated structure), *perm* (permanent wave), and *zoo* (zoological garden).

Apart from the above four types, other irregular clippings are *bike* (bicycle), *mike* (microphone), and *pram* (perambulator). Clippings with *-y*, *-ie* or *-o* suffixes include *hanky* or *hankie* (handkerchief), *comfy* (comfortable), *telly* (television), *Aussie* (Australian), *bookie* (bookmaker), *commie* (communist), *veggies* (vegetables), *ammo* (ammunition), *dyno* (dynamic), and *aggro* (aggression).

4.3.2　Blending

Blending is the process of word formation in which a new word is made by combining the meanings of two words, one of which is not or neither of which is in its full form: *videophone* (video + telephone), and *smog* (smoke + fog). Blends may fall into four types:

1. The first part of the first word + the last part of the second word

brunch (breakfast + lunch)

beautility (beauty + utility)

botel (boat + hotel)

motel (motor + hotel)

telecast (television + broadcast)

multiversity (multiple + university)

coronacation (coronavirus + vacation)

2. The first part of the first word + the first part of the second word

Amerind (American + Indian)

comsat (communication + satellite)

hi-fi (high + fidelity)

sci-fi (science + fiction)

sitcom (situation + comedy)

telex (teleprinter + exchange)

hi-tech (high + technology)

3. The first word + the last part of the second word

cablegram (cable + telegram)

lunarnaut (lunar + astronaut)

travelogue (travel + catalogue)

sportscast (sports + broadcast)

slimnastics (slim + gymnastics)

netizen (net + citizen)

4. The first part of the first word + the second word

hi-rise (high + rise)

autoroute (automobile + route)

medicare (medical + care)

Eurasia (European + Asia)

sociolinguistics (social + linguistics)

Brexit (British exit)

Blending is a very productive process, especially in commercial and journalistic coinages. Some blends are short-lived novelties but many become well-established as in *dish-mobile* (dishwasher + mobile), *Egg-a-Matic* (egg + a + automatic), *garbax* (garbage + bag), *moped* (motor-assisted + pedal-cycle), *dawk* (dove + hawk), and *stagflation* (stagnation + inflation).

Others again achieve a brief surge of productivity under the impact of a remarkable social event. In the years following the Washington Watergate scandal, the name Watergate became a model for such blends as *Irangate* and *Dianagate*. All of these denote specific cases of social events taking place at a specific time.

Science and technology are always the main source of blends, as in *telex* (teleprinter + exchange), *skylab* (sky + laboratory), and *lidar* (light + radar). Politics, finance, and culture also give rise to many blends: *Commart* (Common + market), *Euro-currency* (Europe + currency), *Eurovision* (European + television), *Chinglish* (Chinese + English), and *Oxbridge* (Oxford + Cambridge). Ever since the publication of Lewis Carroll's *Through the Looking Glass*, a novel full of blends, the number of blends is on a great increase.

4.3.3 Acronymy: Initialisms and Acronyms

Acronymy denotes a word-formation process whereby a proper name or a phrase is formed from the initial letters of words. As a device of shortening, to avoid saying or printing long titles or names of organizations, acronymy is as old as language itself. But acronymy has undergone a sudden rapid growth since the 1930s with American President Roosevelt's New Deal and "alphabetic agencies" such as *NIRA* (National Industrial Recovery Act) and *WPA* (Works Progress Administration). World War Ⅱ provided many, but some of them were short-lived, for example, *CARE* (Committee for American Relief in Europe) and *SHAPE* (Supreme Headquarters of the Allied Powers in Europe) which were the war products and have ceased their existence today. However, the number of acronymy has been on a constant increase in recent years. There are two types of acronymy: initialisms and acronyms.

Initialisms, also called "alphabetisms", are pronounced as sequences of letters: *VOA* (Voice of America) and *BBC* (British Broadcasting Corporation).

The usual practice in the past was to put a period after each letter of an initialism, but the tendency today is to omit periods, especially for the names of well-established organizations or conventional titles, e.g., *CBE* (Commander of the British Empire) rather than *C.B.E.*; *FRS* (Fellow of the Royal Society) rather than *F.R.S.* Some initialisms, however, appear both with or without periods: *C.O.D.* or *COD* (Concise Oxford Dictionary).

There are three types of initialisms:

(1) The letters represent full words. For example, *IOC* (International Olympic Committee), *IMF* (International Monetary Fund), *NSF* (National Science Foundation), *PC* (Peace Corps), *ASAP* (as soon as possible), *MVP* (most valuable player), *IQ* (intelligence quotient), *IT* (information technology), *WTO* (World Trade Organization), *VR* (virtual reality), *UFO* (unidentified flying object), *PLA* (People's Liberation Army), *PRC* (People's Republic of China), and *GDP* (Gross Domestic Product).

(2) The letters represent elements in a compound or just parts of a word. For example, *GHQ* (General Headquarters), *ID* (Identification Card), *ETV* (Educational Television), and *CCTV* (China Central Television).

(3) A letter represents the complete form of the first word, while the second word is

in full form. For example, *D Notice* (Defence Notice), *N-bomb* (Nuclear bomb), *G-man* (Government man), and *D-Day* (the day of the allied invasion of Western Europe in World War II). Examples like *V. J. Day* (Victory over Japan Day) also belong to this type. Some linguists call this type "semi-acronyms".

Acronyms differ from initialisms in that they are pronounced as words rather than sequences of letters, for example, *laser* is pronounced /ˈleizə/ rather than /el-ei-es-iː-aː/. For examples *TESL* /ˈtesl/ (Teaching English as a Second language), *TOEFL* /təʊfl/ (Test of English as a Foreign Language), *NATO* /ˈneitəʊ/ (the North Atlantic Treaty Organization), and *UNESCO* /juˈneskəʊ/ (the United Nations Educational, Scientific and Cultural Organization).

Some acronyms are usually spelled in small letters, e.g., *laser* and *radar*.

Initialisms and acronyms are mainly used in the following fields:

(1) The names of organizations and places. For example, *NPC* (National People's Congress), *CPPCC* (Chinese People's Political Consultative Conference), *APEC* (Asia-Pacific Economic Cooperation), *EU* (European Union), *LA* (Los Angeles), and *AE* (Arizona).

(2) The titles of technical or professional posts. For example, *MA* (Master of Arts), *BA* (Bachelor of Arts), *TA* (Teaching Assistant), and *MP* (Member of Parliament).

(3) Occupational jargons. For example, *ESP* (English for Special Purposes), *COLA* (cost-of-living adjustment), and *ECM* (electronic countermeasure).

(4) The names of the mechanisms. For example, *ICBM* (intercontinental ballistic missile), *NS* (nuclear ship), *SLV* (satellite launch vehicle), and *SST* (supersonic transport).

(5) Words of daily life. For example, *OK*, *O.K.*, or *Okay* (probably standing for Old Kinderhook, the nickname of Martin van Buren, an American ex-president, whose birthplace was Kinderhood in the state of New York), *ID* (identification card), and *VIP* (very important person).

Organizations are fond of using initialisms and acronyms to make themselves vivid and impressive, e.g., *NOW* (National Organization of Women) which implies that "Now it is the time to struggle for women's rights"; *SCARE* (Students Concerned About a Ravaged Environment) which connotes the students' worry about the scaring environment; *PEN* (Poets, Essayists, Novelists) which is a society of literates; *GASP* (Great Alliance to Stop Pollution) which implies that air has become so polluted that we are gasping for breath.

Moreover, initialisms and acronyms are also used for euphemisms, e.g., *DOA* (dead on arrival) and *PNG* (persona non grata) which help to avoid mentioning unpleasant things in a straight-forward way.

4.3.4 Back-Formation

Back-formation refers to a type of word formation by which a shorter word is made by deleting a supposed affix from an already existing longer word. For example, the verb *televise* has been produced by back-formation from the noun *television*, though the *-ion* is an integral part of the word; the verb *burgle* is back-formed from the noun *burglar* on the assumption that the *-ar* was a suffix like the *-er*. Hence, back-formation reverses the more common process of derivation and is itself a process of shortening.

Back-formation is particularly productive in creating de-nominal verbs. When people come across nouns ending in *-er*, *-ar*, *-or* and *-sion*, they often take it for granted that what precedes these endings must be verb bases, so they unconsciously create new verbs by deleting the supposed suffixes. For example: *beg* from *beggar*, *cobble* from *cobbler*, *edit* from *editor*, *denote* from *denotion*, *loaf* from *loafer*, and *lase* from *laser*.

A particularly productive type of back-formation occurs with the noun compounds in *-er* and *-ing*. For example: *baby-sit* from *baby-sitter*, *brain-wash* from *brain-washing*, *bulldoze* from bulldozer, *caretake* from *caretaker*, *chain-smoke* from *chain-smoker*, and *sight-see* from *sight-seeing*.

Less common are verbs back-formed from adjectives, such as *cose* from *cosy*, *frivol* from *frivolous*, *laze* from *lazy*, and *peeve* from *peevish*.

A now obsolete adverbial suffix *-ling* was removed from *darkling*, *groveling*, and *sidling* to produce the verbs *darkle, grovel* and *sidle*. The verb *gangle* is coined from *gangling*, which was originally not an adverb but a participial adjective.

English has a few nouns back-formed from adjectives such as *gloom* from *gloomy*, and *greed* from *greedy*.

Less common are words formed by dropping prefixes. A recent example is *flappable* (from *unflappable*) meaning "easily upset or confused, especially in a crisis", which is labeled "slang" by *The Random House College Dictionary* published in 1988.

Interestingly, back-formation may even occur with proper nouns. For example, the verb *to bant* comes from a Canadian doctor Frederick Banting (1891–1941), who created a healing method of slimming down by dieting; the verb *to maffick* is derived from *Mafeking*, a place in South Africa where a carnival was once held on May 17, 1900; *to deep-freeze* comes from the trademark "Deep Freezer".

No doubt many back-formed words are fully acceptable in contemporary English, but a few of them are dubious, at least to some scholars. For example, in *The Random House College Dictionary*, *to enthuse* from *enthusiasm* "is felt by many to be poor style, and in formal writing, it would be best to paraphrase it". Other examples may be *to liaise* from *liaison* and *to reminisce* from *reminiscence*. Besides some back-formed words, we have a humorous and nonce character, as in *bish* with the sense of "officiate as bishop" in "When does the bishop bish?" During the ruling period of King Edward VII (1900–1910), the question "Do you kipple?" meant "Do you like reading Kippling's novels?"

4.3.5 Words from Proper Names

A great number of common words have been created from proper names in English. The transition from proper names to common words occurs not only with names of people and places, but also with book titles, literary characters, and trademarks. Several types of them are classified according to their sources as follows:

1. Words from the names of scientists

It is a usual practice to name scientific inventions and diaries after the inventors and discoverers. For example, the word *newton*, the derived SI unit of force, is named after Sir Isaac Newton, a great English scientist and formulator of the law of gravity. *Aldrin*, an insecticide, originated from Kurt Aldrin, a German chemist. A more recent example is *Alzheimer's disease*, a progressive organic disease involving degeneration of the brain's nerve cells, resulting in confusion and disorientation. The term comes from its discoverer Alois Alzheimer, a German doctor. *Pasteurization* and *pasteurize* are two words from Louis Pasteur, who is a French chemist and biologist. His research showing that the fermentation of milk and wine was due to the multiplication of bacteria and other microorganisms led to the discovery of the role of microorganism in human and animal disease. From these findings, he developed immunization by inoculation of attenuated microbes, and the process of pasteurization. Pasteurization is a process that renders milk free of disease-producing bacteria and helps to prevent it from spoiling without destroying the vitamins or changing the taste. It involves heating the milk to 62℃ – 65℃ for 30 minutes. To pasteurize is to sterilize by pasteurization.

Other familiar instances are the terms of electric energy—*watt*, *volt*, *ohm*, and *ampere* which are respectively from four distinguished 18th century scientists James Watt, Alessandro Volta, Georg Ohm, and Andre Ampere.

2. Words from the names of politicians and celebrities

A card game called *napoleon* is named after Napoleon Bonaparte, an emperor of France.

Ngugi, a beverage of wine and hot water with sugar, nutmeg, and lemon, is named after its inventor Colonel Francis Negus who died in 1732. A kind of bread sandwich comes from the fourth Earl of Sandwich. Even a girl name Nelly has come to denote a cheap red wine called *nelly*. *Nicotine*, a poisonous alkaloid found in tobacco leaves, is named after Jean Nicot, a French diplomat who introduced tobacco into France in the 16th century.

3. Words from place names

Places have been a rich source of this word-formation process. For example, *annabergite*, a mineral occurring in apple-green crystalline mass, is named after Annaberg, a town in Saxony, Germany. Another two German places name Homburg and Hamburg have helped to produce a man's felt hat *homburg* and the food *Hamburg* steak. The wine *champagne* was originally made in the region of Champagne, France. Now books are bound in *morocco leather*, and plates are made of *china*.

4. Words from literature

Literature is always a main source of new words, including words from proper names. *Odyssey*, for example, meaning "any long series of wanderings", comes from Homer's epic poem *Odyssey* in which the hero Odysseus wandered for ten years after the Trojan War. From the Bible, we get a *Judas* meaning a traitor and a *Solomon* meaning a wise person. From Shakespeare, we get a *Shylock*, a cruel and greedy man, and a *Romeo*, a lover. Greek and Roman myths beget words such as *Hercules*, a man of unusual strength, and *Neptunian* from Neptune, the god of the sea. The following are more examples:

Tantalize: It comes from Tantalus, a king in Greek mythology who is punished for his misdeeds by having to stand in water that recedes when he tries to drink it and under fruit that moves away as he reaches for it.

Argus: Argus is a giant with 100 eyes in Greek mythology. After he was killed, his eyes were transferred to the Peacock's tail. From Argus comes the word *Argus-eyed*, which means "keen-sighted; observant". For example, "We have decided it is impossible to cheat when that *Argus-eyed* professor gives an exam."

Narcissus: Narcissus, in Greek mythology is the name of a beautiful youth who fell in love with his reflection in a pool, hence comes the word *narcissism* and the meaning: of an interest in or admiration for oneself.

Munchausen: He was a German soldier. After his retirement from his service in the Russian Army against the Turks, he told exaggerated stories of his campaigning adventures, thus the meaning "a person who boasts; exaggerated".

Christopher Pinchbeck: He was a British jeweler. He invented an alloy of copper, zinc formerly used for cheap jewelery, hence the meaning: specious and spurious goods.

Frankenstein: He is a character in the novel written by the famous British woman writer Mary W. Shelley. He is a medical researcher, who created a robot monster, brought it to life, and finally was killed by the monster. For example, "the United States is raising a *Frankenstein* by providing hardware to that country."

This word-formation process even occurs with some book titles. *Alice-in-Wonderland* by Lewis Carroll comes to mean "something illusive, illogical or paradoxical"; *The Razor's Edge* by Somerset Maugham now denotes a difficult position between success and failure, as illustrated by the phrase "a razor's edge situation between peace and war".

5. Words from trademarks

Some trademarks have become generic, for example, *Kodak*, formerly a trademark, now means a portable camera introduced by George Eastman in 1888; *nylon*, a strong elastic material, was also formally a trademark.

"Hoover", "Whiteout", and "Mace" are the trademarks respectively for a type of vacuum cleaner, a white correcting fluid and a liquid causing tears and nausea, used as a spray for riot control. Again, these trademarks have undergone communization and picked up ordinary meanings: *to hoover* a floor, *to white out* a mistake, *to mace* demonstrators. The same applies to *picturephone*, *xerox*, *frisbee*, *kleenex*, and *vaseline*, which were formally trademarks.

As shown by many of the above examples, when a proper name joins the common vocabulary, it tends to lose its capital letter. Some may even change their spellings, e.g., *bowler* from a hat merchant Mr. Beaulieu; *calico*, a type of heavy cotton cloth, is from the Indian city Calicut; *maccaboy* or *maccabaw*, a kind of snuff, is produced in a West Indian island Macouba; *cashmere*, a kind of fine soft wool, is made from the long hair of a type of goat in Kashmir. More examples:

Irenic (peace-loving) comes from Irene, the Greek goddess of peace.
Stentorian (uncommonly loud) comes from Stentor, whose voice is loud.
Morphine comes from Morpheus, the god of sleep.
Solecism comes from Soloi, an Athenian colony of Cilicia where the inhabitants spoke another form of Greek.

Some words from proper names can adopt the plural form, e.g., *Wellingtons*, a leather boot with the front part of the top extending above the knee, is originally from Duke of Wellington, a British general who defeated Napoleon at the Battle of Waterloo. *Nylons*, a kind of nylon stockings, is another ready example.

Words from proper names can develop into clipped forms (mackintosh → mack, Wellingtons → Wellies, Coca-Cola → Coke), blends (beef + hamburger → beefburger, cheese + hamburger → cheeseburger), and back-formed words (Mafeking → maffick, Banting → bant, Quisling → quisle).

4.3.6　Miscellaneous

So far, there are still some minor word-formation processes unmentioned. One of them is neo-classical formation, which refers to the process of using Latin and Greek elements to form new words. The majority of such formations are in learned and scientific fields. Some scientific vocabularies are almost entirely made up of them. Chemical names are, for example, basically neo-classical in form. These are the stems of *benz-* and *chlor-*, the prefixes of *di-* and *para-*, and the suffixes of *-ene* and *-me*. The reason why this has come to be so is related to historical and psychological factors. The renewed study of classics in the Renaissance (14th–17th centuries) resulted in the influx of many Greek and Latin words, most of which were literary, technical, and scientific words. It was the usual practice then to receive ideas as well as words from classical authors. When new ideas and new objects developed and demanded linguistic expression, scholars were still accustomed to drawing upon the Greek and Latin vocabulary in preference to their own native stock of words. They believed that the use of Greek and Latin elements might add dignity and seriousness to new words. Today, this type of neo-classical formation is still productive. We have observed that many new branches of science adopt their names with Greek elements: *codicology*, *cytology*, *aeroacoustics*, *astrochemistry*, *embryology*, and *psychopharmacology*, to mention only a few.

The neo-classical formation is productive not only in English but also in French, Spanish, Russian, and some other languages. Some of the neo-classical scientific terms are labeled ISV (International Scientific Vocabulary) in *The Third Webster* published in 1961 to denote that "they are known to be current in at least one language other than English", so it can be predicted that the number of neo-classical words will keep increasing with the exploding growth of science and technology.

A less productive word-formation process is reduplication, by which a compound word is formed from two or more elements, either identical or slightly different, e.g., *goody-goody* and *criss-cross*.

The common uses of reduplicative are:

(1) to imitate sounds, as in *tick-tock* of a dock and *bow-wow* or *woof-woof* of a dog.

(2) to suggest alternating movements, as in *flip-flops* of slippers, *ping-pong* of table tennis, and *zig-zag* of a line or pattern.

(3) to disparage by suggesting instability, nonsense, insincerity, or vacillation, as in *higgledy-piggledy* (in disorder, mixed together without system), *hocus-pocus* (trickery, deception), *wishy-wash* (without strength, weak) and *silly-shally* (waste time without reaching a decision or taking actions).

(4) to intensify, as in *teeny-weeny* (very small) and *tip-top* (of the highest quality).

The process of analogical creation has also begotten many new words. For example, *Jane Crow* is derived from *Jim Crow*; *workaholic* from *alcoholic*; *wordsmith* from *blacksmith*; *girlcott* from *boycott*; *brawn drain* from *brain drain*; *househusband* from *housewife* by analogy. Such familiar terms as *missile gap* and *environmental pollution* have given rise to a long series of new terms in contemporary English: *cultural gap, development gap, credibility gap, research gap, information gap,* and *generation gap; cultural pollution, graffiti pollution, noise* or *sound pollution,* and *visual* or *eye pollution.* This shows the important role of analogy in word formation.

To sum up, words formed by these minor processes we have dealt with so far account for over 26% of the new vocabulary after World War II. They are therefore very active in English word formation today.

Exercises

I. **Combine the two sentences in each group into one sentence by turning one of them into a noun phrase.**

1. The worker perfected the operation rapidly.
This astonished the technician.

2. The engineer explained the technique brilliantly.
This impressed all of us.

3. This pipe was eroded quickly.
This surprised everyone.

4. The professor determined the value correctly.
This made the experiment possible.

5. Advantages and disadvantages exist in each case.

We know it clearly.

II. Tell the semantic difference between the two words in each pair.

1. astronaut, astronomer

2. astrology, astronomy

3. anthropoid, anthropomorphic

4. homochromous, heterochromous

5. homogeneous, heterogeneous

6. historic, historical

7. politic, political

8. psychiatrist, psychologist

9. pediatrics, paedeutics

10. parenthood, parentage

III. Pick out the converted words in the sentences below and state the word class of the converted words and their meanings and to what word class the base of each of the converted words belongs.

1. Bill chaired the meeting.

2. They gifted him with a watch.

3. Let's get on with the clean-up.

4. They downed tools in protest.

5. This speech was to be a Nixon original.

6. Mary bottled the juice and canned the pickles.

7. If you uh-uh again, I won't go on with my story.

8. There will be a repeat of this program next week.

9. This book is a must for the student of English.

10. People crowd the glittering neon shopping districts at night to window-shop and people-watch.

IV. Express each of the following in one compound word.

1. an owner of one or more shares in a business

2. a dog kept to guard property

3. sick when in a moving car

4. written on a typewriter

5. someone who is both the producer and director of a film

V. Write out the complete words of the following clips.

1. prefab	2. pram	3. zoo	4. vet	5. combo
6. quotes	7. bike	8. gym	9. dorm	10. hanky
11. gas	12. kilo	13. flu	14. biz	15. comfy

VI. Explain the formation and the meaning of the following blends.

1. medicare   2. telecast   3. comsat   4. Eurasia   5. cinerama

VII. Write out in full the following initialisms.

1. CPC   2. GMT   3. IMF   4. YOLO   5. BRB

Chapter 5

Word Meaning, Polysemy, and Homonymy

This chapter will deal with the relationship between form and meaning, main types of word meaning, and semantic features of words. It will also study polysemy and homonymy.

5.1 Motivation

Motivation refers to the relationship between name and sense, form and meaning. Most English words are non-motivated, since they are conventional, arbitrary symbols. There is no way to explain this or that word has this or that meaning beyond the fact that the people of a given speech community have traditionally agreed to use one to stand for the other.

The non-motivated character of words can be illustrated by the fact that different speech communities may employ different names for the same object. For example, what the English call *bed*, *chair*, *window*, and *wall* are the Frenchmen's *lit*, *chaise*, *fenêtre*, and *mur*. A further illustration is offered by the polysemous nature of words, e.g., the English word *bed* cannot only mean "a piece of furniture upon which a person sleeps", but also mean "a piece or area of ground in a garden or lawn where plants are grown" and "the plants in such areas". The non-motivated nature of most English words can be further depicted by homonyms which are identical in sound or spelling but different in meaning.

Nevertheless, there exist a small number of words whose creation is based on a certain motivation.

5.1.1 Phonetic Motivation

Words motivated phonetically are called onomatopoeic words or echoic words, which are coined in imitation of the sounds associated with the things named. Onomatopoeic words show a close relation of sound to sense: the *baa-baa* of a sheep, the *coo* of a pigeon, the *miaow* of a cat, the *quack* of a duck, and the *woof-woof* or *bow-wow* of a dog.

Since natural sounds such as cries and calls of some animals may be "the same or almost the same in all parts of the world, words created directly from the sounds may share a universal linguistic feature. For example, a bird called *cuckoo* in English is *coucou* in French, *kuckuck* in German, *cuclillo* in Spanish, *cuculo* in Italian, *kakuk* in Hungarian, *kokyx* in Greek, and *bùgu* in Chinese, etc. Here, the referent is more or less closely imitated by the phonetic structures of different languages.

However, the imitative effect of onomatopoeic words is more often than not conventionally symbolic rather than acoustically accurate, as Henry Bradley put it that the resemblance which an imitative word is felt to bear the inarticulate noise which it names consists not so much in similarity of impression on the ear as in similarity of mental suggestion. Quirk (1963: 43) also pointed out: "And even these (echoic words) are conventional to quite a large extent... If you throw a stone into water, the sound you hear is by no means the same as when you say 'splash'."

The symbolic nature of onomatopoeic words may be partly due to the phonetic or morphological restraints. We have observed the fact that different languages may employ different phonetic structures in imitation of the cries of the same animals. For example, the cry of a dog is *wang-wang* in Chinese, but *woof-woof* in English, *gnaf-gnaf* in French, *guau* in Spanish, *amh-amh* in Irish and *wung-wung* in Japanese. We say "狗吠，鸡鸣，鹤唳，猿啼，马嘶，狼嗥，虎啸，狮吼", but dogs *bark*, cocks *crow*, cranes *whoop*, apes *gibber*, horses *neigh* or *snort*, wolves *howl*, tigers *snarl* or *growl* and lions *roar* in English.

5.1.2 Morphological Motivation

Many derivatives and compounds in English are motivated in that their meaning can be inferred partly or entirely from their morphological structures. For example, if one knows the meaning of the agentive suffix *-er* and the root *work*, then one can immediately tell that the meaning of the word *worker* is "a person who works"; if one has learned the words *note* and *book*, then he can certainly infer from the compound *notebook* the meaning "a book in which notes are written". We say that words such as *worker* and *notebook* have a morphological motivation, for a direct association can be observed between their morphological structures and meaning. Besides derivation and compounding, other word-formation processes like blending, back-formation, and words from proper names are also morphologically motivated to a more or less extent. Neo-classical compounds originated from Greek and Latin elements, whose morphological motivation is interpretable only to linguistic experts.

However, one should not take it for granted that words of the above types are always interpretable. The word *inflammable* means the same as *flammable*; *unloosen* is synonymous with *loosen*; *redcap* refers to a military policeman in Britain or a porter in the US; *night-hawk* is not a nocturnal bird but a person with the habit of staying up and doing things at night.

5.1.3 Semantic Motivation

Semantic motivation is based on semantic factors. It is a kind of mental association. When we speak of the foot of a hill, we are comparing the base of a hill to the lower part of a leg below the ankle; when we say the eye of a needle, we are comparing the hole in a needle to man's organ of sight.

Interestingly, we find the Chinese equivalents "山脚" and "针眼". This is no doubt due to the universality of modes of human thought, but it is also natural that different nations may name objects from different angles. The Chinese word "蚯蚓", for example, is so named according to the wriggling movement of the worm; the English *earthworm* (土虫) is named according to the worm's living environment; the German *Regenwurm* (雨虫) is named according to the weather under which the worm comes out to work. Although the same kind of worm is called by different names in the three different languages, these names are all based on the typical features of the referent.

 5.2 Main Types of Word Meaning

Word meaning is made up of various components, which are commonly described as types of meaning. Two main types of word meaning are grammatical meaning and lexical meaning.

5.2.1 Grammatical Meaning

Grammatical meaning is that part of meaning which indicates a grammatical relationship. The meaning of a sentence is not the total of the semantic meanings of the constituent words, because, in addition to the semantic meanings of the words that make up a sentence, words also have grammatical meanings. Let's look at the following examples:

- Mary criticized John.
- John criticized Mary.

The words that make up the above two sentences have the same semantic meanings and references, but the two sentences mean differently. It is the differences in the grammatical meanings of the words that make the two sentences different in meaning. The grammatical relation of *Mary* to the verb *criticized* in the first sentence is different from the grammatical relation of *Mary* to the verb *criticized* in the second sentence.

As stated in Chapter 2, words can be divided into functional words and content words. Grammatical meaning is dominant in functional words. Functional words are determiners, conjunctions, prepositions, and auxiliaries. They do not have much lexical meaning and some of them have no lexical meaning of their own. Their main function is to express various grammatical relationships in and between sentences.

Grammatical meaning also refers to such grammatical concepts as tenses, numbers, cases, comparative degrees, etc. that a word indicates when used in communication. The grammatical meanings of these kinds are often indicated by inflectional morphemes.

The same word may have different grammatical meanings as indicated in the uses of the word *criticize* in the following sentences:

- He criticized me.
- He has criticized me.
- He was criticizing me.
- He often criticizes me.

Different words may have the same grammatical meaning. *Books*, *desks*, and *children* are different words, but their grammatical meaning is the same because all of them indicate the same plural meaning.

5.2.2　Lexical Meaning

Lexical meaning of a word includes the intrinsic meanings of a word and the meanings realized in communication. Lexical meaning may be subdivided into denotative meaning, connotative meaning, social or stylistic meaning, affective meaning, reflected meaning, collocative meaning, and contextual meaning.

1. Denotative meaning

Denotative meaning is sometimes called cognitive or conceptual meaning. In order to communicate with each other, the first thing that human beings have to do is to cut up the world in which human beings are living and use symbols to refer to the things cut up so that they can talk about them using these linguistic symbols. In this sense, denotative meaning is what our words denote or refer to. Denotative meaning may be regarded as the central core or basic meaning of a word. It is basic because it is the same to all the members of a speech community.

Semanticists use componential analysis to break the denotative meaning of a word into its meaning components or semantic features. Semantic features or meaning components of a word can be distinctive or non-distinctive. The distinctive semantic features are the meaning components that can define the word in question. In this sense, the distinctive semantic features constitute the denotative meaning of a word. Take *man* for example. The distinctive semantic features that define the word *man* are [+ Male, + Adult, + Human]. As long as the word *man* is used with these three necessary semantic features included, it can be said that the word *man* has been used correctly in its denotative sense. The denotative meanings of such words as *woman, boy*, and *girl* can be analyzed into the following distinctive semantic features or meaning components:

woman [– Male, + Adult, + Human]

boy [+ Male, – Adult, + Human]

girl [– Male, – Adult, + Human]

By breaking the denotative meaning of a word into its meaning components or semantic features, we can better understand the sense relations that hold between different words.

2. Connotative meaning

In addition to the distinctive semantic features of a word, a word can also possess many non-distinctive and non-criterial semantic features. Take *woman* for example. While three distinctive semantic features such as [– Male, + Adult, + Human] provide a criterion of the correct use of that word in the denotative sense, there are, in addition, many additional, non-criterial and non-distinctive properties that we have learned to expect a referent of *woman* to possess. They include not only physical characteristics (biped, having a womb), but also psychological and social properties (gregarious, subject to maternal instinct), and may extend to features which are merely stereotypes (capable of speech, experienced in cookery, skirt-or-dress-wearing, frail, prone to tears, cowardly, emotional, irrational, inconstant). These non-distinctive features of a word make up the connotative meaning of the word in question. Because these non-distinctive features result from the mental associations that a word acquires in the mind of a language user, connotative meaning is also defined as the mental association that a word or phrase suggests in one's mind; it is the additional meaning that a word or phrase has beyond its denotative meaning. Connotative meanings have the following characteristics.

1) Connotative meanings vary from age to age

A ready example is a rival between the words *black* and *Negro*. Some decades ago, Negro educators and leaders in America fought a long and finally successful fight to get themselves referred to as Negroes with a capital N. But later they were told that Negro was just the white man's word for nigger and must be eliminated in favor of black. So, in the 1960s and 1970s, we witnessed an effort to effect the abandonment of the word Negro in favor of black. This development is reflected in the instructions in the *Boston Globe* stylebook which say, "Use black (lower case), as a racial designation. Negro (upper case) only in direct quotes. But 'Black Power'."

2) Connotative meanings vary from society to society

The fabulous animal dragon, for instance, connotes "sovereignty and supremacy" to the Oriental nations but "fierceness, ferocity, and violence" to most Occidental races. *Road* is another word with different connotations for people of different cultures. To the Eskimos living in the far north of North America and Eastern Siberia, *road* often connotes snow-covered ground, whereas, to us living in cities, *road* connotes smooth and tree-lined avenues crowded with people and heavy traffic.

3) Connotative meanings vary from individual to individual

In talking about connotation, we are in fact talking about the real-world experience we associate with an expression when we use or hear it. Our physical and mental experiences may be different, therefore, the associations that a word gives rise to in our mind may also be different. For example, the word *mother* generally connotes love, care, and tenderness to a normally-bred child, but the word would lose all such connotations to an abandoned child. While the connotative meanings of the word *home* may be "warmth, convenience, etc." to someone who has pleasant experiences with the family members, in the mind of another who has been maltreated in the family, *home* will certainly conjure up a different mental association, therefore, the different connotative meaning. Because our experiences affect the connotations of a word, connotative meaning is regarded as incidental to language rather than an essential part of it.

In conclusion, connotative meaning is relatively unstable, indeterminate, and open-ended. It varies considerably, according to culture, historical period, and the experience of the individual.

5.2.3 Social or Stylistic Meaning

Social meaning is that which reflects the social circumstance of its use. In part, we work out the social meaning through our recognition of different dimensions and levels of style within the same language.

Take geographical dialect for example. Differences in geographical dialects are the result of geographical barriers. By looking at the kind of geographical dialects that one speaks, we may know something about the geographical origin of the speaker. We may even form some social stereotypes against or for the person in question. If someone speaks a local dialect of a backward region, we may come to the biased conclusion that the speaker is poor.

Just as geographical barriers are the causes of geographical dialects, social barriers are the causes of different social dialects. The greater the social differences, the bigger the differences between social dialects. Social dialects can tell us something about the social origin or social status of the speaker. For example, Queen's English, which is spoken by the Royal family members, displays many characteristics:

In selecting words for communication, the royal family members tend to choose *America, cake, helping, ice, lavatory, looking glass, pudding, relatives, rich, Royalties, scent, scurf, sick, sofa, spectacles, writing paper* instead of *the States, pastry, portion, ice-cream, toilet, mirror, dessert, relations, wealthy, Royals, perfume, dandruff, ill, settee, glasses, notepaper.*

Royal family members also show some peculiarities in the way words are pronounced. Table 5–1 are some examples.

Table 5–1　Examples of the difference in pronunciation between general standard English and Queen's English

Words	General standard English	Queen's English
powerless	/ˈpaʊəlis/	/ˈpɑːlis/
fire	/faiə/	/fɑː/
tired	/taiəd/	/tɑːd/
our	/aʊə/	/ɑː/
really	/ˈriəli/	/ˈrɛəli/
house	/haʊs/	/hais/
hello	/heˈləʊ/	/heˈlei/

In addition, language varies according to different provinces, such as the language of the law, the language of science, etc.

Firstly, Language of the law:

General	Specialist
theft	*larceny*
beat	*assault*
burning	*arson*
crime	*felony*

Secondly, Language of science:

General	Specialist
hole	*orifice/cavity*
speed	*velocity*
force	*intensity*

William Saroyan wrote a novel entitled *The Human Comedy* (1943). The following is a passage selected from the novel:

> *Homer sat chewing the dry candy while the Mexican woman talked. "It is our own candy," she said, "from cactus. I made it for my Juanito when he comes home, but you eat it.*

You are my boy, too.

Mrs. Sandoval, a Mexican woman, lives in America, but she still keeps the Mexican way of life. "Candy from cactus" is a typical Mexican homemade candy. Superficially, the word "come" has been wrongly used here in the sentence "I made it for my Juanito when he comes home." However, the writer has every reason to use the form "come" instead of "comes". By using "come" instead of "comes", the writer wants to convey social meaning: Although the old woman lives in America, she has not been well-acculturated into mainstream American society. If "comes" is used, then this social meaning will be lost.

I. V. Morris, in his short story, "The Sampler" (1933), describes a gentleman whose family has come down in the world. The gentleman was short and advanced in age and often suffered from hunger. He always took advantage of the free sampling offered by shops at Christmas and free-sampled the puddings without intending to buy the puddings. Out of sympathy, a young man offered to buy him some puddings. The following are taken from the short story:

> *"Pardon me, sir, will you do me a favor? Let me purchase you one of these puddings. It would give me such pleasure."*
>
> *"Excuse me," he said, … "I do not believe I have the pleasure of knowing you. Undoubtedly, you have mistaken me for someone else." … "Kindly pack me up this one here. I will take it with me."*
>
> *The girl took down the pudding from its stand and started to make a parcel of it, while he pulled out a worn little black pocketbook and began counting out shillings and pennies onto the counter. To save his "honour" he had been forced into a purchase which he could not possibly afford.*

It is not difficult for us to see why the old gentleman has used formal words and structures to talk to the young man. The social meaning that the old gentleman wants to convey is that he comes from the upper class, is well-educated, enjoys high social status and is rich enough to buy the puddings himself.

Other features of language can tell us something about the social relationship between the speaker and the hearer. Very often, we can work out the social relationship between the speaker and the hearer because of the different stylistic meanings that words have. Take the word *mother* for example. It has varied forms used in different dialects or social classes: *mom* (American English [AmE], informal), *mum* (British English [BrE], informal), *mama* (old use, upper class), and *ma* (informal, especially working class). As a general rule, the more formal the words are that participants use for communication, the greater the social distances there are between the participants, the less intimate the social relations between them. The more informal the words that participants use for communication, the more intimate the social relations between the participants in the communication.

Let's look at another example:

- Hey, baby, love those threads. How about doin' the town tonight?

The man who approaches a woman with the above utterance may not be an inner city youth. Although his own usual dialect does not normally greet with "Hey, baby," or use "threads" to mean "clothes", he still may choose that terminology as a way of asserting his masculinity. His "hey, baby" lets the woman know that he does not want their encounter to be formal. It is an invitation to intimacy. Of course, she may not be in accord. If she is not, she responds in a style appropriate both to her status and to the degree of intimacy she prefers. As in:

- I am busy tonight, thank you.

She does not need to comment overtly on his style. Rather, by her responding with a formal style, she instructs him to keep his distance. Her style alone says, "Back off, Jack", although her words do not.

In fact, it would be downright odd if she said something explicit like "I do not want you to be so familiar to me. I do not consider myself a sexually available woman, nor do I wish to be intimate with you." Such messages are usually given by the stylistic meanings of words. Actual words are used only on the rare occasions that the offending party is too obtuse to "get the message".

English is rich in synonyms, and this inevitably leads to stylistic differentiation. There are in English countless pairs of synonyms in which a native term exists side by side with the one borrowed from French, Latin, or Greek. In most cases, the native word is more informal and unpretentious, whereas the foreign word is more learned and bookish.

A set of synonyms such as *steed*, *nag*, *gee-gee*, and *horse* denote the same kind of equine animal, but each term contains its particular shade of stylistic meaning. *Steed* is often used in poetry, and has an archaic ring; *nag* is a slang term and sounds pejorative; *gee-gee* smacks of either racing slang or babytalk; *horse* is a neutral term. Another set of synonyms *residence*, *domicile*, *abode*, and *home* differ in that *residence* belongs to formal style; *domicile* sounds officialese; *abode* is a poetic term and *home* is a neutral term.

Language uses are sometimes inappropriate because of the conflict found in the stylistic meanings expressed. Let's look at the following examples:

- Let's dine on fried chicken.

- Hey, baby, wanna dine tonight?

- Me and Bob are dinin' out.

- Wouldja dine with me tonight?

- Would you dine with me tonight?

- Mrs. Whitmore wishes you to dine with her.

The first four sentences are usually unacceptable. "Fried chicken" is food eaten with the fingers, therefore it is not an appropriate object of *dine*. "Hey, baby" implies that the speaker is a young male trying to put forth a macho image. Since, in English society, being macho is not associated with refinement, such speech forms clash with formal *dine*. In the third sentence, the grammatical variant "me and Bob" is a marker of nonstandard speech. People who use "me and Bob" are not likely to speak of dining no matter how well they eat. The pronunciation of *dinin'* is humorous because the *-in'* replacement for *-ing* is reserved for informal speech, but *dine* is formal. Similarly, *wouldja* is a more casual pronunciation than *would you*. The last two sentences are not humorous because they are entirely formal, hence appropriate for *dine,* although they too could be used facetiously by, say, a person adopting the formal tone for comic effect. In short, as a social indicator, language reflects a speaker's living place, educational background, social status, and social relationship with each other. One's way of speaking can more or less classify him.

5.2.4 Affective Meaning

Affective meaning is concerned with the expression of feelings and attitudes of the speaker or writer. It is largely a parasitic category in the sense that to express our emotions and attitudes, we rely upon the mediation of other categories of meaning such as denotative, connotative, or stylistic meanings. We can feel the strong feeling of hatred in the utterance "I hate you!", because of the denotative content of the word "hate". Most of us have a positive attitude to "home", because of the connotative meanings that the word "home" has in the minds of most of us. These connotative meanings arise from our pleasant experiences when we live at "home". Emotional expression through style comes about, for instance, when we adopt an impolite tone to express displeasure, or when we adopt a casual tone to express friendliness.

Lakoff did an experiment by instructing her students to act too formally to their friends. Their results illustrate how affective meanings can be conveyed by stylistic meanings:

- (In the dormitory)
  Trish: Would it be possible for you to wait for me after class?

Ann: Yes, of course, it's possible. Why are you talking so properly?

Ann responded to both the linguistic and stylistic messages. She answered the question, then attempted to find out why the style was wrong. Notice that when Ann answered the question, she matched Trish's formal style. "Yes, of course, it's possible." is not a usual college girl's response to her roommate. "Yeah, sure." is more likely. Ann felt offended because Trish's formal style implies Trish's maintenance of social distance from Ann and a lack of intimacy.

- (In a car on a date)

  Pat: Jacques, could you tell me how far we are from our destination?

  Jacques: (sarcastically) Yes, Patricia. We are about fifty miles from our destination. Are you satisfied?

Pat used a very formal style to talk to Jack. Jack felt the lack of intimacy in Pat's utterance. He felt hurt. In retaliation, he used the formal variant of his girlfriend's name: Patricia. Even the "yes" is a formal answer. He continued in a super-formal style, to the point of actually mimicking Pat's words.

S. I. Hayakawa, in his book *Language in Thought and Action* published in 1978, described a story. A black sociologist went out for a journey. He was warmly received by a white couple and was provided with all the conveniences that he needed. But the white couple always called the sociologist "nigger". Although the sociologist felt deep gratitude for the white couple for the help they had offered, he was hurt by the address term "nigger":

"Who's insulting you, son?" said the man.

"You are, sir—that name you're always calling me."

"What name?"

"Uh... you know."

"I ain't callin' you no names, son."

"I mean your calling me 'nigger'."

"Well, what's insultin' about that? You are a nigger, ain't you?"

From the above conversation, it can be seen that the conflict results from the failure of the white man to recognize the pejorative feelings caused by the word "nigger". Affective meaning varies in different word classes. Interjections such as *Aha! Alas!* and *Wow!* are charged with emotion, whereas conjunctions, for example, lack the emotive charge.

There are countless pairs of synonyms that may share the same denotation but differ in affective meaning. In the table below, the words in the left column are appreciative, expressing the speaker's approval of the referent; the words in the right column are derogatory, showing disapproval or contempt on the part of the speaker. The words in the middle column carry no emotive charge.

Appreciative	Neutral	Derogative
slim	thin	skinny
loyalty	adherence	partisanship
bachelor girl	single woman	old maid; spinster
innovative	new	newfangled

Besides, a few English suffixes also carry affective meanings. For example, -y and -ie (*daddy*, *auntie*, *girlie*, and *dearie*) express an intimate feeling; *-ard*, *-art*, *-eer*, *-ling* and *-ster* (*drunkard*, *dullard*, *braggart*, *profiteer*, *routineer*, *hireling*, *underling*, *weakling*, *gamester*, *gangster*) are generally charged with a pejorative meaning, expressing disapproval or contempt on the part of the speaker.

Affective meanings of a word may vary with the context:

- He was *proud* and was criticized by the teacher. (pejorative)
- He was *proud* of the achievements that China has made in recent years. (positive)

A word that has an appreciative meaning in one culture may arouse a pejorative feeling in another culture. The affective meanings of the words *individualism* and *collectivism* are certainly different in Chinese culture and English culture. Affective meanings may vary from age to age.

5.2.5 Reflected Meaning

Reflected meaning is the meaning which arises in cases of multiple denotative meaning when one sense of a word forms part of our response to another sense. Some words evoke mental association. In a church service, the synonymous expressions *The Comforter* and *The Holy Ghost*, both refer to the Third Person of the Trinity, but the reactions to these terms can be conditioned by the everyday non-religious meanings of *comfort* and *ghost*. The Comforter sounds warm and "comforting" (although in the religious context, it means "the strengthener or supporter", while *The Holy Ghost* sounds awesome.

Words with unpleasant associative meanings often turn into taboo words. When a student writes such a sentence "Human language is a tool of social intercourse.", his teacher will correct it with the word *communication*. It is because the word *intercourse* calls up a sexual implication. Leech (1987: 23) points out that it becomes more and more difficult for people to use *intercourse*, *ejaculation*, and *erection* without any sexual implications. For the same reason, we now say *rooster* instead of *cock* to denote a species of farmyard bird. When we drink someone's health at a banquet, we now say "Cheers!" instead of "Bottoms up!".

Years ago, China exported a kind of cell with the trademark *White Elephant* and was surprised to find that the product didn't sell in the market. The reason was simple: In *Longman Dictionary of Contemporary English* published in 1978, the phrase *white elephant* means "a usually big object not useful to its owner, though perhaps having cost money, or being given as a present, which the owner wants to get rid of". No one would buy a costly and troublesome thing without any value. We should learn from this lesson that we must pay enough attention to the reflected meaning of a word to guarantee the success of our communication, including business transactions.

5.2.6　Collocative Meaning

Collocative meaning refers to the semantic restriction that determines the collocative relationship between two words, say, an adjective and a noun. For example, the adjectives *addled*, *rancid*, *rotten*, and *sour* are synonymous, all denoting a bad quality of food. But they habitually collocate with different kinds of food; *addled eggs*, *rancid bacon* or *butter*, *rotten butter* or *egg*, and *sour milk*. Hence these adjectives have developed their collocative meanings. The following are more examples:

- *sail a small boat*
  navigate a liner

- *teach arithmetic*
  inculcate doctrine

- *offering to a church*
  dole to the unemployed

Collocative meaning is simply an idiosyncratic property of individual words.

5.2.7　Contextual Meaning

As a word or phrase appears in a sentence, it interacts with other words and acquires part of its meaning from them. For instance, we cannot give a vague word a definite and precise meaning until we see it operating in the given context: "Then one day it (= accident) happened. He reached for a cable, and had had it (= died from the accident)." Another example is the expression "You're welcome (to [do] something)", which generally expresses the speaker's permission to let the addressee use or enjoy something, but which, in certain situations, may suggest the speaker's reluctance or unwillingness to give his permission.

Independent of context, language users may often find it difficult to interpret the meaning of words or expressions.

Here is a celebrated utterance recorded in actual conversation by Pamela Downing: "Please sit in the apple-juice seat."

In isolation, this sentence has no meaning at all since the expression "apple-juice seat" is not a conventional way of referring to any kind of object. But the sentence makes perfect sense in the following context in which it was uttered:

An overnight guest came down to breakfast. There were four place settings, three with orange juice and one with apple juice. It was clear what the apple-juice seat was. And even the next morning, when there was no apple juice, it was still clear which seat was the apple-juice seat.

Contextual meaning may be the same as the denotative meaning, but in some cases, contextual meaning may not be the same as the denotative meaning. In some cases, it may be the opposite of the denotative meaning. For example, if a student did not work hard and got 30 marks out of a total number of 100 marks in an examination, when his parent commented on his performance by saying "You are clever!", in that context, "clever" could be taken to mean "stupid".

Since most words are polysemous, the best way to find the particular meaning you want in the dictionary is first to bear in mind the context (whether sentence or paragraph) in which the word appears; secondly, to read carefully all the definitions listed for the word; and finally, to choose the definition which most nearly fits your context.

But what if the meaning that you need is not listed in the dictionary? What if your dictionary is not available at the moment? The solution to the problem lies in your guessing technique. In many cases, you can guess the meaning of a word by relying on the clues furnished by the context. We can reason easily, for example, that *edifice* means "building" in this context: "The edifice is striking architecturally, but it seems abstract and cold." When a word is used ironically, we understand the contextual meaning rather than its literal meaning. We may hear people saying, "Oh, how I love queuing up!" when in fact they hate it.

5.3 Componential Analysis and Semantic Features

Words can be analyzed and described in terms of their semantic components, which usually come in pairs called semantic oppositions. Componential analysis, also called feature analysis or contrast analysis, refers to the description of the meaning of words through structured sets of semantic features, which are given as "present", "absent" or "indifferent with reference to feature".

5.3.1 Componential Analysis on the Basis of Semantic Contrast

Componential analysis is the analysis of word meaning that "is often seen as a process of breaking down the sense of a word into its minimal components" (Leech, 1981: 84), which are known as semantic features or sense components. For example, the word *man* is made up of the features [+ Human], [+ Adult], and [+ Male] (as mentioned in 5.2.2).

Semantic features are established on the basis of binary opposites and can be stated in terms of [+] and [–] to express the presence or the absence of a given semantic feature. For example:

man [+ Male, + Adult, + Human]
woman [– Male, + Adult, + Human]
boy [+ Male, – Adult, + Human]
girl [– Male, – Adult, + Human]

Usually, componential analysis is applied to a group of related words which may differ from one another only by one or two components.

By way of introducing semantic components, we can distinguish between the nine words in the following componential table (Table 5–2) by the features [± Adult], [± Male], [Galline], [Anatine], and [Equine]:

Table 5–2　Componential analysis of the features of nine words

	+ Adult + Male	+ Adult ± Male	± Adult ± Male
Galline	*rooster*	*hen*	*chicken*
Anatine	*drake*	*duck*	*duckling*
Equine	*stallion*	*mare*	*foal*

Thus, the meaning of each word is defined and is at the same time distinguished from others by its semantic features. More examples:

A feature of "belongingness" distinguishes *to return*, when it takes an object, from *to take back*. "We took Junior back to the zoo." might refer to letting him visit the place again, but "We returned Junior to the zoo." calls him an inmate.

A feature "enemy" distinguished *U-boat* from the neutral *submarine* in World War Ⅰ.

5.3.2　The Role of Componential Analysis in English Lexical Teaching

In the 1950s, semantics was still regarded by many linguists as metaphysical and unfit for the kind of scientific inquiry into observable language structures. The early writers on componential analysis first applied the method to the study of kinship terms and showed that their study could be carried out using approved methods of distinctive feature analysis. Nowadays, componential analysis is favored not only by many linguists in their study of word meaning but also by many teachers in their vocabulary teaching. This is no doubt due to the following advantages of this approach:

(1) Componential analysis enables us to acquire an exact knowledge of the denotative meaning of words. For example:

hippopotamus: [+ Quadruped + Animal + Mammal + Plant-eating + Heavy + Thick-skinned + Short-legged + Semi-aquatic]

giraffe: [+ Quadruped + Animal + Mammal + Plant-eating + Tall + Long-necked + Long-legged + Terrestrial]

(2) Componential analysis is useful in explaining the meaning relations of polysemous words. For example:

man 1: [+ Human + Adult + Male]
man 2: (= human being) [+ Human ± Adult ± Male]
child 1: [+ Human – Adult ± Male]
child 2: (= descendants) [+ Human ± Adult ± Male + Younger generation]

(3) Componential analysis can define clearly the sense relations such as hyponymy, synonymy and antonymy. For example:

plant: [– Animate + Living + Concrete + Vegetative]
tree: [– Animate + Living + Concrete + Vegetative + Trunked]
kill: [± Intend + Cause + Die]
murder: [+ Intend + Cause + Die]
man: [+ Human + Adult + Male]
woman: [+ Human + Adult – Male]

Tree is a hyponym of plant as it belongs to a type of plant, and *plant* is a general term that includes tree and other types of plant. *Kill* and *murder* all refer to a causative action, but they differ in that the act of killing may be intentional or unintentional. *Man* differs from *woman* by the feature [+ Male].

(4) Componential analysis can help us to choose the right word or collocation.

Some verbs like *assemble* require a plural subject [+ Plural] and thus cannot go with a singular subject: "The girl assembled." Some other verbs require a human subject [+ Human] and so cannot collocate with inhuman nouns: "The giraffe arrested the mob."

In the set *fall* and *topple*, we find they distinguish themselves in the semantic feature [Intentionality]. *Fall* can either be intentional or unintentional. Lacking any indication to the contrary, we would assume that "Jane fell" meant that it happened without her intending it. Yet this feature is not permanently stuck to *fall*. We can say "She fell on purpose" but not "She toppled on purpose" because *topple* has the semantic feature [– Intentionality] and is completely unintentional, therefore it cannot collocate with *on purpose*.

So far, much space has been devoted to the discussion of the useful role played by the approach of componential analysis. Nevertheless, we should realize its defects as listed below:

Many words, especially abstract words, can hardly be segmented into their semantic features because we are not sure of them and because different people may have different understandings of them. For example, it is difficult to define "friendship", "happiness", "beauty" and "privacy" in terms of semantic features or components.

The analysis of word meaning into its semantic features is not enough. For instance, the componential definition of woman is [+ Human + Adult – Male], which is, in fact, only a biological definition. It does not include its connotative meaning at all. It fails to explain the implied meaning of *woman* in the sentences "Anyway, she is a woman." and "Don't cry like a woman!"

Exercises

I. **The synonyms in the following groups carry different connotations, although their denotations are roughly similar. Can you detect any difference in their meanings?**

1. fastidious, fussy, particular

2. critical, fault-finding, picky

3. adventurous, foolhardy, rash

4. dull, stolid, impassive

5. runty, petite, little

II. Match the name of each animal in Column A with its proper onomatopoeic word in Column B.

A	B
apes	bellow
asses	bleat
bears	bray
bulls	cackle
cats	buzz
ducks	croak
flies	coo
frogs	gibber
geese	gobble
goats	growl
larks	hoot
lions	howl
wolves	mew
mice	warble
owls	quack
pigeons	roar
turkeys	squeak

III. Analyze the following words by using the semantic features: [± Male], [± Adult], and [± Human].

1. bachelor   **2.** spinster   **3.** boy

4. girl   **5.** stallion   **6.** mare

IV. Explain how polysemous words are used in the following sentences.

1. He'll have a fit if you don't *humor* him.

I have a sense of *humor* but I just don't think it's funny.

2. The *panel* was called to appear in Judge Long's court at 9 a.m.

I am going to *panel* the wall in Philippine mahogany.

3. When the radio signal comes on again, I'll take a *fix* on our position.

What a *fix* I'm in.

The drug addict was desperate for a *fix*.

4. I have a major in math but a *minor* in science.

Minors are not permitted in this establishment.

It was such a *minor* matter that I did not report it.

5. After counting off, those with *odd* numbers take one step forward.

The dessert left an *odd* taste in my mouth.

I wish that I could find a mate for the *odd* shoe.

V. Write a pair of homonyms in the blank spaces to complete each sentence. An example has been given for you. One word is provided in the bracket at the end of each sentence.

Sample: John <u>won</u> only <u>one</u> prize at the carnival. (one)

1. The catcher _____ the ball _____ the infield and a runner scored. (through)

2. Mary _____ the _____ coat was too expensive. (new)

3. Bill _____ the title "The _____ Baion Flies Again". (red)

4. The pilot decided to land the _____ on the smooth _____ beyond the river. (plain)

5. He felt a sudden _____ as his arm broke the _____ of glass. (pain)

Chapter 6

Sense Relations Between Words

Words may be classified according to the relationships between their senses. The semantic relations of similarity, oppositeness, and inclusion classify words respectively into synonyms, antonyms, and hyponyms. Words may also be joined together by some common semantic features and belong to different semantic fields. Below is a brief account of them.

6.1 Synonymy

Synonymy means the relationship of sameness or close similarity of meaning between lexical items (including words and phrases). Lexical items that possess the same or nearly the same denotative meaning but differ in connotation, application, or idiomatic use are synonyms. As separate lexical items, synonyms naturally differ in morphemic structure and phonological form. When we decide whether two words are synonyms or not, context plays an important role. Words, which are synonyms in one context, may not be synonyms in another context. For example:

- He is well-known for his wide *range* of knowledge.
- What a nice *range* of flowers in this shop!

In the first sentence, when we substitute *scope* and *breadth* for the word *range*, the sentence meaning remains unchanged. Therefore, *range* in the first sentence is synonymous with *scope* and *breadth*. In the second sentence, if we substitute *scope* and *breadth* for the word *range*, the sentence meaning is unacceptable. However, we can replace the word *range* by *choice* and *selection* without changing the sentence meaning. Therefore, the word *range* in the second sentence is synonymous with *choice* and *selection*.

Synonyms can generally be classfied as complete synonyms, relative synonyms and other types of synoymys.

6.1.1 Complete Synonyms

Complete or absolute synonyms are rare as English has few pairs of words that are fully identical in both denotative and connotative meanings and are interchangeable in all contexts. Two expressions may denote the same referent, but it doesn't mean that they are total equivalents on all occasions. Ogden & Richards (1946: 92) remarked, "The two symbols 'the King of England' and 'the owner of Buckingham Palace' have the same referent. They do not, however, symbolize the same reference, quite different psychological contexts are involved in the two cases. Accordingly, they are not substitutes one for another."

Many words, which we regard as synonyms, are not absolute synonyms because they are not identical in all aspects of meaning. Superficially, *scarlet fever* and *scarlatina* could be thought of as absolute synonyms in medicine, but in fact, they are not, because *scarlatina* sounds more technical than *scarlet fever*.

However, complete or absolute synonyms, though rare, do exist. They are mainly technical terms, such as *word formation* and *word building* in lexicology, *breathed consonant*, and *voiceless consonant* in phonetics.

6.1.2　Relative Synonyms

Relative synonyms are those synonyms that are interchangeable only in certain contexts and which show differences in the following aspects.

1. In shades of meaning

The words *smile*, *beam*, *giggle*, *grin*, *chuckle*, *chortle*, and *laugh* all express a pleasant and happy facial expression, but differ in their shades of meaning. *Smile* is a facial expression with the mouth turned up at the ends and the eyes bright; *beam* means "to smile brightly and happily", *giggle* denotes high-pitched sounds and is usually associated with children and especially girls; *grin* is a smile which shows the teeth; *chuckle* and *chortle* denote quiet laughter. *Chuckle* is generally low-keyed, reflective, and masculine, whereas *chortle*, coined from *chuckle* and *snort* by Lewis Carroll in *Through the Looking-Glass*, has a suggestion of high glee or impishness that is lacking in *chuckle*. *Laugh*, the most general term of this synonymous group, describes the inarticulate, explosive sounds that people make to express joy and happiness.

Chat, *gossip*, *nag*, *gabble*, *prattle*, *babble*, and *chatter* are synonyms, but they are different in certain aspects of meaning.

chat: to talk in an easy familiar way, e.g., We had a *chat* over coffee yesterday.

gossip: to talk casually, idly, and maliciously about other people, e.g., I don't like people who *gossip*.

nag: to scold or annoy constantly, e.g., She *nagged* (at) her husband about their lack of money.

gabble: to utter words rapidly and indistinctly, e.g., The lady was obviously upset as she *gabbled* out her story to the policeman.

prattle: to talk in a foolish or childish way, e.g., She *prattled* on about nothing.

babble: to talk foolishly, incessantly, or irrelevantly, e.g., The speaker was *babbling* in a language I couldn't understand.

chatter: to speak (about unimportant matters) rapidly and incessantly, e.g., The children *chattered* when the teacher left the room.

2. In degrees of a given quality

Relative synonyms may show differences in degrees of a given quality. Take *surprised, amazed, astonished, astounded, flabbergasted*, and *stunned* for example. According to *Use the Right Word: A Modern Guide to Synonyms* (Hayakawa, 1982), these words mean "filled with wonder or incredulity because of a confrontation with something unexpected". *To be surprised* is to meet with something that momentarily, at least, sets one back; *astonished* is a stronger word, indicating that a person has had more than an ordinary reaction to the unexpected; *amazed* suggests great wonder or bewilderment in the face of something that seems impossible or highly improbable; *astounded* and the informal *flabbergasted* express extreme difficulty of belief; *stunned* indicates shock and even speechless.

3. In affective meaning

Synonyms may be identical in their denotative meaning but different in their affective or emotive meaning. Such nouns as *statesman, intellectual* and *black* are appreciative or favorable in meaning, while *politician, egghead*, and *nigger* are derogative or unfavorable in meaning. So with the following pairs of adjectives: *slender and skinny, thrifty* and *niggardly, firm* and *pigheaded, resolute* and *stubborn*.

4. In stylistic meaning

There are many words that possess the same denotative meaning but carry different stylistic meanings: neutral, colloquial, literary, slang, vulgar, scientific, technical, and so on.

For example, *horse, charger, courser, palfrey, steed, nag*, and *plug* have the same referent but differ in their stylistic references. The word *horse* belongs to a neutral style; *charger, courser, palfrey*, and *steed* belong to a formal or poetic style; *nag* and *plug* belong to an informal or colloquial style. Other examples are *diminutive* (formal), *tiny* (colloquial), *wee* (dialectal); *cast* (literary), *throw* (neutral), *chuck* (slang); *pass away* (formal), *die* (neutral), *pop off* (informal); *gentleman* (polite), *man* (neutral), *chap, fellow* or *bird* (colloquial), *guy* or *bozo* (slang); *an obnoxious effluvium* (formal), *a nasty smell* (neutral), *a horrible stink* (colloquial). Let's look at the following passage:

> *Florence Nightingale manifested unprecedented attributes of dogged determination and drive during the hideous holocaust of the Crimean War and at lots of other times too. It was then that she had to put her shoulder to the wheel and come to grips with an awful*

lot of really tough jobs, which, it goes without saying, took a lot out of her. At Scutari, the stricken warriors were languishing in a foul den which was really falling to bits and wasn't at all suitable for a hospital. A ministering angel, she descended upon them, armed with medicines and detergents and supported by a devoted band of dedicated heroines.

In the above passage, the writer of this passage has used many formal words such as *manifested, unprecedented, attributes, dogged, determination, drive, hideous*, and *holocaust*. However, in the same passage, these formal words are mixed together with some informal words and expressions such as *lots of, It goes without saying, wasn't, didn't*, and also some archaic expressions and clichés such as *to put one's shoulder to the wheel* and *ministering angel*. The mixture of words and expressions with different stylistic meanings makes this passage very odd.

5. In collocation and distribution

Relative synonyms may be used in different collocations. For example, *good, strong*, and *high* are synonyms when used to modify such words as *likelihood, probability, possibility*, and *chance*, but their collocations are different:

good likelihood	strong likelihood	*high likelihood[1]
*good probability	strong probability	high probability
good possibility	strong possibility	*high possibility
good chance	*strong chance	*high chance

very, really, quite, perfectly, well, and *totally* are synonyms. When *able* is used predicatively, or when it is used as a modifier of another noun, only *very, really*, and *quite* can be collocated with *able*, not the words *perfectly, well, totally*. For example:

- Mary is very (really, quite) *able*.
  Mary is a very (really, quite) *able* student.

- *Mary is perfectly (well, totally) *able*.
  *Mary is a perfectly (well, totally) *able* student.

In the pattern, *be able to do something, very* cannot be collocated with *able*. It can, however, collocate with the words *really, quite, perfectly, well*, and *totally*. For example:

- *Mary is very *able* to give the lecture.
  Mary is really (quite, perfectly, well, totally) *able* to give the lecture.

High and *tall* are synonyms. We can say either *high building* or *tall building*, but we can

---

1   The symbol * means that such collocations are not acceptable.

only say *a tall man*, not *a high man*. On the other hand, we can only say *high spirits*, not *tall spirits*.

Sometimes distribution (syntactic positions) of two synonyms may be different. Take the synonymous pairs *lonely* and *alone*, *living* and *alive*, *sleeping* and *asleep* for example. We can say *a lonely man*, *a living fish*, and *a sleeping child*, but the second word with the prefix *a-* in each pair can only serve as a complement, e.g., "The man is alone.", "The fish is alive.", and "The child is asleep.".

6. In their associative meanings

Attract and *tantalize* are synonyms, but they might give rise to different associations. Look at the following examples:

- The advertisement is *attractive*.
- The advertisement is *tantalizing*.

Both *attract* and *tantalize* have the denotative meaning of "to cause somebody to notice". However, *tantalizing* reminds us of a Greek myth in which a king called Tantalus was punished for his misdoings by being forced to stand in water that receded when he tried to drink it and under fruit that moved away as he reached for it. Because of this association, *tantalizing* suggests the arousing of expectations that are repeatedly disappointed.

Hooverize and *economize* are synonyms. They carry different associative meanings. *Hooverize* suggests Herbert Clark Hoover, who was a US statesman, and the 31st president of the US. He organized relief for Europe during and after World War Ⅰ. As president, he made great efforts to reduce government expenses and lost favor after his failure to alleviate the effects of the Depression.

7. In their origins

The English vocabulary is noted for its wealth of synonyms, which can be largely accounted for by abundant borrowings. Quite a number of words in synonymous sets are usually of Latin, Greek, or French origin. Thus, two synonymous patterns exist side by side in English, namely, double-scale and triple-scale patterns.

1) The double-scale pattern

There are many pairs of synonyms in which a native word exists side by side with the one borrowed from Latin, Greek, or French. In most cases, the native word is more informal and spontaneous, whereas the loan word is more learned and formal. Their stylistic differences may give rise to emotive differences. Since a native word is usually more informal and familiar than a loan word, the former may consequently sound warmer and more homely than its synonym of foreign origin. For example, we feel that *a hearty welcome* is warmer than *a cordial welcome*, which sounds official, stiff, and cold.

The following are some examples of the double-scale pattern:

Native	Latin
answer	reply
bodily	corporeal
brotherly	fraternal
buy	purchase
hearty	cordial
help	aid
outer	external
same	identical

In a few cases, the native word is more formal than the loan word:

Native	Latin
dale	valley
deed	action
meed	reward

The double scale pattern is found in many set expressions such as *end* and *aim*, *honest* and *true*, *act* and *deed*, *food* and *sustenance*. They are used mainly for emphasis.

2) The triple-scale pattern

Native	French	Latin or Greek
ask	question	interrogate
begin	commence	initiate
bright	brilliant	resplendent
end	finish	conclude
fast	firm	secure
fear	terror	trepidation
food	nourishment	nutrition
kingly	royal	regal
time	age	epoch

In most of these sets, the native words are felt as more colloquial, the Latin or Greek ones are more bookish, whereas the French words stand between the two extremes.

It is generally believed that we do not react to words of native origin the way we do to words of foreign origin. In most situations, we react more strongly to our native words than to words of foreign origin. An interesting case to notice is that in daily communication, a student who studies a foreign language often feels shy about talking about tabooed subjects such as sex directly in his mother tongue. Very often, he code-switches between his mother tongue and the foreign language that he has learned. It seems that when he uses a foreign language to talk about a taboo subject, he may feel less awkward and more natural. Because the stimulus that a native word poses to our mind is much stronger, we find many euphemisms are made by borrowing words from other languages—terms that are less freighted with negative associations. Thus, we use Greek and Latin expressions for many bodily parts and functions. We have coined *halitosis* (bad breath) from the Latin *halitus* for *breath* and we have substituted *urination* for the more vulgar Indo-European *piss*.

6.1.3　Other Types of Synonymy

So far we have dealt with synonyms of the same word class, but it should be noted that synonymy covers a much wider sphere. Synonymy may concern words of different word classes (such as *to move* and *movement*, *patient* and *patience*), phrases (such as *to try* and *to make an attempt*, *to interfere* and *to take a hand*), and different sentence patterns expressing the same idea, the last of which is especially useful in developing our writing skill. For example:

- It is not only our responsibility but also yours.
- It is your responsibility as well as ours.
- It is as much our responsibility as yours.
- It is both our responsibility and yours.

Leech (1987: 366) regarded the following expressions as synonymous:

- Bert collects stamps.
- Bert is one who collects stamps.
- Bert is a stamp collector.
- Bert is a philatelist.

However, different sentence patterns and choices of words often belong to different styles:

- When his dad died, Peter had to get another job. (informal)
- After his father's death, Peter had to change his Job. (neutral)
- On the decease of his father, Mr. Brown was obliged to seek alternative employment. (formal)

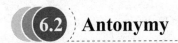

6.2 Antonymy

The term "antonymy" denotes the relationship of semantic oppositeness between two or more lexical items. Words that are opposite in denotative meaning to one another are antonyms.

6.2.1 Types of Antonyms

Antonyms can be classified into three types on the basis of semantic contrast: contraries, complementaries, and conversives.

1. Contraries

Contraries or contrary terms express a type of semantic contrast, illustrated by such pairs as *hot* and *cold*, *old* and *young*, *rich* and *poor*, *love* and *hate*, etc. They display the following features:

(1) They can be seen in terms of the degrees of the quality involved. A man may be old or very old and a man may be older than another. The weather may be hot or very hot and the weather of today may be hotter than that of yesterday. These show a gradation of age and temperature. The semantic contrast between the opposites is therefore gradable.

(2) Since contraries are gradable, their semantic polarity is relative. This means that contraries can be placed at both ends of a scale, between which there may be intermediate terms. Thus, between the two opposites *hot* and *cold*, there are such gradations as *warm*, *tepid*, *lukewarm*, and *cool*; between the two opposites *love* and *hate*, there are such intermediate terms as *attachment*, *liking*, *indifference*, *antipathy*, and so on. Contraries are also called gradable antonyms or antonyms proper. Some linguists use the term "antonym" to mean only gradable antonyms.

(3) Denial of one of the pair does not mean the assertion of the other. Because contraries are gradable, very often, there exists a middle ground between the two extreme points. When we negate one of the pair, it does not necessarily mean that we assert the other of the pair. For example, "He is not rich." does not necessarily mean "He is poor." If a person were asked whether he is rich, he could possibly answer "I am neither rich nor poor. I am comfortably off."

(4) Their meanings are relative to each other. The meaning of one of the pair is determined in reference to the meaning of the other of the pair. Without a reference, the meanings of the contraries can hardly be decided upon. For example, *fast* is often defined in

a dictionary as "swift", or "quick". But how swift a runner must be before we can say that he is fast? It is not easy to answer that question. With reference to one person, you may be slow. However, in comparison with another, you may be fast.

2. Complementaries

Complementaries or contradictories represent a type of binary semantic contrast that admits of no intermediate terms. In a complementary pair, the contrast between the two terms is absolute, i.e., the assertion of one of the items means the denial of the other or vice versa, e.g., *alive* and *dead*, *male* and *female*, *single* and *married*, *present* and *absent*, etc. To say that someone is alive, male, single, or present is to say that he is not dead, female, married, or absent.

Complementaries differ from contraries in that the former cannot be modified by adverbs to convey the degree of its intensity, nor can it be treated in terms of comparison. For example, one cannot say, except ironically, "He is very alive." or "He is more alive than dead". Another difference is that complementaries permit no intermediate terms, whereas contraries allow them. Because there is no overlapping allowed between the two concepts indicated by the two extreme points, these antonyms generally cannot be used in the pattern "neither...nor...":

- I am neither present nor absent.

In Chinese, very often we hear the expression " 半死不活 " or " 不死不活 ". These expressions are accepted only in the pragmatic sense. A person cannot be neither alive nor dead. Physiologically speaking, even if we describe a person by using the expression " 不死不活 ", he is still alive. No one would use that expression to talk about someone who has died in the literal sense. In the use of language, there is a figure of speech, which is called an oxymoron, in which apparently contradictory terms are combined to produce an epigrammatic effect. Many people treat oxymorons as examples of metaphorical transfer. For example, a *female man* is regarded as a man possessing some characteristics of a woman. For another example:

> *Jim Hall was right. He was innocent of the crime for which he was sentenced... When the doom of fifty years of living death was uttered by Judge Scott, Jim Hall... rose up and raged in the courtroom until dragged down by a dozen of his blue-coated enemies.*

In the above example, *living* and *death* are semantically contradictory because, as has been said above, if someone is alive, he is not dead; if someone is dead, he is not alive. The two contradictory terms cannot be used to refer to the same entity. When looked at from the angle of semantic transfer, the above expression *living death* is reasonable. Jim Hall was innocent of the crime for which he was sentenced to fifty years of imprisonment. The fifty-year imprisonment meant to him a life so unpleasant that it was worse than death.

3. Conversives

Conversives show the reversal of a relationship between the two items, as seen in such relational opposites as *sell* and *buy*, *give* and *take*, *husband* and *wife*, *teacher* and *student*, *up* and *down*, *left* and *right*, and so on. If someone A sells to another B, then B buys from A; if A is B's husband, then B is A's wife; if A is on the left of B, then B is on the right of A. The same applies to other pairs mentioned above.

Conversives display such an interdependence of meaning that one term of the pair presupposes the other.

- I am a good husband; I have a wife.

The above sentence sounds not natural enough, because of the redundancy in the semantic meaning expressed. *Husband* and *wife* indicate the reversal of a relationship. "I am a husband" presupposes "I have a wife".

Conversives differ from complementaries in that the latter lacks such symmetry of relative dependence; conversives also differ from contraries in that the former admits of no intermediate terms.

6.2.2　Different Antonyms of One Word

A polysemic word has different antonyms for its different meanings. For example, when the word *fine* is used in the sense of "beautiful" (*a fine woman/house/view*), its antonym will be *ugly*; when *fine* means "very thin" (*fine hair/thread*), then its antonym will be *thick*; when *fine* means "healthy and comfortable" ("I'm fine.", in reply to "How are you?"), then its antonym will be "ill and uncomfortable". When we analyze the semantic contrast of an antonymous pair, we can deal with only a single "semantic continuum".

Different contexts also require different collocations with different antonyms:

fresh air	*stuffy air*
fresh bread	*stale bread*
fresh flowers	*faded flowers*
fresh meat	*frozen meat*
fresh newspaper	*stale newspaper*
fresh water	*salt water*

The antonym of *handsome* in the phrase "handsome boy" is *ugly*, but the antonym of *handsome* in the phrase "handsome income" is *meager*.

6.2.3 Marked and Unmarked Members

Marked and unmarked were originally the terms used to analyze the grammatical meaning of a word. For example, the word *books* is a marked word because *books* contains *-s*, which is a marker of plurality; *book* is an unmarked word, because we cannot find any marker. Then, the concept of markedness has been applied to the analysis of the meanings of words. An unmarked word is a word, whose meaning is more inclusive and comprehensive than a marked word, whose meaning is specialized. Take the words *lady* and *woman* for example: A lady is certainly a woman, but a woman may not be a lady. Compared with *woman*, *lady* is a marked word, because not all women are ladies. Only those with special qualities can be called ladies. In the 19th century, George Eliot, in her *Silas Marner*, described a lady as "She had the essential attributes of a lady high veracity, delicate honour in her dealings, deference to others, and refined personal habits."

The concept of markedness is applicable to the analysis of the meanings of antonyms. The members of certain antonymous pairs appear to be in an unmarked–marked relationship: one member of the pair being marked and the other member unmarked for a certain feature. For example, the word *man* may include *woman* so that the generic *man* is unmarked and sexless, whereas the generic *woman* is always marked. The markedness is sometimes indicated by the feminine suffixes such as *-ess* and *-trix* with some names of people and animals.

It is not difficult to see the differences in the semantic inclusion of gradable opposites. Let's look at another pair of antonyms—*well* and *badly*. When asked "How well do you speak English?", you can either answer by saying "Very well", or "Very badly"; when asked "How badly do you speak English?", you can answer by saying "Very badly", but not "Very well".

The concept of markedness is often applied to antonymous pairs of adjectives such as *old* and *young*, *heavy* and *light*, *big* and *small*, and *long* and *short*. The first member in each pair is unmarked and it can always denote the common quality shown in these pairs; *old* denoting age, *heavy* denoting weight, *big* denoting size, and *long* denoting length. The second member in each pair is marked, and it always carries a certain implication of distinctiveness. Normally we employ the unmarked member of an antonymous pair for comparison. So when we compare two persons' age, we usually say, "A is older than B." The statement doesn't mean that A is old; it merely means that A's age is greater than B's age. On the other hand, the statement "A is younger than B" would imply that both A and B are not old. Again, we usually use the unmarked members for an ordinary inquiry. For example, we always use "How old are you?" to inquire about a person's age no matter whether he is an adult or a child. In contrast, the question "How young is he?" would sound unusual. The speaker must assume that the addressee is quite young. This also applies to "How small is it?" and "How short is he?", which would imply that the object is very small and the person is very short. By the way, it should be noted that of the three types of antonyms, only contraries can be used in the "How…?" question. One cannot say "How true or right is…". This is due to the fact that the "How…" question can only occur with gradable antonyms.

6.2.4 Asymmetry in the Pragmatic Uses

Some of the antonyms, especially those that show contrast in the semantic feature of gender, may show asymmetries in their pragmatic uses.

(1) A word once reserved for female persons in high places is generalized to refer to people of all levels in society.

The titles of women are more likely to undergo this generalization than the titles of men. For instance, under the entry *lord* in *Collins COBUILD English Language Dictionary*, ten meanings are listed, all associated with nobility, authority, and power. However, its counterpart *lady* is not so fortunate as to be reserved especially for females of nobility. For example, in George Eliot's description of a lady in her *Silas Marner*, as quoted earlier, "She had the essential attributes of a lady high veracity, delicate honor in her dealings, deference to others, and refined personal habits.", the connotation of woman of refinement can be felt. However, now, the connotations of the word *lady* are rather different from those of the word *gentleman*. As far as use is concerned, *lady* is in many respects actually an equivalent to *man*. Shop assistants in Britain may be referred to as *sales ladies*, but not *sales gentlemen. Ladies' wear* can be found for sale alongside *men's wear*.

(2) Some female terms reserved for female persons in high places have slipped past respectable women, and acquired obscene references, while their counterparts still retain reputation.

Mistress is a title that used to be the counterpart of *master*. For example:

- Is your *mistress* at home?

In the children's rhyme, we often hear "Mistress Mary quite contrary. How does your garden grow?" Once again, "Mistress" here is the counterpart of "master."

In modern English, however, the word "mistress" has gone pejoration in meaning. According to *Collins COBUILD English Language Dictionary*, a man's mistress is now "a woman who he has a sexual relationship with, but is not married to", as is shown in the example:

- For all these years, he has regarded me as his *mistress*, and not his wife.

What is worth noting here is that the terms for females in authority have taken on sexual meaning. However, those terms for noble males have remained the same. In *Collins COBUILD English Language Dictionary*, there are eight definitions given about the use of the word *master*. None of the meanings of the word *master* is pejorative in sense. All the meanings are related to *power*, *ability*, and *authority*.

King and *queen* are antonymous. A king is either a crowned head or a top dog. A queen is a woman who rules a country as its monarch. But in language use, *queen* has an unfavorable and sexual meaning. The first, most common today, at least in America, is "male homosexual who acts like a woman". A female homosexual who acts like a man is not called a king, however. Rather, she becomes a butch, an older nickname for a tough, lower-class boy. An outcast male who acts like a woman is called a queen, the highest ranking for a woman. A woman who acts like a man becomes a lower-class boy, not even a man, much less a king.

Governor and *governess* are counterparts. In *Oxford English Dictionary*, the term "governor" refers to a man who "exercises a sovereign authority in a colony, territory, or state". A governess, on the other hand, is chiefly "a nursemaid", operating in a realm much diminished from that of Queen Elizabeth I, who was acknowledged to be "the supreme majesty and governess of all persons".

Uncle and *aunt* are antonymous. *Aunt* was generalized first to mean "an old woman" and then "a bawd or a prostitute". It is the latter meaning that Shakespeare's *The Winter's Tale* draws upon in lines:

Summer songs for me and my aunts
As we lie tumbling in the hay.

6.2.5 The Rhetorical Use of Antonyms

Antonyms are often used for the sake of contrast to impress one's listeners or readers. Hence it is widely used in English proverbs and idioms. A few examples are given as follows:

- United we stand, divided we fall.
- Hope for the best and prepare for the worst.
- More haste, less speed.
- Light come, light go.
- Few words, many deeds.

As shown by the above examples, antonyms can achieve antithesis—the deliberate arrangement of contrasting ideas in balanced structural forms for emphasis. Here is another example from Shakespeare's "A Madrigal":

Youth is full of pleasure, age is full of care;

Youth like summer mom, age like winter weather;

Youth like summer brave, age like winter bare:

Youth is full of sport, age's breath is short,

Youth is nimble, age is lame:

Youth is hot and bold, age is weak and cold,

Youth is wild, and age is tame:—

Age, I do abhor thee; Youth, I do adore thee;

O! My love, my love is young!

Antonyms are also used to achieve oxymoron—a kind of paradox formed by the conjoining of two contrasting, contradictory terms, as in Shakespeare's *Romeo and Juliet*:

His honour rooted in dishonour stood

And faith unfaithful kept him falsely true (Tennyson)

My only love sprung from my only hate!

Too early seen unknown, and known too late.

Other familiar examples are *bitter-sweet* memories, *proud humility*, *orderly chaos*, *living death*, and *friendly hostility*.

6.3 Hyponymy

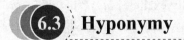

Hyponymy is the relationship between specific and general words, in which the meaning of the specific word is included in the meaning of the general word. From a viewpoint of semantic features, hyponymy exists between two words if all the features are present in the other. Thus, *woman* is hyponymous with *grown-up* because the two features making up the meaning of *grown-up* [+ Human + Adult] are both present in the meaning of *woman* [+ Human + Adult – Male]. Here the word *grown-up* is a general term, linguistically called a superordinate or upper term, whereas the word *woman* is a specific term, linguistically called a subordinate or lower term. As seen from the semantic analysis of *grown-up* and *woman*, the subordinate terms naturally have at least one more feature than their superordinate terms.

Structurally, hyponymy displays a paradigmatic and hierarchical relationship between words as illustrated in Figure 6–1:

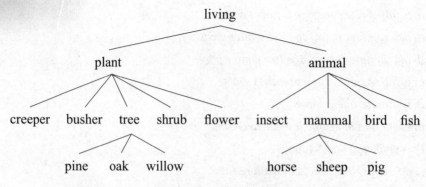

Figure 6–1　The hierarchical diagram of "living"

The word *plant* in the diagram is a hyponym of the more general term *living*, but the plant itself is also the superordinate or upper term, having such co-hyponyms as *creeper*, *bush*, *tree*, *shrub*, *flower*, and so on. The word *tree*, in turn, owns a list of trees of various kinds such as *pine*, *oak*, and *willow*. Other terms in the diagram may also possess some hyponyms of their own.

Lyons observed that in Classical Greek there is a superordinate term to cover a variety of professions and crafts, *carpenter*, *doctor*, *flute player*, *helmsman*, *shoemaker*, etc., but none in English. The nearest possible term is "craftsman", but that would not include *doctor*, *flute player* or *helmsman*. Similarly and rather strangely, there is no superordinate term for all color words, *red*, *blue*, *green*, *white*, etc.; the term "colored" usually excludes *black* and *white* or else means *nonwhite*.

The same term may appear in several places in the hierarchy. This is, of course, possible only if it is polysemic; in one of its meanings, it may be superordinate to itself in another meaning. Thus *animal*, as mentioned in the diagram of the previous section, may be used (1) in contrast with plant to include *insect*, *fish*, *bird* as well as *mammal*; (2) in the sense of "mammal" to contrast with *bird*, *fish*, and *insect*, to include both *humans* and *beasts*; (3) in the sense of "beast" to contrast with *human*. Thus, the term "animal" occurs three times in the hierarchical diagram, as shown in Figure 6–2:

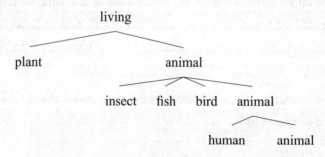

Figure 6–2　The hierarchical diagram of "animal"

Interestingly, the Polish language contains a superordinate term conveying both humans and beasts, and also a superordinate term covering man and woman. The use of specific words is a great aid to exactness and vividness of expression and it is a good writing practice to find specific words for general ones. Take the following line by Bunyan for instance: "I am resolved to run when I can, to go when I cannot run, and to creep when I cannot go."

If Bunyan fails to use different hyponyms to depict different manners of bodily movement, then this well-known line will become senseless.

It should not be supposed, however, that general words always had better be avoided. On the contrary, general terms often suffice for our ordinary purposes. For instance, in reply to the question "What are you going to do tonight?", the answer "We are going to the cinema." will be fit and proper. It will be unnecessary to describe how to get to the cinema because this additional information is not asked for.

6.4 Polysemy

6.4.1 Definition

Polysemy means literally a plurality of meanings, and it refers to a word that has two or more different meanings. Such a word is called a polysemous word. In English as in any other language, polysemy is the rule and monosemy (a word with only one meaning) is the exception. Most of the common words denoting familiar objects in our daily life have various meanings. Take the word *head* for example. *Head* can mean: (1) the part of the body which contains the eyes, ears, nose, and mouth; (2) the mind or brain; (3) a ruler or leader; (4) a measure of height or distance; (5) a person (in the phrase *so much a/per head*); (6) the top or front, highest or furthest point; (7) a body of water at a certain height and so on. A medium-sized *Longman Dictionary of Contemporary English* (1978) lists altogether 45 meanings under the entry *head*. In contrast, monosemous words are few and they are often those denoting specific plants and animals such as *peony*, *forget-me-not*, *sunflower*, *giraffe*, and *zebra*; or those denoting technical and scientific concepts and elements such as *oxygen* and *hydrogen*. In fact, common and old words are more likely to be polysemous, whereas new words denoting rare objects are more likely to be monosemous.

6.4.2 Two Processes Leading to Polysemy

Polysemy occurs through the two processes of radiation and concatenation.

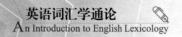
1. Radiation

Radiation refers to a process of meaning development in which the original or primary meaning of a word stands at the center in the form of a hub while secondary meanings radiate from it like the spokes of a wheel.

Take the word *foot* for illustration. Its primary and central meaning is (1) "the movable part of the body at the end of the leg, below the ankle", and from it, the following meanings have developed; (2) (a measure of length equal to) 12 inches; (3) the bottom part; base; (4) the lower end (of anything) where feet lie; (5) manner of walking, step; (6) the part of a stocking or sock that covers the foot; (7) a division of a line in poetry; (8) soldiers who march and fight on foot; infantry.

The primary meaning "the movable part of the body at the end of the leg, below the ankle" stands at the center, and all the secondary meanings are derived from it in every direction like rays. Each of the secondary meanings might easily have developed from the primary meaning without regard to any of the others.

2. Concatenation

Concatenation (from Latin *catena* meaning "chain") refers to a process of meaning development in which the meanings of a word move gradually away from the original meaning by successive shifts until there is no trace of connection between the sense that is finally developed and the original meaning.

A good example is the word *board*. Its original meaning is "a long thin piece of cut wood", then it has acquired through different historical stages such additional meanings as "a flat piece of hard material used for putting food on" and "meals" as in *board* and *lodging*. The successive shifts of sense from "a piece of cut wood" to "dining table" and then to "meals" illustrate the process of concatenation well.

Besides, we observe the fact that the two processes of radiation and concatenation may interact in the sense development of a word. For example, the word *board* develops its meanings from "a piece of cut wood" to "table" and then to "meals" by successive shifts, but meanwhile, the sense "table" of *board* applies to such objects as dressing-board and side-board. This example shows the processes of radiation and concatenation are intertwined with each other.

 Homonymy

Homonymy is a relation holding between two or more lexical items that have the same phonological or spelling form but a different meaning. The lexical items in such a relationship are called homonyms.

6.5.1 Types of Homonyms

English homonyms are classified as follows:

1. Perfect homonyms

Words that have the same pronunciation and the same spelling but differ in meaning are called perfect or complete homonyms. For example:

- ear *n.* the organ of hearing

  ear *n.* the part of a cereal plant that contains the flowers, grains or kernels
- fair *n.* an exhibition and sale of goods

  fair *adj.* beautiful or attractive
- nap *n.* a brief period of sleep

  nap *n.* any downy coating, as on plants

  nap *n.* a card game

2. Homophones

Words that are pronounced alike but are different in spelling and meaning are called homophones. For example:

{ *air* / *heir*	{ *ant* / *aunt*	{ *bare* / *bear*	{ *berry* / *bury*	{ *bough* / *bow*	{ *heal* / *heel*
{ *knight* / *night*	{ *loan* / *lone*	{ *mail* / *male*	{ *meat* / *meet*	{ *rain* / *rein*	{ *sail* / *sale*

3. Homographs

Words that are identical in spelling but different in sound and meaning are called homographs. For example:

- bow /baʊ/ *n.* the forward part of a ship

  bow /bəʊ/ *n.* a device for shooting arrows
- mare /meə/ *n.* a female horse or donkey

  mare /ˈmɑːreɪ/ *n.* any of several large dark areas on the surface of the moon or Mars, which look like seas
- mate /meɪt/ *n.* a fellow worker or partner

  mate /ˈmɑːteɪ/ *n.* a tealike South American beverage

- lead /li:d/ *v.* to guide or direct

  lead /led/ *n.* a heavy, soft, easily melted, bluish-grey chemical element

There are more homophones than homographs in English. This is partly due to the complicated and asymmetric relationship between the phonological and orthographical systems in English. As we know, a letter may be pronounced differently in different situations, e.g. the letter *a* is pronounced /æ/ in *cat*, /eɪ/ in *came*, /ɑ:/ in *calm*, /ɔ:/ in *call* and /ə/ in *rota*. The long vowel /i:/ has the following spellings: *meet, mete, seat, seize, niece, key, quay*, and *police*. Bernard Shaw once said humorously that *ghoti* should be read as /fɪʃ/ (fish) because *gh* may be read as /f/ (*cough*), *o* as /i/ to the fact that in the 16th and 17th centuries printers, who contributed much to the standardization of English words which have the same pronunciation but regarded homophones as the lesser evil.

6.5.2 Sources of Homonyms

1. Phonetic convergence

Homonyms may arise from phonetic changes. For example, homophones *sea* and *see* were once /saese/ and /see/ respectively before the time of the great English vowel shift, and later became /seɪ/ and /si:/ respectively in Shakespeare's time. The following poetic lines illustrate the point:

God moves in a mysterious way, ...
He plants his footsteps in the sea.

Here thou, great Anna! whom three realms obey.

The study of the rimes of such poems reveals that the old pronunciation of *ea* was evidently not /i:/, but /eɪ/. It was later in the 17th century that /eɪ/ was raised to /i:/. Therefore, words such as *sea* and *see*, *tea*, and *tee* are homophones today. The same phonetic change occurs with such pairs as *bean/been, flea/flee, heal/heel, read/reed, seam/seem, steal/steel*, etc.

2. Semantic divergence

Homonymy may also arise from diverging meaning development. When two or more meanings of the same word drift apart to such an extent that there will be no obvious connection between them, polysemy will give place to homonymy. For example, the homonyms *flower* and *flour* originally were the same word in Old English, meaning "flower" and "the finest part of wheat". Now the original polysemous word has split into the two words *flower* and *flour* and distributed one of the two meanings to each word respectively. The pair *draught* and *draft, metal* and *mettle, mantle* and *mantel*, and *gate* and *gait* have undergone a similar semantic diverging process. They were originally single words, but are now regarded as homophones.

3. Foreign influence

Loan words have enriched the number of homonyms in English. For instance, *sound* meaning "channel of water" is from Old English and Old Norse *sund*; meaning "healthy; secure" is from Germanic *gesund*; meaning "noise" is from Old English and Old French *son*. Again, the adjective *fair* meaning "attractive, beautiful" is from Old English *feeger*, whereas the noun *fair* meaning "an exhibition and sale of goods" comes from the Latin term *fena* (holiday). Judging by the above examples, we can know that foreign influence is a special form of phonetic converging development.

4. Shortening

Homonyms may also be created by the word-formation process of clipping. The following are a few examples:

- fan: any device meant to make a flow of air

  fan: fanatic, an enthusiastic devotee, or a follower
- cab: (especially AmE) taxi

  cab: cabriolet
- rock: a large mass of stone

  rock: rock'n'roll, a kind of popular modern dance music

6.5.3　The Rhetorical Features of Polysemy and Homonymy

Polysemous words and homonyms are usually kept distinct in meaning in actual utterances by the constraints of the context in which they are used. The proper context will impose an unambiguous interpretation on them. When ambiguity arises, it is usually intentional, for polysemy and homonymy are often employed for rhetorical purposes such as "punning". A pun is a play on words, or rather a play on the possibility of ambiguity provided by polysemy and homonymy so as to achieve humor. Some familiar examples read as follows:

- A: waiter!

  B: Yes, sir.

  A: What's this?

  B: It's *bean* soup, sir.

  A: No matter what it's *been*, what is it now?
- A man sits down at a table in a restaurant and asks, "Do you *serve* (= sell, supply) crabs here?". The waiter replies, "Sure, sit down. We *serve* (= are at your service) anybody."

Such punning may also achieve a satirical or emphatic effect. For example:

- On Sunday they *pray* for you and on Monday they *prey* on you.
- We must *hang* (= unite) together, or we shall *hang* (= be put to death with a rope) separately.

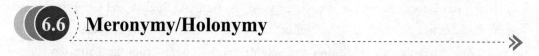

6.6 Meronymy/Holonymy

6.6.1 Definition

According to Murphy (2003), meronymy refers either to the directional relation from whole to part or collectively to that relation and its converse, holonymy. For example, *finger* is a meronym of *hand* and *hand* is a holonym of *finger*; *leaf* is a meronym of *tree*, and *tree* is a holonym of *leaf*. The relation between these two items is meronymy. Therefore, meronymy denotes a part-whole relationship between lexical items. A meronym may be a holonym of another meronym, which is illustrated in Figure 6–3 (Jackson & Amvela, 2007: 120).

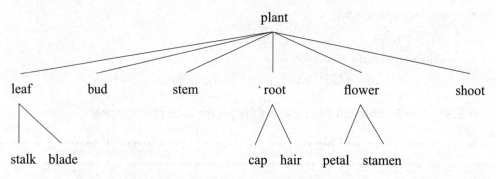

Figure 6–3   Illustration of a meronym

It can be seen in the diagram above that *flower* is a part (meronym) of *plant* and a holonym of *petal* and *stamen*.

6.6.2 Distinction Between Meronymy/Holonymy and Hyponymy

Both meronymy/holonymy and hyponymy deal with sense relations that relate words hierarchically (Jackson & Amvela, 2007). In both types of relation, one word has a more general meaning, and the other has a more specific meaning while referring to the same object. For example, *horse* and *mammal* can be used to refer to the same animal, but *horse* is a more specific word to refer to the same animal than *mammal*. Of course, *mammal* can be used to refer to animals that are not horses. Similarly, a man from *Beijing* and a man from *China* may refer to the same person, and the first is merely a more specific way of designating where the man is from.

However, meronymy/holonymy and hyponymy deal with different types of hierarchical relations. To be specific, hyponymy is a "kind of" relation. For example, a horse is a kind of mammal. However, meronymy/holonymy is a "part of" relation, as illustrated by the relation between *finger* and *hand* that a finger is a part of the hand.

6.6.3 Types of Meronymy

Winston et al. (1987) classifies meronymy into the following types, as shown in Table 6–1.

Table 6–1 Types of meronymy

Relation	Examples
Component < Integral Object	*pedal < bicycle* *puchline < joke*
Member < Collection	*member < committee* *card < deck*
Portion < Mass	*slice < pie* *grain < rice*
Stuff < Object	*flour < cake* *glass < bottle*
Feature < Activity	*swallowing < eating* *dating < adolescence*
Place < Area	*oasis < desert* *London < England*

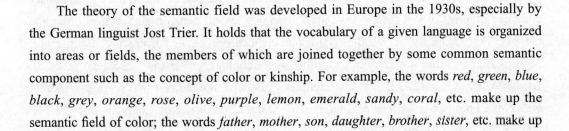

6.7 Semantic Field

The theory of the semantic field was developed in Europe in the 1930s, especially by the German linguist Jost Trier. It holds that the vocabulary of a given language is organized into areas or fields, the members of which are joined together by some common semantic component such as the concept of color or kinship. For example, the words *red, green, blue, black, grey, orange, rose, olive, purple, lemon, emerald, sandy, coral*, etc. make up the semantic field of color; the words *father, mother, son, daughter, brother, sister*, etc. make up the semantic field of kinship.

Word frequency in a semantic field varies. Take color terms for illustration. Words of high frequency are *green, blue, black, gray, red,* and *yellow*; the next group is *orange, rose, pink, olive, and purple*; words of the least frequency are *lemon, emerald, sandy,* and *coral*. Words of high frequency like *green* also have great collocative ability (e.g., *green hill, green winter, green corn*) and are likely to create derivatives and compounds (e.g., *greenly, greenness, green-blind, greenhouse*). In contrast, words of low frequency such as *coral* lack so great collocative ability and are rarely used to form derivatives or compounds.

Words within a semantic field interrelate and define each other. In other words, such words are semantically interdependent; the meaning of one word in a semantic field is limited by the meaning of its neighbors. As Quirk (1963: 131–132) points out, "we know what *captain* means only when we know whether his subordinate is called the 'mate' or 'first officer' (merchant service), 'commander' (navy), 'lieutenant' (army)."

This is actually related to the polysemous character of most English words. The various meanings of a polysemous word usually belong to various semantic fields. *Rose*, for instance, is related to *peony, herbaceous peony, lily, canna, azalea,* and *cockscomb* in the semantic field of plants; it goes with other color terms such as *lemon, grange, emerald,* and *coral* in the semantic field of color.

The scope of semantic fields varies from one language to another. The English kinship terms *grandfather, grandmother, grandson, granddaughter, uncle,* and *aunt* make no difference between the relatives on the father's or mother's side, whereas Chinese employs different terms for them.

Though useful in recognizing the sense relations between words, the theory of semantic fields is found true only of a number of highly integrated sectors such as colors, kinships, social ranks, and intellectual and emotive qualities. It is restricted in scope, and far from capable of covering the entire vocabulary.

In spite of the limitations, the theory of semantic fields has turned out some useful products. One of them is *Roget's International Thesaurus* (Kipfer, 2016), which is a dictionary compiled in terms of this theory. Instead of arranging lexical items in alphabetical order, the compiler Peter Mark Roget classifies words into eight categories, i.e., abstract relations, space, physics, matter, sensation, intellect, volition, affection, and further into subcategories (I, II, III, …; A, B, C, …; 1, 2, 3, …). The dictionary contains altogether 1,040 sections. Another widely-used product is *Lexicon of Contemporary English* published by Longman in 1981. The lexicon has only 14 semantic fields involving 129 subtopics and 15,000 lexical items. These two dictionaries will help readers to choose the right words from a series of related terms so as to make their expressions more exact and forceful in meaning.

Exercises

I. Define the following terms.

1. semantics   **2.** sense   **3.** reference   **4.** synonymy

5. polysemy   **6.** homonymy   **7.** homophones   **8.** homographs

9. hyponymy   **10.** componential analysis

II. Choose one from the four selection words that is closest in meaning to the given word.

1. grumble

    A. giggle   B. scold   C. complain   D. sneer

2. drowsy

    A. lazy   B. sleepy   C. exhausted   D. sad

3. alien

    A. exclusive   B. foreign   C. tropical   D. fickle

4. penalize

    A. compensate   B. charge   C. tax   D. punish

5. conference

    A. congregation   B. congress   C. negotiation   D. association

6. meditative

    A. desire   B. spectacle   C. thoughtful   D. desperate

7. synopsis

    A. discussion   B. summary   C. report   D. preview

8. confidential

    A. important   B. secret   C. interesting   D. alarming

9. proficient

    A. efficient   B. effective   C. gifted   D. skilled

10. shrill

    A. thrill   B. shriek   C. sharp   D. shout

III. How far can you carry the search for the precise synonym? Is there only one good choice in the following sentences, or would you agree that several choices might fit in each sentence? Check these synonyms in your dictionary and discuss the suitability of each.

1. The horizon stretched before us in one _____, unbroken line.
  (continual, continuous, constant, eternal, perpetual)

2. He was not a professional. He dabbled in the arts, collecting sculpture, attending exhibitions, and trying his hand at oils. He could be called a(n)_____.
  (amateur, dilettante, novice, neophyte, tyro)

3. The dictator rode in a bulletproof car lest someone attempt to _____ him.
  (kill, dispatch, assassinate, execute, murder)

4. She called for a witness in order to _____ her story.
  (confirm, substantiate, corroborate, authenticate, validate)

5. This paper is an exact _____ of the document, but reduced in size,
  (reproduction, facsimile, replica, copy)

IV. Choose one from the four selection words that is opposite in meaning to the given word.

1. barbarous
  A.polish   B. civilized   C. primitive   D. decorative

2. prudent
  A. decree   B. discreet   C. preview   D. careless

3. latitude
  A. attitude   B. longitude   C. conclude   D. altitude

4. defection
  A. departure   B. joining   C. invitation   D. affection

5. sophisticated
  A. philosophical   B. complicated   C. naive   D. naval

6. exasperate
  A. calm   B. separate   C. provoke   D. stimulate

7. inconspicuous

   A. ambiguous   B. remarkable   C. superficial   D. insignificant

8. contempt

   A. humble   B. conceit   C. perspect   D. respect

9. humane

   A. potent   B. exotic   C. offensive   D. barbarous

10. transparent

   A. remiss   B. hoary   C. trodden   D. opaque

V. Fill in the blanks with words antonymous to those given on the left.

1. to decline: to _____ his offer

                             to _____ towards the hill

2. peculiar: _____ customs

                             _____ taste

3. light: a _____ blue dress

                        a _____ box

4. fresh: _____ bread

                             _____ flowers

5. dull: _____ books

                             _____ boys

VI. Choose one from the four selection words that is the subordinate term of the given word.

1. fruit

   A. food   B. spinach   C. persimmon   D. celery

2. horse

   A. ewe   B. calf   C. sow   D. stallion

3. vehicle

   A. machine   B. van   C. vessel   D. computer

4. profession

   A. trash-collecting   B. farming   C. teaching   D. gardening

5. dessert

    A. ice-cream   B. carrots   C. wine   D. beverage

VII. Find the holonym in Column B for each of the meronyms in Column A.

A	B
wheel	forest
branch	month
flour	body
heel	bottle
books	car
ear	airplane
tree	foot
day	tree
cockpit	library
glass	cake

Chapter 7

Changes in Word Meaning

Words often develop new meanings, and when they do, they sometimes lose their old meaning. When a word loses its old meaning and comes to refer to something (partially or totally) different, the result is a change of word meaning. Vocabulary is the most unstable element of a language as it is undergoing constant changes both in form and content. Comparatively, the content is even more unstable than the form. Of course, some meanings remain much the same for a long time because the referents to which they direct us do not change. Often, an old form or a group of forms is pressed into new service when a new linguistic need is felt.

Anyone who has difficulty in reading and understanding Shakespeare's *Hamlet* will agree that word meanings can change. When Horatio says to Hamlet, "Season your admiration for a while…", he is not telling Hamlet to increase his respect for something but to moderate his astonishment. When Hamlet, resolving to remember and avenge his father's murder, says, "Yea, from the table of my memory I'll wipe away all trivial fond records", he is using "table" in its earlier sense of "a tablet" and "fond" in its earlier sense of "foolish"!

Examples such as these can be found on nearly every page of Shakespeare's play. *Climate* in Shakespeare's day meant "country"; *to enlarge a thrall* meant "to release a slave"; and *closet* meant "bedchamber" rather than "a small room for storing clothing". Such changes in word meanings have been taking place since the beginning of language. They are a part of the natural development of language.

Changing in word meaning has never ceased since the language came into being and will continue in the future. Yet the ways in which changes occur have seldom been systemized. Changes in meaning, though usually unpredictable, are not utterly arbitrary. The changes of meaning in English words would themselves provide enough material for a large volume. In this chapter, all we can do is mention a few of the many causes leading to the development of new meanings, the main tendencies in semantic change, and the change of meaning resulting from the figurative use of words. They will be dealt with in the following sections.

7.1 Causes of Changes in Word Meaning

There are various causes of change of meaning, some social, some psychological, some purely linguistic, and various types of classification of semantic change have been proposed. For instance, the late Gustaf Stern, on the basis of a large amount of material in English, arrived at a more or less empirical system with seven main mechanisms of semantic change which he then justified on psychological grounds. One early semanticist advanced thirty-one possible causes. It is a very complicated process. Below is a brief account of some main causes.

7.1.1 Historical and Social Causes

The history of the social, economic, and political life of the people and the progress of culture bring about changes in notions and things influencing the semantic aspect of language. One reason why a word changes its meaning is that although it retains its original name, the object or concept it denotes changes. In other words, the thing it refers to changes. As Ullmann (1977: 198) put it:

> *"It often happens that language is more conservative than civilization, material as well as moral. Objects, institutions, ideas, scientific concepts change in the course of time; yet in many cases the name is retained and thus helps to ensure a sense of tradition and continuity."*

Turning to present-day English, we may first notice that some changes in meaning are due to changes in things rather than in words. A familiar example is the word *ship* which has been used in English for over a thousand years to denote "a vessel or a long boat traveling on the sea", but the kind of machine actually used for this purpose has changed enormously, the word is now also used to denote "a modern liner, an aircraft carrier or space vehicle". So it is reasonable to say that the meaning of the word *ship* has changed since the object in practice referred to by the word has changed considerably. The same applies to other products of our material culture, such as *car*, *lamp*, *pen*, and *weapon*. The word *car*, for example, derives from the Latin *carrus* which meant "a two-wheeled Celtic war chariot", but now denotes "a vehicle driven by a motor, especially one for carrying people". *Lamp* comes from the Greek *lampe* meaning "torch", but is now used in various types of apparatus for giving light, such as from oil, gas, or electricity. *Pen* is from the Latin *penna* meaning "feather" because in ancient times the writing instrument was made of fowl quills. Later, when the writing instrument was made of a thin short piece of wood with a metal nib at one end, it was still called a pen. Now we use fountain pens and ballpoint pens. Again, we can say that *aeroplane* no longer has exactly the same meaning as it had fifty years ago, in the days of struts and canvas. Similarly, there has in practice been a change of meaning in the words *parliament*, *king*, *law*, and so on, as the institutions denoted by these words have undergone a process of historical evolution.

Such changes of meaning have taken place even in the animal and vegetable kingdom, thanks to selective breeding: medieval sheep and horses differed a great deal from the sheep and horses found on British farms today (the sheep were much longer-legged and the horses smaller), and the rose that Shakespeare wrote about was not much like the typical garden-rose in England today.

Similar diachronic changes have been undergone by many words in more abstract realms—words concerned with concepts, values, and moral and aesthetic judgments. As Charles Barber (1964: 245) (cited from Anderson & Stageberg, 1975: 131) points out, "the words *good*, *virtuous*, *modest* and *beautiful* do not mean the same today as they did in 1600, because our moral and aesthetic standards have changed: our idea of what constitutes virtuous conduct, or a modest woman, or a beautiful painting does not tally with the ideas of Shakespeare and his contemporaries." For example, a modern Englishwoman can wear clothes that would have seemed shockingly immodest a hundred years ago, she can discuss topics that were taboo for women in the Victorian age, she can do things that would have been unseemly in her grandmother's youth, and still not incur the charge of immodesty.

The constant verbal traffic between common words and various technical words also leads to semantic changes. The word *hi-fi*, for example, is a technical term when used for very sensitive sound-reproducing apparatus. But recently we hear people say that someone is a hi-fi, which means that he is a reliable person. By so doing, the term "hi-fi" becomes a common word again. *Catalyst* meaning "somebody or something that helps to bring about change", *angel* meaning "a radar echo caused by something not visually discernible" and conventional meaning "having a power source that is not nuclear" are further instances of conversion from technical words to common words and vice versa.

Words are a reflection of life as life changes, so do the words used to describe it. For example, the original meaning of *feedback* is "the transfer of part of the output of an active circuit or device back to the input". But now it can mean "response" in common use, as in "The teacher likes to have feedback from his students.".

Science and technology as social cause also bring about changes in meaning. Take the word *engine* for example: its origin is the Latin word *ingenium*, meaning "natural ability". But when steam power was developed in the first quarter of the 19th century, the term engine came to mean "a railroad locomotive"; and in contemporary English, it means "any machine that uses energy to develop mechanical power, especially a machine for starting motion in some other machine".

Language faithfully reflects the spirit of the age, so that words of long-standing can readily modify their meaning in accordance with the latest outlook of a given society. It is evident that the word *music* has a wider connotation today than in the 18th century, or even than a generation ago, for we now include within the scope of this same word a number of phenomena which would not formerly have been considered as coming into the musical sphere at all. In 1945, the unleashing of nuclear weapons against the Japanese caused the harmless little word *atom* to take upon itself the terrifying implications of endless destruction. Even the simple words *cold* and *hot* have changed their meanings in the field of politics, as in *cold war* and *hot war*.

7.1.2 Psychological Cause

The psychological cause is also constantly at work in bringing about changes in word meaning. Words can create various mental images and emotive associations in the speaker's mind. For example, words denoting occupation or social rank often develop meanings referring to the moral or intellectual qualities (real or supposed) of people in that station. The word *noble*, from meaning "pertaining to the aristocracy", has come to mean "lofty, magnanimous, imposing, holding high ideals" because these qualities are supposed to be characteristic of noble families. On the other hand, prejudice against countrymen or rustics changed the meaning of the word *villain* from "a farm servant" to "a cruelly malicious person or a scoundrel", and the meaning of the word *boor* from "a peasant" to "a clownish, rude, or unmannerly person".

The psychological cause can be classified into three categories: euphemism, grandiloquence, and cynicism.

1. Euphemism

People have a tendency to use mild, agreeable language when speaking of an unpleasant or embarrassing fact (such as death, unfortunate events, etc.), and of taboo subjects such as sex and the excretive processes of the body. This tendency leads to euphemisms.

Hence, death and things related to death are one of the most common objects of euphemism. We have a long list of expressions concerning death: *pass away, breathe one's last, depart this life, taken or called, go to a better world* or *go west, kick the bucket, be no more*, and many others. The undertaker, who was originally an "undertaker of funerals", is now a *funeral director, mortician*, or even a *funeral counselor*. The coffin is now commonly called a *casket*, and graves are *plots* or *last resting places*. Graveyards are now less bluntly known as *cemeteries* or *memorial gardens*.

It is a general human tendency to avoid using "dirty words" which usually refer to taboo subjects such as sex and excretion, in polite society. Hence for *urinate*, there are many euphemisms such as *to go to the toilet* or *to go to the loo (bathroom, lavatory, toilet, cloak-room, ladies, ladies' room, gentlemen, rest room, W.C.* and so on, not to mention the innumerable phrases such as *to wash one's hands*, *to spend a penny*, etc. Euphemism itself does not lead to a change of meaning, but it often happens that euphemistic expressions, as mentioned in the above context, become so popular that their original and literal senses are completely forgotten, and they come actually to denote what they at first intended to conceal.

Since the spread of democratic sentiments in the British community, people have also found it indelicate or politically inexpedient to mention too bluntly the difference between individuals—differences of endowment, of possessions, of social class. For example, people who are below the average intellectually are described as *dim* or *dim-witted* in popular speech, and *mentally deficient* in official language which is further softened by the use of initials to *m.d.*; another example of initials as a euphemism is *e.s.n.*, used in schools to mean "educationally sub-normal". Nowadays people in western countries are no longer rich or poor: instead, they are placed in a higher or a lower income bracket, and the poor have become the *underprivileged*.

2. Grandiloquence

Grandiloquence refers to the use of long, important-sounding words for effect. The desire to upgrade or raise the social status of a position, occupation, or institution by changing its common name to one felt to confer greater dignity or importance is another psychological factor in the change of word meaning.

For example, during the 1960s *garbage collector* was upgraded to *sanitation man*, but even this title was found wanting and so the more high-sounding one of *sanitation engineer* was invented. Some barbers who at first were satisfied with calling themselves *hair stylists* later chose *hairologists* as a better title. Car salesmen are publicized as car *counselors*, and in at least one school system the people hired to assist with bookrooms and audiovisual aids are called *para-professionals*, a more impressive title than *clerk*.

Similarly, a janitor is often called a *custodian*, and a gardener becomes a *landscape architect*. *Concentration camp* was originally a euphemism referring to a camp where political prisoners and prisoners of war are imprisoned in a place similar to a prison, or even worse. A place of solitary confinement in a prison is called an *adjustment center*. In Great Britain, a reform school is now called a *community home*. In a sense, a grandiloquence is a form of euphemism, too.

3. Cynicism

Another psychological factor that has something to do with semantic change is cynicism, the desire to sneer, and be sarcastic. For instance, the word *pious* may mean "hypocritically virtuous", in addition to its primary meaning, "having, showing deep devotion to religion". *Fanatic*, a Latin synonym for *enthusiastic*, means "unreasonably enthusiastic, almost approaching to madness"; *grandiloquent*, a Latin word for *eloquent*, very soon took on the present sense of "pompous in language; given to beautiful talk". The present meaning of *sanctimonious* is "pretending to be very holy or pious", whereas, it once meant "devout, holy, or sacred".

7.1.3 Linguistic Cause

Sometimes a change of meaning is caused by the form of a word: one word is confused with another that resembles it in some way, or its meaning is affected by the meaning of its components. For example, in early Modern English, *obnoxious* often had the meaning of its Latin original, "liable to harm or punishment, exposed to injury"; its modern meaning "offensive, objectionable" is due to the influence of the word *noxious*. Malapropism, namely the ridiculous misuse of words that are similar in sound, may have played a part in the development of a new meaning for *disinterested* ("not taking an interest" instead of "impartial") and *protagonist* ("supporter" instead of "main character"). The new meaning of *disinterested* is probably due to confusion with *uninterested*. The change in *protagonist* is probably due to the influence of *antagonist*: speakers feel half consciously that these two words contain the prefixes *pro-* ("for") and *anti-* ("against"), and are therefore the antonymous pair. They are unaware of the fact that the first part of *protagonist* is from the Greek *protos* ("first"), and the word originally meant "first competitor" or "first actor". The new meanings of *disinterested* and *protagonist* enjoy current popularity, though they are frowned upon by many literators.

Change of word meaning is also often brought about by ellipsis in English. Omission as a cause of semantic change often occurs in habitual collocations, such as "adjective + noun", or "attributive noun + noun", in which the noun is often deleted and only the first element (the attributive) is left, but retaining the sense of the whole phrase. *Private*, for instance, meaning "a soldier of the lowest rank", comes from the omission of the noun in the phrase *private soldier*.

More instances such as the shortened forms *editorial*, *bugle*, *gold*, *uniform*, *daily*, and *general* as substitutes for "editorial article", "bugle horn", "gold medal", "uniform dress", "daily newspaper" and "general officer" have extended their meanings to cover the meanings of the whole phrases.

The analogical tendency is also constantly at work. New meanings developed in one part of speech are passed on to other parts of speech from the same lexical base. For instance, the adjective *diplomatic* had earlier meant only "skillful in managing international relations", had by 1826 developed the sense of "tactful in the management of relations of any kind; artful management in dealing with others". By 1848, this new meaning had been passed on to the noun *diplomacy* (Waldron, 1967:123). Another interesting example is *fruition*, originally from the Latin word *fruitio* meaning "enjoyment". It is hardly ever used in this sense in contemporary English; in the *Longman Dictionary of Contemporary English* (1978), its meaning is given as "fulfillment of (plans, desired results, aims, etc.)", possibly from connection with the word *fruit*.

7.1.4   Foreign Influences

The influence of foreign words has been another cause of the change of meaning in words. The influx of loan words causes competition between native words and their foreign counterparts. Sometimes a Saxon word that had a general sense has been replaced by a French word or a Latin derivative, and the competition among synonymous words often ended with the result that the native words have survived with a restricted meaning. For instance, the Saxon word *doer* (= deer) meant a wild animal of any sort from a lion to a mouse. The line from *King Lear*, "Rats and mice and such small *deer*", reminds us that this meaning survived at least until Shakespeare's time. But during the Middle Ages, the French word *beste* (= beast) became the general word, and in the 16th century, the Latin derivative *animal* was also adopted into the English vocabulary. Today *deer* has retained only its present meaning.

The native word *stool*, for example, originally meant any kind of seat for one person, and could even be used for a king's seat. It got its present humble meaning because the French word *chair* was adopted to denote a more comfortable piece of furniture. Similarly, *pig*, *sheep*, and *ox* (cow) meant both the animals and their meat in the Old English period, but since the meat was called *pork, mutton*, and *beef* respectively among the Norman conquerors, the original terms are now used only as the names of the animals.

7.2   Four Tendencies in Semantic Change

The meaning of words themselves may shift over time. The classical examples are *knave*, which once meant a young lad and now means someone rather nasty; *deer*, which once meant "wild animals in general (so bears could be considered deer)"; and *couth*, which meant "known or familiar" and now survives only in *uncouth*. The word *broadcast* meant "to scatter seeds" but now is used primarily to refer to "scattering words on radio and television". *Drive* originally referred to "driving cattle" but is now mainly used for "driving cars". Clearly, what a word once meant is not always what it means now.

An amusing example is the word *virtue* which is related to the Latin *vir*, meaning "man". *Virtue*, then, originally meant something like "manliness" in general. Later it came to stand for "warlike prowess". Still later, as it passed into French and then English, it meant "power and noble quality", and then it came to be applied primarily to women as in "May all your sons be brave and all your daughters virtuous."

We have observed that change of meaning follows certain tendencies. Change in the denotational meaning may result in the extension of meaning and the restriction of meaning; change in the connotational meaning may bring about the elevation of meaning and the degradation of meaning. These four tendencies are universal in their application and are not confined to the English language. They will be found at work in every language and at all times.

7.2.1 Extension of Meaning

Extension or generalization of meaning means the widening of a word's meaning until it covers much more than its original sphere. In other words, it is a process by which a word that originally had a specialized meaning has now become generalized. A good example is the word *paper*. It is the same as *papyrus*, the paper-reed of the Nile from the thin strips of which writing-sheets were first made as a substitute for parchment. The name was naturally transferred to paper made of cotton, linen, and other fibers. Today a *paper* may mean a written or printed document, negotiable notes or bills, any written piece of schoolwork, an essay, article, or dissertation on a particular topic, a newspaper or journal, and so on.

Another good example is the word *manuscript*, a word that now refers to any author's copy whether written by hand or typed, but originally meant only something handwritten. Some manufactured articles are still made by hand (which is what the word means), but the word *manufactured* now applies generally to all sorts of mechanical processes. The followings are more examples:

Word	Original meaning	Current meaning
• *bird*	young bird	a creature with wings and feathers
• *pigeon*	young dove	any dove
• *pig*	young swine	any swine
• *place*	square, broad street	any kind of locality

- *butcher* one who slew one animal only, the goat a person who slaughters animals, fish, or poultry for food or market
- *holiday* holy day, a day of religious significance a time of rest from work; a day fixed by law or custom on which ordinary business is suspended in celebration of some event or person
- *rubbish* rubble waste matter, anything worthless
- *salary* salt money a fixed compensation periodically paid to a person for regular work or services

Words often take on a wider meaning when they move out of the language of some special group and get adopted by the speech community as a whole. The word *industry* serves as an excellent example. *Industry* has traditionally meant manufacturing enterprise in a particular field, being named after its principal products. But now almost any profit-making activity is termed an *industry*. The traditional definition is no longer appropriate. Besides *the farming industry*, we have all sorts of industries concerning horticulture, pig, catering, clothing, toy, film, insurance, handknit, newspaper, tourism, and so on. Now we even have *Internet industry, holiday industry, gambling industry, hotel industry, racing industry*, and *football industry*. Similar widenings of meaning can be seen in the popular use of words from other fields: *feedback* from electronics, *dimension* from physics, *catalyst* from chemistry, *allergic* from medicine, *complex* from psychology, and so on.

A recent example of the extension of meaning is *Mafia* (often capitalized). It was the name of a hierarchical society of criminals which arose in Sicily in the 13th century. Sicilians and Italians who emigrated to North and South America in the late 19th and early 20th centuries took the Mafia along with them, and in the US, it grew to be the largest and most powerful of crime organizations. Nowadays the term is applied indiscriminately to any secret society of criminals "engaging in blackmail, illicit trade in narcotics, etc.", and to "a group of people of similar interests or backgrounds prominent in a particular field or enterprise".

The word *cadet* in New Zealand English is applied not only to the military, but also to someone learning sheep-farming. In Australian English, the word *mob* is not restricted to people but also includes animals (*a mob of cattle*) or even mass nouns (*mobs of booze*). Furthermore, it can be used as an intensifier (*it's mobs better*).

We have certain words which have generalized to such a degree that they can mean almost anything. Such words are *thing, business, concern, condition, matter, article, circumstance, deal, fact*, and so on. The word *thing*, for example, used to mean "a public assembly" or "a council" in Anglo-Saxon times. Now it has become a what-you-may-call-it kind of word; it is capable of fitting into a wide variety of contexts on which its sense is wholly dependent. Some linguists have regarded general and vague words as an inevitable and useful feature of a language. They afford us a choice between an exact expression and a vague term: sometimes we do not want to commit ourselves to precise and distinct statements. So both exactness and vagueness in meaning are the *things* we need.

But note that additions of meaning or semantic broadening can also include an extension of the field of collocation, as when *buy into* (normally: *a business*) is extended, for example, to buying into an argument in Australian English.

7.2.2 Restriction of Meaning

Restriction or specialization of meaning is the converse of semantic broadening, which is also called semantic narrowing, which means that a word acquires a narrower, more specific meaning than it formerly had. The process is the opposite of the extension of meaning and occurs much more frequently. There are two main reasons for this tendency, as indicated by the well-known psychologist Heinz Werner:

> *"... One is that the predominant developmental trend is in the direction of differentiation rather than of synthesis. A second reason, related to the first, is that the formation of general concepts from specific terms is of lesser importance in non-scientific communication though it is rather a characteristic of scientific endeavour. In other words, language in everyday life is directed toward the concrete and specific rather than toward the abstract and general" (Ullmann, 1977: 229).*

Meat, as in *sweetmeat* and as in the archaic phrase *meat and drink*, meant any kind of food. It now means "edible flesh", a sense formerly expressed by *flesh* and *flesh meat*. Another example is the verb *starve* which originally meant simply "die". In Middle English, it was sometimes specialized to mean "die of cold" (and in modern Yorkshire dialect a body can still "starve of cold"), but a 16th-century specialization, "die of hunger", is the meaning that has survived in the current English. *Girl* meant "young person of either sex", but is now restricted to "a young and unmarried female person". Interestingly, we find that in Chinese "子" formerly denoted both son and daughter in ancient times, but now it refers only to a son in one's family.

Several names of animals have been restricted from genus to species; for example, *fowl* denoted "bird" in general as in Chaucer's *Parlement of Foules* and Biblical "fowls of the air", and as in traditional names of large birds such as *sea fowl, water fowl*, and *wild fowl*. But now *fowl* normally means a domestic cock or hen, especially when full grown. Interestingly, we find the same narrowing of meaning happening in the Chinese word " 禽 ". It could denote both hair-grown animals and feather-grown ones in ancient times, but now it means only birds with feathers, especially farmyard birds.

Here are more examples of specialization:

Word	Original meaning	Current meaning
• *disease*	any kind of discomfort, lack of ease	illness
• *undertaker*	one who undertakes to do a particular work	a person whose job is to arrange funerals; a mortician
• *liqueur*	any liquid	strong alcoholic drink
• *garage*	a place for storage	a place where motor vehicles can be kept
• *grocer*	one who sells in the gross; a wholesale dealer	a shopkeeper who sells food and other household things
• *wife*	woman	married woman especially in relation to her husband
• *success*	result, outcome	a favorable or satisfactory outcome or result

Moreover, words used in special trades or occupations often lose their general meaning and take on specialized meanings. The French term *chauffeur*, which meant a man who "stokes a fire" acquired the general meaning of "driver", but has now been specialized to mean "driver of a motor vehicle".

As new words move into the language, they may develop special meanings. For instance, the meaning of *readable* has moved from something being simply, able to be read to something that is easy or pleasant to read; *washable* does not simply mean that something is able to be washed; it means something, especially clothing, that can be washed in water without being spoiled. *Breakable* means something quite special too; to say something is *breakable* means it is easily broken. The word implies that one has to take good care of it and handle it carefully.

What are the factors that account for the restriction of meaning? One is the competition among synonymous words. The borrowing of the Latin *animal* and the French *beast* meant that with the native *deer*, English would have possessed three exactly synonymous terms for the one and same referent, thus for the sake of linguistic economy the word *deer* has restricted its reference to one particular species of animal. *Animal* and *beast* have also differed in their shades of meaning. According to *Longman Dictionary of Contemporary English* (1978), *animal* means "a living creature, not a plant, having senses and able to move itself when it wants to: snakes, fish, and birds are all animals" whereas *beast* denotes "a 4-footed animal, especially a large 4-footed farm animal". *Bird* and *fowl*, *dog* and *hound* are further instances of words that were once synonymous but have differed in meaning by the specialization of *fowl* and *hound*.

Another factor is that as society changes, one aspect of the general meaning of a word surges to the fore, and becomes more important than the rest of the meaning. This explains the specialization of the word *doctor*. Originally the title *doctor* was given to one who was skilled in any learned profession. But today *doctor* normally means only the man of medicine, the man who becomes of some importance to people when they are ill.

7.2.3 Elevation of Meaning

The two phenomena of extension and restriction are not enough to cover semantic change adequately. There are also changes in which associations, or connotations, of a word, take on a new character. When a word is upgraded it adopts a more positive meaning. Words often rise from a humble beginning to a more dignified status. This developing process is called elevation or amelioration of meaning. Elevation of meaning is often the result of a general change in social or cultural attitudes. Some words early in their history signified something quite low or humble but changed as time went by to designate something agreeable or pleasant. Take a common word *nice* for example. Its original meaning was "ignorant", then changed to "foolish" and now elevated to mean "delightful, pleasant". In the late 17th century, the words *enthusiasm* and *zeal* were pejorative, implying violence and fanaticism, because of their association with revolutionary Puritanism, but as English society changed and the civil wars were forgotten these associations were lost.

A more recent example is the word *job*, which was a slang term or colloquialism in the 1930s. The various household tasks such as cooking, washing, sweeping up, and so on were known as "jobs". A job was not supposed to denote any paid employment which should be called a "post" or "situation". Once upon a time, school teachers used to warn their students against the use of the word *job* in their written applications for employment. But since 1930s, the term has gained greatly in prestige and is capable of being used in quite dignified circumstances. This upward movement of an original slang word left a gap for a term describing household tasks and this has been filled by "chores" (Foster, 1981: 130).

The word *witch*, for example, is traditionally connected with evil and magic, and witches are generally conceived of as old and ugly women. Evidence for this lies in the appearance of and the role attributed to witches in fairy tales. But it also picks up the positive connotation, stressing only the practice of magic, the enchanting or charming activities of an enchantress.

Here we have amelioration. The following are more examples:

Word	Original meaning	Current meaning
• *angel*	a messenger	a messenger of God
• *martyr*	witness	a person who chooses to suffer death rather than renounce his religion
• *paradise*	park	heaven
• *pretty*	sly	beautiful
• *nice*	ignorant; foolish	pleasant, acceptable
• *fond*	foolish	affectionate
• *chamberlain*	room-attendant	a high official of a royal court; an official appointed to direct the housekeeping affairs of a king or nobleman's court
• *minister*	servant	a person in charge of a particular department of the government
• *constable*	stable-attendant	a policeman
• *governor*	pilot, steersman	a person who controls an organization or a person who rules a colony
• *steward*	sty-guardian	a person who serves passengers on a ship or plane

No one today would resent being described as *shrewd* or *nimble*, yet these words were at one time highly pejorative. A *shrewd* person used to be associated with "evil" or "wickedness", and a *nimble* one was thought to be good at taking things without permission. *Chamberlain*, now a "high official of royal courts", was formerly a "servant".

7.2.4　Degeneration of Meaning

It is much more common for word meanings to change from neutral to derogatory than it is for them to go the other way. This tendency, the opposite of elevation, is called degradation or pejoration of meaning. Many terms that are now descriptive of moral degeneration were once quite without this suggestion. An example is *lust*, which in Old English meant "desire, pleasure", but which today means "illicit or intemperate sexual desire". Another example is *lewd*, which was merely "ignorant", but now means "impure, dirty, obscene".

Words once respectable or neutral may shift to a less respectable, or even derogatory meaning. For instance, the neutral word *accident* once meant an occurrence, an event, as shown in Swift's *Journal to Stella*: "I'll... confine myself to the *accidents* of the day." It has since been degraded into its modern sense "an unplanned or chance event with unfortunate consequences".

Social prejudice against certain classes and occupations has also caused the word meanings to degenerate. For example, the names associated with farming have in general declined in dignity. A *villain* was a farm servant in feudal times but is now a scoundrel. Words like *boor*, *churl*, and *peasant* have also undergone deterioration from "a farm hand" into "an uncouth, ill-bred fellow in the low society". So we can see that *peasant* means something different from the Chinese "农民" which is usually appreciative or at least neutral in affective meaning. The English equivalent of "农民" should be a farmer or a farm worker.

The overuse of particular words on unsuitable occasions may also lead to the degeneration of meaning. Many people tend to use a few adjectives to describe everything they approve or disapprove of. These adjectives may be excellent in themselves, but if they are used too often, they will undergo deterioration and become mere symptoms of approval or disapproval without any particular meaning of their own.

Adjectives seem particularly susceptible to degradation. *Homely* originally meant only "pertaining to the home in any way". Since homes were most simple, unpretentious, and even plain, the word *homely* comes to mean "not beautiful, unattractive, not having elegance or refinement". *Notorious* and *egregious* have declined from the meaning of "well known or outstanding in a good way" to the meaning of "well known in a bad way or infamous". *Pompous* changed from "magnificent, splendid" to "foolishly solemn and self-important". *Sly*, *crafty*, and *cunning* all implied the compliment "skillful", but now connote "clever in deceiving, dishonest".

Euphemism is also an important factor leading to pejorative sense change. The figurative force of euphemism fades with constant use and faded euphemism results in the deterioration of meaning. The word *accident* mentioned above is euphemistic in origin, although the word had ceased to be so felt. Once a euphemistic expression ceases to be felt as such, it comes actually to denote the very same unpleasant fact or reality that it was intended to disguise; the result is a permanent degeneration of its sense.

Degradation of meaning indicates not only the changes of meaning from good to bad, but also the loss of intensity or weakening of meaning resulting from the habitual use of some strong modifiers and superlatives on light occasions. So *fair* comes to mean "passable" and "moderately good" (e.g., He has a fair chance of success); the adverb *quite* has passed, at least in some contexts, from "entirely" of "completely" to "moderately" (e.g., I think she is quite good). Similar weakening has occurred in the words *dismal*, *dreadful*, *fearful*, *frightful*, *horrible*, *horrid*, *monstrous*, and so on. Many intensifying adverbs such as *awfully*, *dreadfully*, *excessively*, *fantastically*, *immensely*, *incredibly*, *horribly*, and *monstrously* have had the same fate.

Degradation of meaning may result from changes in social or cultural attitudes. *Propaganda*, which now implies an organized and vicious distortion of facts for a particular purpose, has suffered depreciation in the present century. The word has been in frequent political circulation as a smearword, far removed from its use by the Roman Catholic Church in 1622 when Pope Gregory XV founded a special Committee or Congregation of Cardinals for the Propagation of the Faith, in Latin *Congregatio de Propaganda Fide* (Anderson & Stageberg, 1975: 127). Now when English-speaking people say "That's all *propaganda*", they mean something rather different from the Chinese term "宣传".

Another example is *apartheid*, originally an African word, meaning "separation". But it has taken on a derogative connotation owing to the policy of racial segregation adopted by South African authorities.

Connotative meaning extends to evaluation, as when the association of black with evil may lend this word a Pejorative connotation (*the black arts*, *blackguard*, *black magic*, *black mail*, *Black Mass*, *or black sheep*). However, since *black* also has numerous positive connotations, its pejoration is counterbalanced by ameliorating associations (to be in the black, black is beautiful, black gold, black tie). Consequently, there is hardly any likelihood that the word *black* will undergo general or permanent pejoration. The same is true of *white*: it suggests both something positive (white knight, white lie) as well as having negative associations (white elephant, white-livered).

7.3 Semantic Changes Resulting from the Figurative Use of Words

Words are used in two ways: literally and figuratively. When they are used literally, they have a nonliteral suggestive meaning. Figures of speech are variations from the literal or ordinary forms of expression to a more attractive or more striking form. They appeal to the imagination, make for clarity, and for beauty.

Change of meaning may result from the figurative use of words. This section is devoted to the discussion of several figures of speech that often cause semantic changes of words.

7.3.1 Metaphor

Metaphor is a figure of speech containing an implied comparison based on the association of similarity, in which a word or a phrase ordinarily and primarily used for one thing is applied to another, a process which often results in the semantic change or figurative extension of meaning; e.g., *a heart of stone*; *thunderous applause*; and a beautiful woman may be described as a *vision*.

Large numbers of word meanings are created through the process of metaphor. What this process means is that words are given additional meaning through an imaginative extension of their literal sense. "The first man to speak of the *foot* of a hill or of the *mouth* of a river was consciously coining a metaphor; but, by constant use, these innovations have ceased to be figurative. They are simply two common meanings of the words *foot* and *mouth*" (Anderson & Stageberg, 1975: 137). English is rich in this kind of dead metaphor which borrows from parts of the human anatomy: the long *arm* of the law, the *hands* and *face* of a clock, the *brow* of a hill, the *tongue* of a shoe, the *teeth* of a comb, the *lip* of a cup, the *head* of a hammer, the *nose* of a car, the *leg* of a table, the *elbow* of a pipe and the *ribs* of a boat, etc.

Another source of metaphors comes from the names of animals. Such a metaphorical use is called zoosemy. Some examples are an *ass* (a foolish person), a *cat* (a nasty person), a *fox* (a cunning or crafty person), a *pig* (a person who eats too much, is dirty or ugly in manner), a *duck* (a person one likes), an *ape* (a person who imitates the behavior of others) and a *parrot* (a person who, without thought or understanding, merely repeats the words or imitates the actions of others).

Metaphor can also be found at work in the following expressions: to *pump* somebody for information, to *squeeze* the rich, to *eat* one's words, to *ape* that one admires, to *dog* a criminal, to *freeze* somebody's assets or credit; time *flies*, anger *burns*, the *spring* and *autumn* of one's life, and the *apple* of somebody's eye.

Skillful speakers often employ metaphors that are drawn from the occupations of their listeners. For example, a political speaker might want to say that the promises of the other party sound fair but are not to be trusted. Here is the way he might express this idea metaphorically to different audiences (Anderson & Stageberg, 1975: 427):

- (To bankers) The Republicratic promises are nothing but watered stock.
- (To airplane pilots) The Republicratic promises are nothing but bent beams that will lend you to a crash on a mountainside.
- (To Texas ranchers) The Republicratic promises are nothing but loco weeds. They look edible and nourishing, but if your stock eats them, you will lose your herd.

- (To housewives) The Republicratic promises are the good berries on top of the basket.

All the above examples show that the semantic range of words is changed as a result of their being used metaphorically. Many words have been used so frequently as metaphors that their metaphorical senses have become well-established in people's minds. They are called faded metaphors; they were metaphors once but are no longer felt as such. When we speak of "at the *foot* of the page", we do not feel that we are comparing a foot to the bottom of a page. The sense "bottom" of *foot* is just one of this word's meanings, listed in any standard dictionaries.

7.3.2　Synaesthesia

Synaesthesia refers to a psychological process of transposition from one sense to another, as the hearing of a certain sound induces the visualization of a certain color. Synaesthesia is a special type of metaphor based on the association, mental or physical, between the two organs of sense. For example, colors can be cold or warm, and voice can be hard or soft. We can say so because we perceive some kind of similarity between colors and temperatures, voices, and the hardness of objects. The following stanzas from Shakespeare's *The Merchant of Venice* illustrate the use of this device:

Soft music like a perfume, and sweet light
Gold with audible odours exquisite
Swathe me with cerements for eternity.
(Arthur Symons, The Opium Smoker)
I heard, I looked, two senses both at once.
(Keats, Hyperion)
Here will we sit, and let the sounds of music
Creep in our ears: soft stillness and the night
Become the touches of sweet harmony.

The synaesthetic words in the above stanzas become widened in their ranges of meaning, having acquired their additionally figurative senses. The adjective *soft* acquires its extended meaning of "low or subdued in sound" in *soft music*; *sweet* is usually associated with taste or flavor, but means here "pleasing to see" in *sweet light*; *audible* usually means "able to be heard, hearable", but obviously acquires a different sense when used for the organs of smell in *audible odours*. The shift of meaning also occurs with some other words in the rest of the above examples.

7.3.3 Metonymy

Metonymy is another factor in semantic changes of words. It is a figure of speech that involves the substitution of the name of one thing for that of another closely associated with it. Change of meaning is brought about by a transfer of names between two things.

Here are two definitions for metonymy. Metonymy is, broadly defined, a trope in which one entity is used to stand for another associated entity. More specifically, metonymy is a replacive relationship that is the basis for a number of conventional metonymic expressions occurring in ordinary language. For example, "The pen is mightier than the sword." Pen and sword represent publishing and military force, respectively. The following examples illustrate the controller-for-controlled metonymy:

- *Nixon* bombed Hanoi. (*Nixon* stands for the armed forces that Nixon controlled.)
- A *Mercedes* rear-ended me. (*Mercedes* stands for a car manufactured by German Mercedes-Benz Automobile Corporation)

In most of the metonymic expressions listed above, the associations have become so close and so well-established in popular usage that people have no difficulty understanding the association. When we say "Poor John is on *the bottle* again" (= Poor John is addicted to alcoholic liquor again.), we do not feel that we are speaking of the container "bottle" for the thing contained "alcoholic liquor". This use of *bottle* is simply one of the word's senses that can be found in any standard dictionary.

Metonymy can be derived from various sources: names of persons (*John Bull* for England, *Uncle Sam* for the United States); animals (*British Lion* for England, the *Bear* for the former Soviet Union); professions (the *bench* for the office of judge or magistrate, the *press* for newspapers and magazines in general); locations or place names (*Hollywood* for American film industry, *Wall Street* for the US financial circles).

Metonymy also includes the following types:

(1) sign for the person or thing signified, e.g., *sceptre and crown* for a king, the *Cross* for the Christian religion

(2) container for its contents, e.g., *kettle* for water in the kettle, *cup* for a cup of tea or coffee

(3) the abstract for the concrete or vice versa, e.g., *pride* for the person or thing one feels proud of, *brain* for intellectual power

7.3.4 Synecdoche

Synecdoche is a figure of speech in which: a term denoting a part of something is used to refer to the whole thing, or a term denoting a thing (a "whole") is used to refer to the part of it, or a term denoting a specific class of thing (a "species") is used to refer to a larger, more general class (a "genus"), or a term denoting a general class of thing (genus) is used to refer to a smaller, more specific class (species), or a term denoting a material is used to refer to an object composed of that material. In a word, synecdoche is a figure of speech that involves the substitution of a part for the whole, or the whole for a part. We can note its use in a *sail* for a ship and *bread* for food, and in such proverbs as "Two *heads* are better than one." and "Many *hands* make light work." in which the words *heads* and *hands* substitute for persons. Here is another example of synecdoche from Shakespeare:

> *Return to her?*
> *No, rather I abjure all <u>roofs</u>, and choose...*
> *To be a comrade with the <u>wolf</u> and <u>owl</u>...*

The words *roof*, *wolf*, and *owl* in the above lines denote the whole house, the whole kingdom of beasts and birds.

On the other hand, the examples of the substitution of the whole for a part are not far to seek: the *army* for a soldier, a *country* for a team or delegation representing the country, and the smiling *year* for spring.

Change of word meaning cannot only result from such rhetorical devices as metaphor, synaesthesia, metonymy, and synecdoche, but also come from some other rhetorical devices such as euphemism, hyperbole, and litotes. Euphemism is the substitution of a word with a more pleasant connotation for one with an unpleasant connotation. To call someone poor is to speak pejoratively of his condition, while the substitution of *disadvantaged* or *underprivileged* indicates that poverty isn't his fault. Psychological necessity accounts for large numbers of euphemisms in English. But these euphemisms will often acquire a new meaning, e.g. *disadvantaged* and *underprivileged* which have a figurative meaning when applied to the condition of poverty.

Allied to euphemistic substitution is the use of hyperbole or exaggeration. They all spring from the same human motive to speak better of something. The set formulas "I beg a thousand pardons." and "I'd give worlds to see you." sound impressive, but the listener should never take them literally. Likewise, expressions like *absolutely unique*, *awfully disgusting*, and *vastly pretty* have their adjectives much weakened in force. So, hyperbole causes word meaning to change in value.

As a sharp contrast, litotes is a figure of speech that contains an understatement for emphasis and is the opposite of hyperbole. In litotes, the affirmative is expressed by the negative, e.g. "not bad" meaning "very good", and "not right fat" meaning "right lean". Litotes is actually a special type of euphemism as it is a roundabout way of speech.

We can observe from the above examples that the figurative use of words often expands word meanings, either denotational or connotational. Thus, figures of speech are an important area of semantic change and development.

Exercises

I. Give examples to illustrate four major tendencies that lead to the change of meaning.

II. For each word in the following table, you are shown an earlier and a later meaning. Label the semantic change of each with one of these symbols.

G. (Generalization or extension of the meaning)

S. (Specialization or restriction of the meaning)

A. (Amelioration or elevation of the meaning)

P. (Pejoration or degradation of the meaning)

Word	An earlier meaning	A later meaning
fame	common talk	renown
saloon	elegant dining room	inelegant drinking joint
marshall	groom, stableman	high official
citizen	city dweller	a member of a country
stink	smell	bad smell
campus	field, plain	college grounds
reek	to smoke	to smell bad
mansion	residence	sumptuous residence
front	forehead	the forward part of anything
wife	woman	married woman

III. Explain the following terms with examples and describe how they cause the change of meaning.

1. metaphor   **2.** synaesthesia   **3.** metonymy   **4.** synecdoche

5. euphemism   **6.** hyperbole   **7.** litotes

IV. Give a euphemistic substitute for each of the following words or expressions.

1. insane   **2.** toilet   **3.** drunkards   **4.** poor people   **5.** old people

V. How have the following words become specialized in meaning?

1. plant   **2.** bird   **3.** holiday   **4.** salary

VI. Find out the original meanings of the following words by consulting an etymological dictionary; suggest explanations as to how they have acquired their present meaning.

1. cunning   **2.** clue   **3.** style   **4.** horrible

VII. Describe the process of elevation or degradation of the meaning of the following words.

1. steward   **2.** shrew   **3.** villain   **4.** cunning   **5.** lewd

Chapter 8

Meaning and Context

From the previous two chapters, we know that most words have more than one meaning and some meanings change over time. Therefore, it is often impossible to tell the meaning of a word before it is used in context. By context, we mean the total environment in which a word appears. Context contributes a great deal to the meaning of a word, an utterance, or a passage and the interpretation of the precise meaning of a particular language unit depends very much on a particular context. Meaning involves both linguistic and extra-linguistic factors where the context of language use is essential. This contextual use of language is what makes language unique to humans. In this chapter, we will discuss different types of context, the relationship between meaning and context, and the way in which context affects the meaning of words.

8.1 Types of Context

Context derives from Latin, *contextus*, and refers to everything that surrounds, either physically or symbolically, an event. From the context, therefore, a fact can be interpreted or understood. The notion of context encompasses two broad categories: linguistic context and extra-linguistic context. Linguistic context or verbal context is the context in a narrow sense and refers to the linguistic environment in which a word is used, such as an utterance, a paragraph, or a passage where a certain word occurs. Extra-linguistic context or non-linguistic context is the context in a broad sense and covers such circumstances as time, place, background knowledge, etc. shared by both the speaker/writer and the listener/reader.

8.1.1 Linguistic Context

Linguistic context can be subdivided into lexical context, grammatical context, and textual context.

1. Lexical context

Lexical context is created by the words before and after a definite word. So in essence, it refers to word collocation, the combination of certain words and a particular word. A word may have various meanings, the exact of which is very often affected and determined by the neighboring words. For instance, the word *introduce* may mean "to make known to/familiar with; usher in/bring in; bring forward; bring into use/adopt; insert; etc." But its specific meaning comes only from its collocation with particular words, as indicated in the following sentences:

- The sophomore took on himself to *introduce* (= make familiar with) the freshman to campus life.

- He is apt to *introduce* (= usher in) new ideas into the business.
- Dressing designers *introduce* (= bring forward) new fashions each year.
- They have *introduced* (= adopted) a new job contract system into the factory's reform project.
- The electrician *introduced* (= inserted) an electric wire into the conduit.
- The well-known speaker *introduced* (= added) a humorous note in his speech.

Now, let's take the word *stage* as another example. Collocated with different words, it carries different meanings, as shown below:

- They are adding another *stage* (= a section of a space rocket with separate means of propulsion) to the rocket.
- He is a star of *stage* (= platform where plays, etc. are performed before the audience), screen, and television.
- At this *stage* (= point of development) of the game, Denver is ahead.
- We will *stage* (= organize and carry out) the next track meet in June.

The same is true of polysemic verbs such as *do*. Used as a notional verb, *do* conveys a large number of meanings and only context will determine exactly what is meant. For instance, we can say "*do* a sum" (work out the answer to a mathematical question), "*do* one's teeth" (brush), "*do* science at school" (study), "*do* fish" (cook), and "*do* a museum/country/city" (visit). Apart from these, we can also use *do* in such sentences as "a car can *do* 80 miles an hour", "Tom is *doing* well in school", "I'll *do* you if you don't stop" and so on. In each case, *do* has a different meaning. Examples like these can multiply in numbers.

2. Grammatical context

In some cases, different syntactical structures determine different meanings of a polysemous word. Such syntactical structures in which a word occurs are what we call grammatical context. For instance, the word *keep* can be used in different syntactic structures, and its meanings are different.

(1) *keep* + a gerund, meaning "continue to do", e.g. Ross kept staring at Nadia's decolletage.

(2) *keep* + an adjectival phrase, meaning "continue to be", e.g. Nadia kept calm and made a cutting remark.

(3) *keep* + a noun phrase, meaning "maintain", e.g. Ross wrote of his embarrassment in the diary that he kept.

Word class and inflectional paradigms contribute a great deal to the task of determining word meanings. Many words are marked at least with one word class in the dictionary. For example, the sentence "They saw her duck." may present two possible syntactical analyses, resulting in two different interpretations. Usually, we treat *her* as a possessive case and *duck* as a noun, and take this meaning for granted: "They saw the duck that belonged to her." However, we can also treat *her* as an objective case and *duck* as a verb, acting as the object complement, meaning "bob down, especially to avoid being seen or hit". Thus, we may well interpret the sentence as "They saw her lower her head."

Moreover, we have known that words will appear in different forms when used in actual speech, for example, play-plays-played. For the form *-ed*, if it stands alone, it is difficult to discern whether the form is past tense or past participle. In the sentence "They played basketball in the morning", *-ed* is the form of past tense, while in "They have played basketball since morning", *-ed* is the past participle. Putting these words into context is an easy way to distinguish their inflectional paradigms.

It should be mentioned that grammatical context alone is not always sufficient to supply a ready choice among the various senses of a particular word. It needs to be combined with lexical context to arrive at the right meaning. Take the pattern "*keep* + a noun phrase" for instance, *keep* may take on different senses if different noun phrases are used, as illustrated in the following examples:

- They *keep* (employ) a maid and a butler.
- Jack *keeps* (breeds) several heads of cattle.
- It is their custom to *keep* (observe) the Sabbath.
- The shepherd boy *kept* (watched) sheep on the moors at night.
- The foster parents *kept* (provided for the sustenance of) the child for a year until his real parents could be found.
- The chairman was not there to *keep* (manage) the yearly assembly.

3. Textual context

Textual or discourse context goes beyond the sentence and may cover an entire paragraph, an entire passage, or even an entire book. For example, the word *retire* in the sentence "He was compelled to retire again" cannot be correctly understood for it may mean "leave office or employment; go to bed; or withdraw". However, interposed in the following paragraph "when the enemy seemed falling back before him and his fellows, he went instantly forward, like a dog who seeing his foes lagging turns and insists upon being pursued. And when he was compelled to retire again, he did it slowly, sullenly, taking steps of wrathful despair.", *retire* definitely means "withdraw".

The famous American writer F. Scott Fitzgerald once made a vivid description in *Babylon Revisited*—"The Place de la Concord moved by in pink majesty". Here, the word *pink* is very confusing. But from the initial sentence of the paragraph "It was late afternoon", we realize that *pink* refers to the sunset glow. For another instance:

> "Frequently <u>his intention</u> operates through and satisfies itself in a combination of <u>the other functions</u>. Yet <u>it</u> has effects not reducible to their effects. It may govern the stress laid upon points in an argument, for example, shape the arrangement, and even call attention to itself in such phrases as 'for contrast's sake of 'lest it be supposed'. It controls the 'plot' in the largest sense of the word and is at work whenever the author is 'hiding his hand'. And it has special importance in dramatic and semi-dramatic literature. Thus the influence of his intention upon the language he uses is additional to and separable from <u>the other three influences</u>, and its effects can profitably be considered apart."

In the above paragraph, *it* cannot be exactly understood in each sentence where *it* occurs. But when the whole paragraph is taken into account, *it* clearly stands for *his intention*. "Whose" intention it is and who *he* is we cannot tell even from the whole paragraph. And neither can we tell the precise meaning of *the other functions* and *the other three influences* even though the entire paragraph is considered. So naturally, we have to go beyond the paragraph to look for the precise meaning. Skimming through the paragraphs before the cited one here, we get to know *his intention* is "the speaker's or the author's intention" and *he* of course is "the speaker or the author"; and *the other functions* and *the other three influences* refer to "sense; feeling; and tone" which the author thinks together with *intention*, form part of "the total meaning readers or listeners are engaged with".

8.1.2 Extra-Linguistic Context

When we talk about context, we usually study linguistic context instead of non-linguistic context. In fact, non-linguistic context often has more impact upon the meaning of words than we realize. Extra-linguistic or non-linguistic context is the largest context which may include such factors as time, place, subject matter, participant relations, or the entire cultural background. In everyday life, word meaning is more often dependent on the actual situation in which a word is used rather than on verbal context. For instance, when walking in the street, you may suddenly hear somebody shouting "Careful!" Only the situation could tell you whether the voice is warning you against being run over by a car or against being hit by a falling tile. Another example is that "Fire!", if used alone, bears various meanings. But it carries a specific meaning when shouted aloud in the dead of night and when pronounced by an officer in presence of his troops.

With the change of contextual factors, the same linguistic form may convey a different meaning. For example, the sentence "I'm sorry to trouble you, but could I ask you to close the door for me, please?" indicates courtesy if said to a stranger. But the polite form manifests irritation and displeasure if the participants are familiars.

The above examples show that the meaning of a word is decided by the actual speech situation in which a word (or an utterance, a speech event, etc.) occurs. In other cases, the extra-linguistic context may lead to an even broader view of context embracing the entire cultural background against which a word, an utterance, or a speech event has been set. For example, in the inaugural address by President John Fitzgerald Kennedy, there is such a paragraph: "We dare not forget today that we are the heirs of *that first revolution*. Let the word go forth from this time and place, to friend and foe alike that *the torch* has been passed to a new generation of Americans born in this century, tempered by war, disciplined by a hard and bitter peace, proud of *our ancient heritage* and unwilling to witness or permit the slow undoing of *these human rights* to which this nation has always been committed and to which we are committed today at home and around the world."

The italicized parts may turn out to be snags to people of other cultures, but to the American audience, their meanings were clear enough: "that first revolution" (the American war of Independence), "the torch" (the torch of the first American revolution ignited by the forebears), "our ancient heritage" (the Declaration of Independence), "these human rights" (the unalienable rights of life, liberty, and the pursuit of happiness) written in "the Declaration of Independence". Obviously, it is not a linguistic context that constitutes the comprehension barrier so much as extra-linguistic context.

Further, because of discrepancies in cultural background, the same lexical item may not carry the same meaning to people from different countries. There are words such as *propaganda* whose counterpart "宣传" in Chinese is by no means derogatory, but the English word is often used disparagingly to connote deception or distortion. The word *liberalism* whose Chinese version "自由主义" is quite unfavorable while the English original is favorable.

There are also words such as the English *Christmas* and the Chinese "春节" (the Spring Festival) which are similar in their denotations in both English and Chinese but dissimilar in their connotations in their respective originals and their corresponding version. To Westerners, the word "Christmas" is fully packed with feelings and emotions, and everything good while it means nothing more than a Western festival to the Chinese. Similarly, to the Chinese, "春节" means a great deal whereas it means just a Chinese traditional festival to Westerners.

When the extra-linguistic context extends to refer to the entire cultural background, it is often called the context of a culture, which is mainly concerned with cross-cultural communication. These cultural differences are important for non-native speakers to know in order to gain a better understanding of the cultural significance of English vocabulary.

8.2 Role of Context in Deciding Word Meaning

Having addressed the different types of context and their respective importance, we will look into the actual functions of context. Context is a tool by which a better understanding of meaning can be achieved and communication can be carried out smoothly and properly. To be specific, context can provide us with great help in eliminating ambiguities, removing vagueness, indicating referents, conveying emotional overtones, and supplying information omitted through ellipsis.

8.2.1 Eliminating Ambiguities

By ambiguity, we mean the phenomenon that a word, phrase, or sentence carries two or more than two possible interpretations or meanings. There are two main types of ambiguity: lexical ambiguity which is caused by the semantic properties of words that are phonetically identical and structural ambiguity which involves the superficial similarity of different syntactic structures. Both types of ambiguity may be readily eliminated by context as can be verified below.

1. Disambiguating a lexically ambiguous language unit

Lexical ambiguity is caused when two words have the same form (homonymy or homophony) or when a word has more than one meaning (polysemy). Some researchers prefer the term "semantic ambiguity" as this makes it clear that it is the meaning of the word that is ambiguous and not its form or grammatical properties (Vitello & Rodd, 2015), but these terms are largely interchangeable. This chapter uses the term "lexical ambiguity" due to its more widespread use.

A classic example of lexical ambiguity involves the word *bank*. The sentence "I went to the bank" is ambiguous because the word *bank* can mean either a type of financial institution or an area of land next to a river. Another example is the sentence "Pass the port", in which *pass* may mean "go across", or "give by hand" and *port* has the meaning "harbor" or "a kind of wine". Hence the sentence can mean: "(The ship) went across the harbor", or "Please hand me the wine".

Lexical ambiguity is sometimes used deliberately to create puns and other types of wordplay. For example, in the joke "What did the fish say when he swam into a wall? Dam", both meanings of the ambiguous word form "dam/damn" (i.e., wall of a reservoir vs. expression of anger) are partially consistent with the sentence context and in order to understand the humor of the pun, both meanings must be accessed. Another joke is cited from *The Linguistic Analysis of Jokes* (Ritchie, 2003), which goes like this: "Do you believe in clubs for young people?" someone asked W. C. Fields. "Only when kindness fails," he replied. Lexical ambiguity lies in the fact that the speaker was referring to nightclubs, while Fields—kiddingly—took it to mean something along the lines of a wooden bat.

2. Disambiguating a structurally ambiguous language unit

Structural ambiguity results when an utterance might have more than one grammatical structure. For example, the phrase *young men and women* can be analyzed either as "young / men and women /" (i.e., both men and women are young) or "/ young men / and women" (i.e., only the men are young).

One widely-cited example is the sentence "Flying planes can be dangerous.", from Noam Chomsky's (1965) *Aspects of the Theory of Syntax*. This sentence is structurally ambiguous because the phrase *flying planes* might refer to the activity of flying or to the machines, planes when they are flying. In the first case, the sentence means "It can be dangerous to fly planes." while in the second it means something like "While flying, planes are dangerous." These two meanings reflect two different grammatical structures, but on the surface, the sentences look and sound alike.

Now let us examine another sentence "The fish is ready to eat." This sentence carries an ambiguous infinitive, of which "the fish" may be either the logical subject or object, thus resulting in two possible interpretations: "The fish is ready to eat something else" or "The fish is cooked and ready to be served". However, when we read "What a nice smell! I think the fish is ready to eat." We will take the latter sense. In this example, it is the linguistic context that disambiguates the ambiguous "to eat".

Let's see another example: "I found John an experienced doctor" with the shared knowledge of John's identity (or occupation). The hearer could positively take this statement to be either "I discovered that John was an experienced doctor" or "I succeeded in finding an experienced doctor for John".

Curiously enough, polysemous words do not create any ambiguity or confusion in the ordinary course of daily life, because the word reaches us already prepared by what precedes and by what surrounds it, interpreted by time and place, and determined by the speaker's relevant features such as personality, age, sex, education, occupation, etc.

Context often makes the meaning of a polysemous word so certain that we do not think of the fact that it has different senses. A good example is the word *man*, a common enough word. Almost anyone knows its different meanings in the following sentences:

- *Man* must change in a changing world. (the human race)
- He tipped the chess board, dumping the *men* to the floor. (a playing piece used in chess)
- Mr. Brown sent his *man* for the luggage. (a servant)
- *Man* the SLA (second language acquisition) laboratory. (supply with a person or persons for service)

The meaning of *man* in the above sentences is the product of its interrelation with the other lexical items in the sentence. Therefore the context generally reveals which meaning out of all its possible meanings is to be attached to the word.

8.2.2 Specifying Referents and the Range of the Meaning

English has a large number of words such as *this/that*, *now/then*, *here/there*, and *these/those*, which are often used to refer directly to people, time, place, etc. Without clear context, the reference can be very confusing. For example, the word *now* always means the time of speaking, naturally referring to a past time when the speech took place in the past or a present moment if the person is speaking. It is the same with all referring expressions. Even a phrase like *the President of the United States* may bring about ambiguity without adequate verbal context, for it can be used to refer to any of the presidents in the US history.

Polysemous words are inclusive of many referents and a variety of meanings. It is context alone that can specify the exact referent and limits the exact range of meaning. In each of the following three sentences, the word *man* is specified by a particular context:

- It is not fit for *man* or beast. (human being without regard to sex)
- Stop crying and be a *man*. (brave person)
- They are *man* and wife. (husband)

A further example can be shown in the following dialogue:

- A: I'm going to *the bookstore*.
  B: Buy me *that book*, please.

Which bookstore is A going to? And what book does B want A to buy for him? The outsiders cannot tell. But as far as the dialogue is concerned, B knows which bookstore A is going to and A knows what book B wants him to buy.

As often as not the subsequent sentence or idea may require re-interpretation of an ambiguous word that has appeared with misleading bias in the previous sentence. For instance, the following two sentences can illustrate this point:

- The CIA called in an inspector to check for *bugs*.
- Some of the secretaries had reported seeing *roaches*.

The first sentence tends to make the reader decide that *bugs* means "hidden microphones", while the second sentence shows it to be "insects".

In conversation, in order to avoid repetition, pronouns such as *I, you, he, she, this*, and *that* are often used instead of a noun or a noun phrase; *do, can, should* can be used in place of a verb phrase; *then* and *there* are used in place of an adverbial phrase of time or place. Context is of great importance in understanding the referents of such words. Take the following dialog by linguist Firth as an example:

- A: Do you think he will?

  B: I don't know. He might.

  A: I suppose he ought to, but perhaps he feels he can't.

  B: Well, his brothers have. They perhaps think he needn't.

  A: Perhaps eventually he may. I think he should, and I very much hope he will.

Without context, these sentences are very difficult to understand. In fact, the modal verbs *will, might*, and *ought to* in the above dialogue are used in place of the verb phrase "join the army".

The determination of the specific referent or meaning of space deixis, time deixis, and most elliptical sentences can be realized only through context. For instance, from the sentence "Johnny lives *upstairs*", we have no idea which floor Johnny lives on. It may be any floor from the second upward depending on the exact floor where the speaker and the listener are. Another example:

- (which *wine* would you like) The red or the white?

Without the preceding question or without the actual situation, it would be impossible to specify the referent of "the red" or "the white", for they may refer to almost anything colorful.

Context is also of vital importance to the efficient comprehension of "conversational implicature", the implied meaning of a sentence. For example, to the question "Where's my box of chocolates?", there may be such possible responses:

- I was feeling hungry.
- I've got a train to catch.
- Where's your diet sheet?
- The children were in your room this morning.

At first hearing, these responses appear to be unduly related to the question. However, on second thoughts, the questioner can clearly understand them in the proper context of course. He may take them respectively to be:

- has eaten them.
- has taken them.
- has hidden them.
- tells him that the children must have eaten them.

8.2.3 Conveying Emotional Overtones

The emotive side of word meaning depends largely on the context, with the exception of those words that have the affective meaning as part of word meaning. Practically every emotionally neutral lexical item can in certain contexts acquire emotional overtones. An ordinary concrete noun like *wall*, for instance, is often used in a neutral and purely objective way; yet it might acquire emotional overtone, as in Shakespeare's *Midsummer Night's Dream* (Act V, Scene I):

"Thou wall, O wall, O sweet and lovely wall,
Show me thy chink, to blink through with mine eyne.
Thanks courteous wall. Jove shield thee well for this...
But what see I? No Thisby do I see.
O wicked wall, through whom I see no bliss;
Cure'd be thy stones for thus deceiving me!"

The word *wall* does not ordinarily occur in combination with such adjectives as *sweet*, *lovely*, *courteous* and *wicked*. This peculiar lexical context accounts for the possibility of emotional overtones.

Considered from the aspect of feelings and attitudes, words are of three kinds, namely appreciatory, neutral and derogatory, as indicated in the following cases:

- She is a *slender* girl. (appreciatory)
- She is a *thin* girl. (neutral)

- She is a *skinny* girl. (derogatory)

Moreover, different linguistic contexts can change a neutral word into a word with different affective meanings, either appreciatory or derogatory meaning. Now, let us take the following statements as an example.

- I like her. She is tall and thin and always walks like a crane.
- I dislike her. She is tall and thin and always walks like a crane.

These two statements are almost the same except for the verbs in their first sentences. According to *Oxford Advanced Learner's English-Chinese Dictionary* (Hornby, 2018), *crane* is "a large bird with long legs, neck, and beak" and has no effective meaning itself. In the first sentence, the word *crane* gives the heroine an elegant image while in the second sentence it becomes a sign of poor health condition and makes a negative impression on the readers' minds. It is the different linguistic contexts that change the meaning of *crane* so greatly and hence make it convey the emotional character of the context.

Words heavily charged with affective meaning can themselves express appreciatory or derogatory feelings and attitudes independent of the context such as the italicized words or expressions in the following two sentences:

- Jane is an *angel* of a girl.
- You're a vicious *tyrant* and a villainous *reprobate* and I hate you for it!

However, context can charge an emotionally neutral word with emotional overtones, as vividly illustrated in the following lines from *Hamlet* (Act I, Scene II) by Shakespeare:

"...
A little month, or ere those shoes were old
With which she followed my poor father's body,
Like Niobe, all tears. why she, even she—
O (God)! a beast that wants discourse of reason
Would have mourn'd longer—married with mine uncle,
My father's brother, but no more like my father
Than I to Hercules. Within a month,
Ere yet the salt of most unrighteous tears
Had left the flushing of her galled eyes,
She married. O, most wicked speed, to post
With such dexterity to incestuous sheets!
It is not nor it cannot come to good.

But break, my heart, for I must hold my tongue."

Here, common nouns such as "tears", "speed", and "sheets" are often used in a natural and objective way to acquire emotional overtones. Through the use of "unrighteous tears", "wicked speed" and "incestuous sheets", Hamlet strongly expressed his indignation at his mother's infamous behavior.

Context can also make an appreciative word carry a derogatory sense, as shown in the sentences which are taken from *G. I. Diary* by David Parks: "We are *lucky*. It's the other side on the thirteenth of December. That makes us *feel real good*."

The writer means exactly the opposite of what he says. The thirteenth is an unlucky number to most Westerners, and therefore they are definitely not lucky. Since on that day (December 13), they will land "on the other side" of the Pacific in Vietnam to fight in the Vietnam war, they don't feel good at all. In fact, they are all quite frightened at the prospect.

8.3 How to Guess Word Meaning from Context

Guessing word meaning from context refers to the ability to infer the meaning of an expression using contextual clues. Context can help us guess the meaning of an unknown word as well as decide the precise meaning of a known word. The importance of context in guessing word meaning can be seen in the following quotation from the renowned Danish linguist Otto Jespersen (1904: 68):

"There are many combinations where the meaning of a word may be "scented" through the context. The ability to arrive at the meaning of an unfamiliar word through the text is valuable and does not deserve to be neglected but should, on the contrary, be cultivated under control of course. The pupil who is acquainted with any two of the three words will be able to reason out the meaning of the third with as great accuracy as in the equation a + b = c. The unknown quantity may be found when the two are given."

Generally speaking, context can provide us with five effective mechanics, with the help of which word meaning can be correctly guessed. These five mechanics include lexical clues, syntactical restrictions, semantic or logical connections, the role of the topic sentence, and the role of background knowledge.

8.3.1 Lexical Clues

More often than not, words around a particular word will give at least a general idea of its sense. There are several different types of lexical clues. The major types include the following ones.

1. Definition

The new term may be formally defined, or sufficient explanation may be given within the sentence or in the following sentence. Clues to definition include "that is", commas, dashes, and parentheses. For example:

- His *emaciation*, that is, his skeleton-like appearance, was frightening to see. ("Skeleton-like appearance" is the definition of *emaciation*.)
- *Fluoroscopy*, examination with a fluoroscope, has become a common practice. (The commas before and after "examination with a fluoroscope" point out the definition of *fluoroscopy*.)
- The *dudeen*—a short-stemmed clay pipe—is found in Irish folk tales. (The dashes setting off "a short-stemmed clay pipe" point out the definition of *dudeen*.)

2. Antonyms and contrast

Antonyms are words with opposite meanings. An opposite-meaning context clue contrasts the meaning of an unfamiliar word with the meaning of a familiar term. Words like *although*, *however*, and *but* may signal contrast clues. For example:

- When the light brightens, the pupils of the eyes contract; however, when it grows darker, they *dilate*. (*Dilate* means the opposite of "contract".)
- The children were as different as day and night. He was a lively conversationalist, but she was reserved and *taciturn*. (*Taciturn* means the opposite of a "lively conversationalist".)

3. Synonyms or synonymous expressions

A synonym is a word or phrase that means the same or is very similar to another word. In some cases, the meaning of an unknown word is expressed in familiar words nearby. Signals of synonyms in the text include *means, called, that is, also known as, is referred to as, by ... is meant ...*, commas, or dashes. For example:

- Flooded with spotlights—the focus of all attention—the new Miss America began her year-long reign. She was the *cynosure* of all eyes for the rest of the evening. (*Cynosure* means "the focus of all attention".)
- The mountain pass was a *tortuous* road, winding and twisting like a snake around the trees of the mountainside. (*Tortuous* means "winding and twisting".)

- Their greatest fear was of a *conflagration*, since fire would destroy their flimsy wooden settlement before help could arrive. (*Conflagration* means "fire".)

But it is rarely the case that two words will be synonymous on every occasion—if they were, there would be little need to have both words in the language. There is no such thing as true synonymy. So, when we use the term "synonymy", we are actually talking about partial synonymy, and the following examples illustrate how synonymy differs.

- flat–apartment (different variety, British English vs. American English)
- kid–child (different style, colloquial vs. neutral)
- skinny–slim (different connotation, pejorative vs. amelioration)
- conceal–hide (different grammar, one is a transitive verb while the other may also be intransitive)

As long as these differences are highlighted, the use of synonyms is often a quick way of explaining words. A more complex example than the ones above involves synonyms with collocational restrictions. For instance, the verb *commit* may be defined as "do" or "make" in the phrases such as *commit a crime* or *commit an error*, but it would need to be pointed out that *commit* only collocates with certain nouns and is not generally synonymous with "do" or "make".

4. Hyponymy or example clues

Sometimes, instead of giving a formal explanation, the author may cite an example that is sufficient to throw light on the meaning of a new word. Superordinates and subordinates often define and explain each other, thus forming an important context clue. Words like *including*, *such as*, and *for example* point out example clues. For example:

- Many United Nations employees are *polyglots*. Ms. Mary, for example, speaks five languages. (Ms. Mary who can speak five languages is a *polyglot*.)
- *Piscatorial* creatures, such as flounder, salmon, and trout, live in the coldest parts of the ocean. (Flounder, salmon, and trout are some of the *piscatorial* creatures.)
- *Celestial* bodies, including the sun, moon, and stars, have fascinated man through the centuries. (*Celestial* objects are those in the sky or heavens.)

Of course, only by hyponyms, we may not get the exact meaning. For example, "flounder, salmon, and trout" does not tell us exactly what "piscatorial" means, but we know at least that it belongs to the same category as the rest and this is adequate because in real situations often a general idea is sufficient.

5. Cause and effect

The author explains the reason for or the result of the word. Words like *because*, *since*, *therefore*, *thus*, and *so* may signal cause and effect clues. For example:

- She wanted to impress all her dinner guests with the food she served, so she carefully studied the necessary *culinary* arts. (*Culinary* means "food preparation".)

6. The component parts of the word

Knowledge of prefixes, roots, and suffixes can tell something about the general meaning of a new word. The power of word parts lies in the ability to combine the roots and affixes with the context in which a word is used to discover the author's meaning. So it is helpful to memorize the most common roots and affixes that help form many English words. For example:

- Copernicus believed in a *heliocentric* universe rather than in the *geocentric* theory. ("Helio-" means "sun", and "geo-" "earth"; " centric" suggests "center".)
- The story is *incredible*. (The root "cred" means "to believe,' and the prefix "in-" means "not". Therefore, if a story is *incredible*, it is unbelievable.)
- The *somnambulist* had to be locked in his bedroom at night for his own safety. (If a reader knows the meaning of "ambular" (walk) and "somn" (sleep) and sees the sentence, the reader may realize that a *somnambulist* is a sleepwalker.)

7. Mood or tone clue

The author sets a mood, and the meaning of the unknown word must harmonize with the mood. For example:

- The *lugubrious* wails of the gypsies matched the dreary whistling of the wind in the all-but-deserted cemetery. (*Lugubrious*, which means "sorrowful", fits into the mood set by the words "wails", "dreary", and "deserted cemetery".)
- She told her friend, "I'm through with blind dates forever. What a dull evening! I was bored every minute. The conversation was absolutely *vapid*." (*Vapid* means "uninteresting" and fits into the mood set by the words "dull", and "bored".)

8.3.2 Syntactical Restrictions

It is true to say that a word may need other words with it to give it context and pin its meaning down. It is also true to say that syntax may impose restrictions upon the meanings of a word. A word receives some of its meaning as it fills grammatical slots in a sentence. Take the word *bull* for example, we cannot tell its particular meaning when it is in isolation. But we can do so in each of the following sentences just from its position or function in it:

- The *bull* chased him. (subject, meaning "male of the ox family")
- He signed the *bull*. (object, meaning "papal edict")
- Let's *bull* our way into the line. (predicate verb, meaning "force")
- We had a *bull session*. (attribute modifier, meaning "free or casual talk")

Now take the word "round" for another example, its meanings vary with the different functions in the following sentences:

- He was knocked out in the first *round*. (noun, meaning "one spell of play in a game, etc. or one stage in a competition")
- *Round* the number off to the nearest tenth. (verb, meaning "make number etc. whole by omitting units, etc.")
- The neighbors gathered *round* our barbecue. (preposition, meaning "so as to encircle or enclose")
- The moon was bright and *round*. (adjective, meaning "shaped like a circle or sphere")
- People came from all the country *round*. (adverb, meaning "throughout")

It should be noted that some words—prepositions like "at", "by", and "of", conjunctions like "and", "but"; and so forth are almost impossible to assign any meaning to the text without talking about their sentence function. For example, the preposition "at" carries specific meanings in the following phrases: *at* a distance (position); *at* dawn (a point in time); *at* war (state); sell *at* each (a value or rate); annoyed *at* failing (with reference to), etc.

8.3.3 Semantic or Logical Connections

Context can also be created out of semantic or logical connections, which may explain the general meaning of a particular word. For example, "The president fears that another wage increase will *escalate* the cost of living to a new high". It is common sense that the cost of living has something to do with the wage increase. Therefore, semantically or logically, "escalate" must carry the meaning "promote/add up to/make... become more intense". For another example: "Do get me a *loquat*." she said, smacking her lips. But her brother, with a scornful glance up at the branches, said that there were none ripe yet. Judging from "smacking her lips", "branches", "ripe" etc., we can rightly guess "loquat" must mean something edible, or to be more exact, it should be a kind of fruit. Likewise, in the sentence "In spite of the fact that the fishermen were wearing sou'westers, the storm was so heavy that they were wet through." the contextual details give sufficient hints for the word sou'wester, that is, something worn by people in storms. The meaning becomes clear.

The following paragraph is from *The Summing Up* (Maugham, 1992: 28–29):

"...Fowler liked simplicity, straightforwardness and common sense. He had no patience with pretentiousness. He had a sound feeling that idiom was the backbone of a language and he was all for the racy phrase. He was no slavish admirer of logic and was willing enough to give usage right of way through the exact <u>demesnes</u> of grammar. English grammar is very difficult and few writers have avoided making mistakes in it..."

How can we guess the meaning of the word "demesnes?" We can do so according to the logical connections it has with the words or sentences before and after it. The expression "right of way" means the right to pass over another person's ground and from this we can be certain that "demesnes" must refer to something like "territory/field" or further. Since it is involved in a paragraph about writing preference and "right of way" is used metaphorically, it must mean something akin to "rules/regulations". As a matter of fact, the whole phrase "to give usage right of way through the exact demesnes of grammar" means that usage should be observed even when it contradicts grammar rules.

8.3.4　The Role of Topic Sentence

Very often we can guess the meaning of a new word with the help of the topic sentence. So it follows that the ability to pick out the topic sentence is relatively important. The topic sentence usually governs one paragraph. In most cases, the topic sentence occupies the initial position, while in some it may appear in the middle or at the end of the paragraph. In still some cases, there may be no topic sentence at all, and we have to draw our own conclusion.

In this paragraph "Charles Goodyear discovered the secret of making rubber when a few drops of a mixture he was working with fell on a hot stove. Alexander Fleming discovered the effects of penicillin when he happened to take a second look at a glass slide he was about to throw away. Modern technology owes much to such instances of *serendipity*. The term comes from the title of a fairy tale 'The Three Princes of Serendip' in which the princes made happy discoveries in a similar manner." We have to infer what the topic is. Apparently, the example shown here illustrate accidental discoveries, which is the topic in question. So, "serendipity" must carry this meaning "making discoveries by chance".

The topic sentence can also help us determine the precise meaning of a familiar polysemous word. For example, "I'm a college professor. As a communications specialist, I train students to become more sensitive and aware of inter personal communication symbolic behavior, use of words, as well as nonverbal behavior. I try to ignite symbols in your mind, so we can come to a point of agreement on language. This is an invisible industry. Since

World War Ⅱ, we've had phenomenal growth. There are seven thousand- plus strong teachers in this *discipline*." The word *discipline* may mean "maintaining of order among those in one's charge; punishment; branch of instruction or learning and system of rules for conduct". However, in this paragraph where the topic is about college education, the precise meaning may very likely be "branch of instruction or learning".

8.3.5　The Role of Background Knowledge

Background knowledge occupies an important position in the language learning process. It constitutes an indispensable portion of the completeness of language acquisition. And it can greatly help guess and determine the particular meaning of a word. As far as English learning is concerned, background knowledge, in a broad sense, covers every aspect of the life and culture of the British people and the American people. Naturally, it includes their social customs, their literature, and arts. Additionally, a little knowledge of the whole European history and literature will be a great help. The following instances will clearly illustrate how background knowledge works efficiently to assist us in guessing and determining word meaning.

What does "Gethsemane" in "In the depths of my despair, I felt that I had reached my Gethsemane" mean? Some knowledge of the Bible will render us timely help: Gethsemane is the name of a garden on the Mount of Olives near Jerusalem, where Jesus Christ was arrested. Thus "Gethsemane" has come to mean a place or occasion of great, especially mental or spiritual suffering. Again, what does the expression "to cross my Rubicon" mean in "Standing before the minister, taking the Vows of marriage. I realized that I was about to cross my Rubicon"? We have to bear in mind this story: Rubicon is a small river in north central Italy which in the time of the ancient Roman Republic formed part of the boundary between Cisalpine Gaul and Italy, and over which Julius Caesar crossed into Italy with his army in 49 BCE against the orders of the government to begin the civil war in which he overthrew Pompey. Now the word Rubicon means a bounding or limiting line, especially one that when crossed commits a person to an irrevocable change or decision. Therefore, the phrase in the above example means "to take a decisive action from which there was no going back" suggesting that by entering into marriage, he was to shoulder the responsibilities it imposed upon him.

In the great speech made by Martin Luther King Jr. on August 28, 1963, there is such a paragraph:

> *"Five score years ago, <u>a great American</u> in whose symbolic shadow we stand today signed the Emancipation Proclamation. This momentous decree came as a great beacon of light and hope to millions of Negro slaves who had been seared in the flames of withering*

injustice. It came as the joyous daybreak to end the long night of captivity."

Any person unfamiliar with American history cannot guess who this great American was. But the Black American audiences on the historic occasion knew clearly that this great American was the 16th American President Abraham Lincoln.

The most serious difficulties arise when similar objects, actions, or points of view have one set of values for the Chinese people and quite a different one for the English-speaking people. For example, to us Chinese, " 窝头 " (*wotou*, a kind of cornbread) has a lower social status than " 馒头 " (*mantou*, steamed bread made of flour); and eating *wotou* can be seen as a sign of poverty. Hence many Chinese people are surprised at the knowledge that Americans sometimes eat "black bread". To Americans, however, eating "black bread" is not a sign of poverty at all; it is only a change of diet or an attempt of getting more of nature's nutriment.

A non-native student therefore should have relevant background information about American and British history and geography, and about the customs and habits of the American and British people. He should also have some knowledge of the English Bible and Christianity, for in the English language there are numerous words with religious connotations. With all this knowledge, he would be better able to grasp the full meaning of many English words.

Exercises

I. Define the following terms.

1. lexical context   **2.** grammatical context   **3.** textual context

4. linguistic context   **5.** extra-linguistic context

II. State the vital roles of context in determining word meaning.

III. Design a proper context to specify the referent of each of the underlined word.

1. The fan broke the <u>glass</u>.

2. John was attracted by the <u>ball</u>.

3. I'll accompany you to the <u>bank</u>.

4. He removed the <u>tick</u>.

5. The view from the window would be destroyed by the addition of a <u>plant</u> out there.

IV. Give two or more interpretations for each of the following sentences.

1. I need some information on getting rid of moles.

2. Each bill requires a check.

3. The suit is too light to wear.

4. I'll give you a ring.

5. The shooting of the hunters surprised no one.

6. The lady you met now and then came to visit us.

7. I saw Mr. Charles Wallace in the classroom.

8. Visiting relatives can be boring.

V. Decide the precise meanings of the polysemous words in the following sentences.

1. He thought how in 1910 a painted woman was said to be <u>fast</u>.

2. The windows and doors were all <u>fast</u> so that thieves could not enter.

3. The patient is <u>fasted</u> and given a mild hypnotic.

4. The acid was chosen because it was <u>fast</u>.

5. He'll have a fit if you don't <u>humor</u> him.

6. I have a sense of <u>humor</u>, but I just don't think it's funny.

7. You are certainly in a terrible <u>humor</u> today.

8. His <u>humors</u> are out of balance. That's why he is melancholy.

VI. Make up a nonsense word and decide its meaning beforehand. Then use it in a context that helps reveal its meaning.

VII. Translate the paragraph below into Chinese. Pay special attention to the specific meaning of the verbs.

We have pursued major-country diplomacy with Chinese characteristics on all fronts. We have promoted the development of a human community with a shared future and stood firm in protecting international fairness and justice. We have advocated and practiced true multilateralism. We have taken a clear-cut stance against hegemonism and power politics in all their forms, and we have never wavered in our opposition to unilateralism, protectionism, and bullying of any kind. We have improved China's overall diplomatic agenda and worked actively to build a global network of partnerships and foster a new type of international relations. We have demonstrated China's sense of duty as a responsible major country, actively participating in the reform and development of the global governance system and engaging in all-around international cooperation in the fight against COVID-19. All this has seen us win widespread international recognition. China's international influence, appeal, and power to shape have risen markedly.

(*source*: Report to the 20th National Congress of the Communist Party of China, October 16, 2022)

Chapter 9

Multi-Word Expressions

Multi-word expressions (henceforth, MWEs) are combinations of words that co-occur frequently. In general, collocations (e.g., *take a photo*), verb-particle combinations (e.g., *put off*), binominals (e.g., *bride and groom*), lexical bundles (e.g., *if you look at*), prefabricated routines (e.g., *What's up?*), and idioms (e.g., *kick the bucket*) are classified as MWEs. They play a crucial role in the process of second language (L2) acquisition and have established themselves as an integral part of L2 teaching and learning. This chapter focuses primarily on the facilitative role of MWEs in L2 learning/use and the pedagogical considerations involved in teaching these units of language in the classroom. To this aim, we first provide a description of MWEs, discussing their key characteristics and how they may affect the ways in which L2 learners acquire and use these sequences. We then outline and discuss the major reasons why MWEs are considered to be of particular importance for the process of L2 learning. Following this, we introduce two most common types of MWEs, i.e., phrasal verbs and collocations. In the final section of the chapter, we turn to the challenges involved in the acquisition of L2 MWEs, proposing the reasons why certain types of these sequences are notoriously difficult for learners to acquire. In the next chapter, we will dwell on one specific type of MWEs, that is, idioms.

9.1 Characteristics of Multi-Word Expressions

While one of the fundamental properties of human language is creativity, we rarely rely on this potential to communicate with others. Rather than creating novel utterances word by word, we tend to rely on prefabricated word sequences (e.g., *I might as well, what's up, on the flip side*) that are generally highly familiar to members of our speech community—MWEs. The term "MWE" encompasses lexical units that are longer than a single word (Siyanova-Chanturia & Omidian, 2019; Wray, 2002). MWEs can be defined as sequences of words that tend to co-occur with each other more often than with other words. They include phrasal configurations such as collocations (e.g., *strong coffee, excruciating pain, seek help*), idioms (e.g., *bite the bullet, break a leg, easy does it*), phrasal verbs (e.g., *get in, break down, go over*), lexical bundles (e.g., *on the other hand, on the contrary, in view of the*) and so on. MWEs are multifarious in nature, taking various forms and sizes. Despite their diversity, however, they share certain key characteristics that set them apart from novel, propositional discourse. The most prominent features of MWEs that have figured in the literature are frequency, familiarity, predictability, and fixedness (Siyanova-Chanturia & Omidian, 2019).

Frequency is one of the most unique statistical aspects of (most) MWEs. It has been argued that the frequency of occurrence of phrasal units is an indicator of their prominence among language users (Ellis, 2002). This is mainly because language users tend to prioritize those linguistic devices that are commonly used in their speech community. Most MWEs (e.g., *in other words, to tell the truth, take your time*) occur with extremely high-frequency rates in natural language production. Research has shown that such high-frequency phrasal elements are typically read and processed faster than lower-frequency, unfamiliar ones by both first language (L1) and L2 speakers (Conklin & Schmitt, 2012; Jiang & Nekrasova, 2007; Siyanova-Chanturia et al., 2011). These observations indicate that language users are highly sensitive to the frequency rates of MWEs. Thus, it can be argued that raising learners' awareness about the commonness of many MWEs may be essential in L2 teaching and learning.

While frequency is an important quality of many MWEs, it is important to keep in mind that some MWEs (e.g., idioms and proverbs) are rather infrequent. Yet, they are highly familiar to L1 and proficient L2 speakers. Thus, another important characteristic of MWEs is their familiarity (or conventionality). It seems reasonable to propose that familiarity should correlate strongly with frequency: the more familiar a phrase is, the more likely it is to be used in discourse. Familiarity and frequency, however, are often considered distinct properties of MWEs, since there is not always a direct correlation between the two. There are MWEs that are highly familiar to language users but are, nevertheless, of low frequency. For instance, the expression *never too late to mend* is a familiar MWE to a L1 speaker of English; but it is of extremely low frequency even in the largest English corpora, occurring only once in the Corpus of Contemporary American English (COCA; Davies, 2008) and twice in the British National Corpus (BNC; Davies, 2004). While infrequent, such MWEs may still be highly familiar to language users due to their specific usage in certain contexts (Hallin & Van Lancker-Sidtis, 2017; Reuterskiöld & Van Lancker-Sidtis, 2013). In addition, Hallin & Van Lancker-Sidtis (2017) recently showed that familiar yet infrequent MWEs, such as proverbs, were spoken at a much faster speech rate compared to novel control phrases (i.e., sequences of the same length, frequency, and grammatical structure). Such evidence indicates that familiarity, regardless of frequency, is another determining factor in how MWEs are processed and used.

Another key characteristic of MWEs is predictability. This particular feature is closely related to familiarity, since easily recognizable word sequences are in most cases highly predictable as well. That is, upon encountering the initial part(s) of a MWE (e.g., *actions speak..., excruciating pain ..., pull yourself...,*), a proficient user of English is highly likely to complete them with *louder than words*, *pain*, and *together*, respectively. Thus, the subsequent parts of a MWE can be said to be somewhat superfluous, in that they are often predicted by the reader prior to reaching them (Siyanova-Chanturia et al., 2011). This particular feature of MWEs has received special attention in psycholinguistic (Underwood et al., 2004) and neurolinguistic studies (Siyanova-Chanturia et al., 2017; Vespignani et al., 2010). For example, Siyanova-Chanturia et al. (2017) found that distinct cognitive mechanisms underlie the processing of predictable and novel word sequences (e.g., *knife and fork* vs. *spoon and fork*) in that reading the initial constituent(s) of a MWE is highly likely to pre-activate a mental "template" that matches the upcoming information about the rest of the sequence (also see Du et al., 2021; Vespignani et al., 2010). These findings provide empirical support for probabilistic models of language processing and acquisition, according to which the probabilistic information about the co-occurrence of certain words (e.g., the word *ins* tends to co-occur with the word *outs* to form the MWE *ins and outs*) is represented in the speaker's mental system (McDonald & Shillcock, 2003). However, acquiring such tacit knowledge about co-occurrence patterns of words requires prolonged and repeated exposure to a language (Omidian et al., 2021; Siyanova-Chanturia & Spina, 2020; Schmitt, 2014). This has important consequences for the acquisition of L2 MWEs, as most learners may never receive such high amount of exposure to a L2 (more on this below).

Finally, MWEs are characterized by their degree of fixedness (Schmitt, 2004; Wray, 2002). While novel utterances exhibit full syntactic flexibility, MWEs are marked by their fixed or semi-fixed nature. Many MWEs (e.g., *by and large, first and foremost*) are rigid in their form; that is, any changes to the structure of such word sequences will result in them losing their original meaning. Not all MWEs are completely fixed, however. There are many MWEs that are semi-fixed and allow for some degree of variation within their structure, such as adding quantifiers (*pull strings → pull a few strings*), adjectival modification (*make a lasting impression → make a big impression*), pluralization (*red herring[s]*), passivization (*spilled the beans → beans were spilled*), and so on. When modified, such expressions do not lose their original, figurative meaning. Therefore, MWEs can differ in terms of the fixedness and invariability of their structures, with some phrases being completely fixed while others being partially modifiable. Raising awareness of this aspect of MWEs (i.e., *fixedness*) is particularly important in the context of L2 teaching and learning, in that learners unaware of the structural invariability of certain expressions may draw on their creativity and attempt to modify such MWEs, resulting in the production of anomalous phrases.

Taken together, frequency, familiarity, predictability, and fixedness should be given careful consideration when teaching and learning MWEs, as they can affect the way in which learners acquire and use these sequences.

9.2 Importance of Multi-Word Expressions

Many studies to date have highlighted the importance of MWEs in L2 learning. There are several reasons why careful consideration should be given to teaching and learning phrasal elements in a L2. First, MWEs have been found to constitute between 20% and 50% of natural language production (Biber et al., 1999; Erman & Warren, 2000; Foster, 2001). Such evidence suggests that communication in a language is not based solely on a creative assembly of single words. Rather, a large and varied repertoire of MWEs is crucial in attaining communicative competence in any language. Considering their pervasiveness in human language, MWEs are believed to be an integral component of L2 teaching and learning.

Second, research has shown that MWEs are processed, and retrieved from memory, considerably faster than novel utterances (Conklin & Schmitt, 2012). The processing advantage of MWEs can give the speaker time to focus on other necessary tasks, such as "generating specific lexical items, planning the next unit of discourse, syntactic processing of novel pieces, and so on" (Wood, 2002: 7). This aspect of MWEs use has been found beneficial for improving speaker fluency (Hallin & Van Lancker-Sidtis, 2017; Pawley & Syder, 1983). In other words, the key to achieving fluency in a language may be dependent on learning and making use of MWEs. Thus, it can be reasonably argued that the processing advantage observed for MWEs relative to novel language can be facilitative to the process of developing L2 fluency. That is, the ability to convey meaning through the use of prefabricated phrases that can be readily pulled from memory—without the processing burden of constructing them word by word—can effectively enhance the fluency with which learners express their ideas in a L2.

Third, research has pointed out a strong connection between MWEs and L2 pragmatic knowledge. Pragmatic knowledge is referred to the ability to express meaning appropriately in a communicative situation (Taguchi, 2009). MWEs are often strongly connected to a particular communicative function (e.g., "How do you do?" performs the function of a greeting in English). MWEs are typically used to fulfill the communicative demands of conventional actions that require specific, commonly used, and highly familiar patterns of linguistic communication (Coulmas, 1979; Siyanova-Chanturia & Nation, 2017; Omidian et al., 2021). Many studies have investigated the functions of the different kinds of MWEs in different communicative and social contexts (e.g., Aijmer, 2014; Bahns et al., 1986; Bygate, 1988, Liu & Siyanova-Chanturia, 2015; Omidian et al., 2018). For example, Bahns et al. (1986) looked at the use of MWEs in conversational interactions between L2 learners. These researchers found that a wide range of L2 MWEs served different pragmatic purposes (e.g., *How come?*

What's that? are MWEs used to elicit information or request for clarification). Therefore, it is believed that the use of MWEs can help learners deal effectively with the complexity of different communicative situations and use language in a contextually appropriate manner. The latter is particularly important in that L2 learners often do not have the linguistic means to perform communicative functions specific to different L2 social situations.

Finally, it has been widely acknowledged that knowing a word involves the knowledge of not only its form, meaning, and pronunciation but also what word(s) or word types usually co-occur with it (Nation, 2001: 27; Schmitt, 2014; Omidian & Siyanova-Chanturia, 2021). This is because the linguistic choices made to create meaning in a language are not based on an independent selection of words; rather, proficient users of a language typically take into account the relations between words to create larger units of meaning which can perform specific communicative functions (Sinclair, 1991; Omidian & Siyanova-Chanturia, 2020). Therefore, one of the most important aspects of knowing a word is the knowledge of the sorts of words that are most likely to be associated with that word. For example, the word *pain* tends to co-occur with verbs such as *cause, suffer,* and *endure* and adjectives such as *sharp, severe, chronic, excruciating,* etc. Acquiring such knowledge about the co-occurrence of words is considered to be an indispensable component of L2 learning (Pawley & Syder, 1983; Wray, 2002). Drawing learners' attention to MWEs can help learners become cognizant of co-occurrence patterns in a L2.

9.3 Common Types of Multi-Word Expressions

Some of the most common and well-studied types of MWEs include idioms, binomials, lexical bundles, collocations, and phrasal verbs. Perhaps, the most quintessential example of MWEs are idioms, which are non-literal expressions, in that the meaning of individual words does not correspond to the overall idiom meaning (e.g., the phrase *tie the knot* means "get married" rather than making a knot). These are often completely fixed expressions that allow for no or minimal changes to their structure. Idioms are also highly familiar to L1 and proficient L2 English speakers. In the next chapter, we will dwell on idioms.

Binomials are phrases that follow the X and Y structure, such as *knife and fork* and *bride and groom*. These phrases are common in the English language and have a canonical word order. That is, one-word order (e.g., *bride and groom*) is more frequent and more acceptable than the reversed order (e.g., *groom and bride*), despite the two phrases having the same (or similar) meaning.

Lexical bundles (e.g., *I might as well*, *on the other hand*, *in accordance with*) are word combinations that frequently recur in language use. They function as "building blocks of discourse" and straddle the boundary of lexis and syntax (Biber et al., 2004). Frequency is the ultimate quality of lexical bundles (Cortes, 2015). That is, they are identified based on their high frequency of occurrence in discourse (Omidian et al., 2021). Lexical bundles are continuous fixed expressions that are both highly predictable and familiar to language users.

Phrasal verbs (e.g., *hang out with*, *look into*) are multi-word verbs composed of a lexical verb and a particle, a construction whose meaning cannot be easily inferred from its constituent parts (Omidian et al., 2019; Siyanova & Schmitt, 2007). For example, *hanging out with someone* means spending time with someone, rather than the action of hanging out something with someone. These verbs are found to be a prominent feature of spoken language (Biber et al., 1999). Phrasal verbs are extremely pervasive in English, such that learners are, on average, expected to encounter one phrasal verb in every 150 words (Gardner & Davies, 2007). Research has shown that learners often find phrasal verbs difficult to learn and tend to avoid them in favor of their roughly synonymous one-word equivalents (e.g., *call off the wedding* vs. *cancel the wedding*; see Siyanova & Schmitt, 2007).

Finally, collocations are a set of two (or more) words that tend to co-occur more frequently than would be expected by chance (e.g., *break a habit*, Stubbs, 1995). Particularly important and frequently occurring collocations in English include verb-noun (e.g., *do a favor*), noun-noun (e.g., *round of applause*), adjective-noun (e.g., *spiritual successor*), and adverb-adjective (e.g., *fully aware*) collocations. Learning collocations requires learners to develop some knowledge about associations between words. As was mentioned earlier, research has repeatedly shown that learners' association knowledge lags behind their general vocabulary and grammar knowledge (Bahns & Eldaw, 1993; Laufer & Waldman, 2011; Schmitt, 1998). Large-scale longitudinal studies have also revealed that learning the myriads of collocations in a L2 is a slow process, requiring extensive language exposure (Omidian et al., 2021; Siyanova-Chanturia & Spina, 2020).

9.4 Challenges of Learning Multi-Word Expressions for L2 Learners

While MWEs have been shown to facilitate L2 learning and use, acquiring and mastering these strings of language have been found to be a complex process that can present major challenges to learners (Omidian et al., 2021; Siyanova-Chanturia & Pellicer-Sanchez, 2019).

Below, we outline and explain three main reasons underlying this complexity based on findings from research conducted in this area.

One of the main reasons why L2 acquisition of MWEs can be complex and challenging for learners is that L2 knowledge of associations between words typically does not develop in parallel with general L2 vocabulary and syntactic knowledge (Bahns & Eldaw, 1993; Laufer & Waldman, 2011; Omidian et al., 2021; Schmitt, 1998; Siyanova-Chanturia & Spina, 2019). This has important consequences for the development of L2 knowledge of MWEs, particularly at the productive level. Research has shown that, due to their insufficient knowledge of associations between words in a L2, learners often make errors when attempting to produce strings of language (Laufer & Waldman, 2011; Nesselhauf, 2005). For example, Siyanova & Schmitt (2008) investigated 810 adjective-noun collocations (e.g., *law-abiding citizens, extenuating circumstances, long time*) extracted from essays written by L2 learners of English. They found that around 50% of the collocations used by learners were inappropriate. In a more recent study, Omidian et al. (2021) explored the longitudinal development of L2 production of verb-noun sequences in essays produced by Chinese learners of Italian before and after a 6-month language program course. The authors found frequent use of certain atypical word sequences (e.g., *cercano storia "[they] look for history", avevo curiosità "had curiosity", ho fatto pianto "I did crying"*) by learners at the end of the language course. They also found that more proficient learners produced fewer distinct verb-noun combinations compared to their beginner-level counterparts. This suggests that higher proficiency learners tend to rely on the phrasal elements they have already mastered (Laufer, 1998; Siyanova-Chanturia & Spina, 2020). Beginner learners, however, tend to rely on creativity and experiment with combinatorial mechanisms of a L2, producing atypical and infelicitous word combinations (Bardovi-Harlig & Stringer, 2017). Such evidence shows that the development of association knowledge about words in a L2 is a multifaceted process that is often very slow and far from being straightforward.

The second main reason why the acquisition of MWEs may be challenging for L2 learners relates to the multifarious nature of these linguistic units. As discussed earlier, MWEs can take various shapes and sizes. The heterogeneity of MWEs results from the numerous co-occurrence possibilities that exist between words. One of the main learning hurdles is to become familiar with such possibilities and the sheer variety of forms they can take (Schmitt, 2000). The problem is further compounded by the fact that some types of MWEs (e.g., idioms, proverbs, phrasal verbs) are highly register-specific (i.e., they are more frequently used in certain communicative situations than others). For example, many phrasal verbs are found to be informal in tone and more common in spoken language than in formal written communication, such as academic writing (Biber et al., 1999: 409). A successful acquisition of different types of MWEs entails knowledge of co-occurrence patterns among words and their usage in various communicative situations. Developing such knowledge requires prolonged L2 exposure and explicit instruction that can raise learners' awareness of various types of MWEs and their L2 usage. While it is not necessary for learners to acquire and fully master all types of MWEs, it is important to draw their attention to commonly used types of these units in the target L2 (more on this below).

Finally, the third reason pertains to the semantic complexity and syntactic peculiarity of MWEs. Research has shown that certain types of MWEs can denote multiple meanings (Gardner & Davis, 2007; Garnier & Schmitt, 2015; Macis & Schmitt, 2017). For instance, Gardner & Davies (2007) observed that the most frequently used English phrasal verbs can carry around 5.6 meaning senses on average. This suggests that the learning load of such MWEs can be greater than that of words and other types of MWEs (Garnier & Schmitt, 2015). In addition, such expressions can convey different evaluative meanings which are often highly abstract. For instance, the phrasal verb *hold up* can carry both positive and negative evaluative meanings (e.g., in the sentence "they are holding up quite well", the verb is utilized to express a positive evaluation of the situation, but when employed in a passive form in "they had been held up by blizzard", the verb serves a negative evaluative function; examples extracted from the COCA and BNC; for further discussion see Omidian & Siyanova-Chanturia, 2020). In a recent study, Macis & Schmitt (2017) showed that a large number of collocations in English are polysemous and can impart both literal and figurative meanings (e.g., *big nose* can have a figurative meaning that is exclusive to the world of wine-tasting). Acquiring figurative meanings of such MWEs can pose major challenges to learners without extensive exposure to their usage as the majority of such meanings are often highly context-specific and cannot be inferred from a word-for-word translation of a phrase. Moreover, as was discussed earlier, while certain MWEs are fully fixed, others may allow for some degree of modification in their syntactic structure. These MWEs may be classified into adjacent (*the extent to which*) and nonadjacent phrases (*in the [capable] hands of*). Cheng et al. (2006) investigated common co-occurrence patterns between two or more words in English and found that the majority of these patterns were nonadjacent (i.e., separated by one or more intervening lexical items). This implies that learning only adjacent MWEs may be insufficient for gaining mastery of these linguistic items in a L2. Psycholinguistic and neurolinguistic studies have also shown that adjacency plays an important role in the learning and processing of phrasal elements. For example, Gomez (2002) and Newport & Aslin (2004) observed a lower degree of learnability for non-adjacent sequences compared to adjacent ones. In a study focused on the processing of adjacent and nonadjacent collocations, Vilkaitė & Schmitt (2019) found that advanced L2 learners of English read adjacent collocations (e.g., *achieve status*) faster than their controls (e.g., *ignore status*), while they exhibited no significant processing advantage for nonadjacent collocations (e.g., *achieve a more secure status*) relative to their controls (e.g., *ignore a more secure status*). On the contrary, L1 speakers read both adjacent and non-adjacent faster than their respective controls. These observations were taken to suggest that since collocations are used frequently in both adjacent and non-adjacent forms, L1 speakers are likely to be exposed and to learn both forms from an early age. Unlike L1 speakers, L2 learners might not receive sufficient exposure to both adjacent and non-adjacent forms of MWEs to strengthen their knowledge of the association between constituent parts of these phrases. Taken together, the above findings indicate that the semantic and syntactic peculiarity of MWEs can make the acquisition and mastery of these word sequences difficult for L2 learners.

Exercises

I. Fill in the blanks with the following verbal phrases in their suitable forms.

take on	break into	bite into	go about	let out
bring up	tear apart	buy off	count on	sink in

1. I was just about to make my little bow of assent, when the meaning of these last words _____, jolting me out of my sad reverie.

2. By the time the trial began on July 10, our town of 1,500 people had _____ a circus atmosphere.

3. Then the court _____ a storm of applause that surpassed that for Bryan.

4. He _____ a Southern war whoop. In a flash, John, McKean, and Franklin crowded around him.

5. 1848 was a year of revolution in Europe; Karl Marx and Frederick Engels published the *Communist Manifesto*, and political demonstration _____ the great cities of Paris, Vienna, Naples, and Berlin.

6. During dinner, Mr. Churchill said that a German attack on Russia was now certain, and he thought that Hitler was _____ enlisting capitalist and Right Wing sympathies in this country and the US.

7. Assuming the hotel man was _____, their only chance—a slim one—lay in removing the car quickly.

8. By 1976, the slump had begun to _____ the bulk-carrier trade.

9. Sailors and officers _____ their chores as usual on these ships, amid pipings and loudspeaker squawks.

10. He traveled to foundling homes, prisons, and lunatic asylums in his search for people with extraordinary heads, and in time _____ a huge catalog of the relationship between particular mental characteristics and bumps on the skull.

II. Choose the expression corresponding to each of the underlined MWEs.

1. I <u>ran across</u> an old friend of mine at the airport.
   A. ran over
   B. ran up to
   C. met... unexpectedly

2. "There's no dinner, madame," he said gravely, "the kitchen staff have <u>downed tools</u>."
   A. gone on strike
   B. put down their tools
   C. begun to work

3. That she will lose all her friends if she continues to gossip about them <u>goes without saying</u>.
   A. goes silently
   B. is useless for saying
   C. is too plain to need talking about

4. You will have to speak a little louder. Mrs. Evans <u>is hard of hearing</u>.
   A. has difficulty in hearing
   B. is difficult to understand
   C. is difficult to be heard

5. She said that he should stop telephoning her late at night, <u>once and for all</u>.
   A. several times
   B. in a final and definite manner
   C. with the hope of pleasing you

6. The plan we were all so enthusiastic about seems less attractive when viewed <u>in the cold light of day</u>.

    A. in the cold day

    B. when considered practically

    C. when the day is light

7. He loves his dog and yet he's unkind to his children; he must have a <u>Jekyll and Hyde personality</u>.

    A. Jekyll and Hyde

    B. Hyde and Jekyll having two personalities

    C. character that has two opposite sides to it

8. My Dad's <u>hopping mad</u> because the dog has just chewed up his Cup Final ticket.

    A. very angry

    B. being mad

    C. going away

9. He <u>made a blooper</u> by starting the food mixer without its lid on, spraying egg all over the kitchen.

    A. made flowers blossom

    B. made a change

    C. made a silly mistake

10. The Inland Revenue has sent me a taxi bill for more than a hundred pounds, but they can't <u>get blood out of a stone</u> because I just haven't got the money.

    A. try to do the impossible

    B. get blood from a pebble

    C. let the blood run free

III. Fill in the blanks with the following appropriate multi-word expressions.

no longer possible	I would appreciate it	delicious food
as soon as possible	As you know	I must admit
unreasonable behavior	express my dissatisfaction	I would be most grateful
from about... to more than	On the other hand	significant change
the following thirty years	It is evident	in terms of

1. Regarding the food, I went to various restaurants and all served mouth-watering dishes but _____ that the most _____ I ate there was in a friend's house.

2. _____ if you could contact me _____, particularly since I need the proposals for a presentation this week. If you could send the bag to me by courier service, _____. I have arranged to pay for the service.

3. I am writing to _____ with my roommate. _____, we share one room. Unfortunately because of my roommate's _____, I feel it is _____ for me to continue with the present arrangement.

4. Although Washington's increase in population between 1940 and 1970 was large, its increase in _____ was even sharper, rising _____ 125,000 in 1970 _____ 240,000 in 2000.

5. The table compares four countries _____ the number of people who watch four different genres of film at the cinema: Action, Romance, Comedy, and Horror. In India and Japan, only 2 to 2.5 million people watch horror films but they are more popular in New Zealand and Ireland. _____, romance films are very popular in India with 7.5 million viewers.

6. The two pie charts compare the percentages of online sales across different retail sectors in Canada in the years 2005 and 2010. For three of the sectors, _____ that over this time frame, there was _____ in their proportion of online transactions.

IV. Complete each of the MWEs with only one word.

1. over and _____

2. wind and _____

3. break and _____

4. top and _____

5. rules and _____

6. ebb and _____

7. wheeling and _____

8. town and _____

9. time _____ time

10. rise and _____

V. The following passage was written by a second language learner. Underline the expressions which are unnatural or not idiomatic.

My typical morning? Well, I never go out on an unfilled stomach, so before class, I usually have a complete English breakfast—I love it. Getting to class can take a big time because it is the rush period. But when I get to class, it is a lot of enjoyment because my classmates come from all over the earth. Anyway, I must go into class right now, but I'll be back in a period.

Chapter 10

Idioms

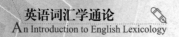
10.1 Definition of an Idiom

The English language abounds in idioms like any other highly developed language.

But what are idioms? Seidle & McMondie (1978: 4) wrote the following in *English Idioms and How to Use Them*.

> *"We can say that an idiom is a number of words which, taken together, means something different from the individual words of the idiom when they stand alone. The way in which the words are put together is often odd, illogical or even grammatically incorrect. Other idioms are completely regular and logical in their grammar and vocabulary... we have learned the idiom as a whole and we often cannot change any part of it."*

In short, an English idiom is a group of words with a special meaning different from the meanings of its constituent words. Idioms are usually semantically opaque, i.e., metaphorical rather than literal. Thus, *a feather in someone's cap* is not at all connected with feather or cap; instead, it means "an honor, success, of which one can be proud". Besides semantic opaqueness, English idioms get their own characteristics which will be discussed later in this chapter.

Many years ago, idioms were only used among the lower class such as farm workers, craftsmen, and factory workers. These people were usually looked down upon by people from the upper class, and idioms used by them faced the same fate. As time passed, idioms came into the language through literary works and by word of mouth, and so many idioms have been used and developed. For centuries, they have enlarged the English vocabulary and enriched the language greatly. In colloquial English, they are still informal sometimes, but most of them have been accepted by those "educated people". Even some celebrated people would use some idioms on formal occasions. Many of them have been taken into all kinds of publications, like *The Oxford English Dictionary* and *The Advanced Learners Dictionary of Current English*, which are considered reputable and trustworthy dictionaries. Yet idioms have been constantly changing and growing, and a good many new ones continue to enter the language; meanwhile, quite a few will not be used again.

English-speaking people from the United States, Australia, etc. have also added a large number of contributions of their own to the English language. Also they are accepted by people much faster than before in modern times. People learn them by means of mass media such as movies, radio programs, newspapers, TV programs, the Internet. Idioms have spread from place to place, from country to country, and from continent to continent. They can also be found in documents, essays, periodicals or magazines, novels, and guidebooks for travelers.

Idioms consist of set phrases and short sentences, which are peculiar to the language in question and loaded with native cultures and ideas. In a broad sense, English idioms include some slangs, colloquialisms, and proverbs. Therefore, idioms are colorful, forcible, and thought-provoking. No clear distinction exists among them nowadays. As the core and essentiality of the English language, idioms are widely used and even have great influence on other languages. If properly and correctly used, they will make the language more vivid and vigorous, greatly enlivening one's style of speaking and making it more interesting and more entertaining. Moreover, idioms reflect the environment, life, history, and culture of native speakers, and are closely associated with their innermost spirit and feeling. This chapter will deal with English idioms in terms of their sources, classification, translation, and characteristics.

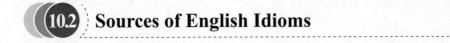

10.2　Sources of English Idioms

As a living language, English has to manage to survive in case it should become extinct; one of the most important ways is to use idiomatic expressions. The abundance and variety of idioms in the English language may be to a great extent accounted for by its historical development. Knowledge of their sources may help us to comprehend what they really mean and to use them correctly.

As commonly known, there are many sources of idioms. All the idioms arise from the people who have created them. They have much to do with customs, culture, history, habits, beliefs, etc. The native people created and used many vivid, interesting phrases out of familiar things while working. They used them all the time and they began to publicize them and then those phrases were taken and used by many people doing other jobs. Idiomatic expressions were thus fixed by wide and long usage and thus idioms have become a very important and essential part of the language.

10.2.1　From Daily Life

When people worked together, they needed short, simple phrases and sentences to convey their thoughts that were related to their jobs and labor. After a long time, these expressions have become fixed idioms, many of which are from the daily life of English people, e.g. *to teach one's grandma to suck eggs* (to tell or show somebody how to do something that they can already do well, and probably better than you can). The following are more examples:

- That girl *was born with a silver spoon in her mouth*.

  (Here it means "be born in a rich family".)

- Bringing an action for defamation may result in having to *wash one's dirty linen in public*.

  (Here it means "have an open discussion about private difficulties".)

- She *wore yellow stockings* when she saw his success.

  (Here it means "be jealous of".)

- Please *throw care to the winds* since all are bygones.

  (Here it means "forget your care".)

- *Make hay while the sun shines*.

  (Here it means "Make use of favorable opportunities when they present themselves.")

- You know "*to err is human*".

  (Here it means "Everyone makes mistakes.")

- He lost his dear wife and was sick for a couple of days. He *was beside himself* at last.

  (Here it means "be out of one's senses".)

- *To the best of one's knowledge*, he is untrustworthy.

  (Here it means "as far as one knows".)

- *Let's drop our enmity and smoke the pipe of peace*.

  (Here it means "Let's stop hating each other and be good friends.")

- Bill slapped George's face and now they *are at it hammer and tongs*.

  (Here it means "fight as hard as they can". It also has the meaning of "study hard and seriously", e.g., Tom had a lot of homework to do and he went *at it hammer and tongs* till bedtime.)

10.2.2   From Food and Cooking

There are many idioms that have to do with food and cooking, e.g. *to eat humble pie* (say and show that you are sorry for a mistake you made), *out of the frying-pan into the fire* (out of one situation of danger or difficulty into another [usually worse] one), *to be in the soup* (be in or get somebody into trouble or difficulties), *sit above the salt* (be in a position of honor). The following are more examples:

- It is difficult to get jobs, but since you have a good job, don't *quarrel with your bread and butter*.

  (Here it means "do something which may result in depriving one of the means of one's livelihood".)

- His words *cooked her goose.*

  (Here it means "put an end to one's hopes".)

- Doing such a job is *a piece of cake* for him.

  (Here it means "very easy".)

- The next time he comes near his house, I'll *put salt on his tail.*

  (Here it means "catch or apprehend somebody".)

- We offered him a lot of help, but what did he offer us for it? *Not a sausage.*

  (Here it means "absolutely nothing".)

- During World War Ⅱ, my uncle was at Dunkirk and he said it was certainly *no picnic.*

  (Here it means "difficult situation".)

- When they organized an evening party, I'm sure Mr. Jones *had a finger in the pie.*

  (Here it means "be one of those who planned the party".)

- He was called names, yet he *shut his pan.*

  (Here it means "keep silence".)

- After they moved to that place they *made a scoop.*

  (Here it means "make a lot of money".)

- After he was promoted, he *thought no beer of himself.*

  (Here it means "be conceited".)

10.2.3　From Body Parts

Many English idioms are derived from parts of the human body, they are called body part idioms or somatic idioms, e.g., *Blood is thicker than water* (your family is more important than any other people). The following are more examples:

- I *had my hands full* when they came to me.

  (Here it means "very busy".)

- Don't *poke your nose into my affairs.*

  (Here it means "to interfere in other's affairs".)

- The old lady made her last will because she was well aware that she *had one foot in the grave.*

  (Here it means "be near death because of old age".)

- You needn't *set your face against my proposal.*

  (Here it means "oppose, not agree with".)

- He *escaped by the skin of his teeth* during that war.

  (Here it means "have a narrow escape from something".)

- His father is easy to *vent his spleen on her.*

(Here it means "fly off the handle".)

- At the police station, Steven made *a clean breast of the crime* he committed.

  (Here it means "confess the crime".)

- *More power to your elbow*!

  (Here it means "May your efforts be effective and successful!")

- He's taken drugs for years and now he *is over head and ears in debts*.

  (Here it means "be deeply in debts".)

- I don't like talking to Jim. He has *a big mouth* and can't keep any secrets.

  (Here it means "to like to spread gossip or cannot keep a secret".)

10.2.4　From Names of Animals

Animals are with people from ancient times. English, like many other languages, is abundant in idioms with names of animals, e.g. *loaded for bear* ("ready for action, prepared and eager"). Such idioms may be related to the appearance, habits, etc. of various animals.

- You'll be *flogging a dead horse* if you expect him to make a contribution. You know well what a greedy guy he is.

  (Here it means "persist in doing something that cannot produce the desired result".)

- Before the war, the Haitian people *kept the wolf from the door*.

  (Here it means "make sure you have enough money to pay for things like food, rent, heating, etc.".)

- He came to shed *crocodile tears* before the dead merchant who was murdered by none other than him.

  (Here it means "insincere sorrow".)

- They even *swallowed a story* that his ship was bombarded in the Persian Gulf.

  (Here it means "believe something too easily".)

- You have to face so many people. Remember to *separate the sheep from the goats*.

  (Here it means "separate good people from evil ones".)

- Last month it *rained cats and dogs* for several days in a row and caused a disastrous flood in Hengyang which had not been experienced for a century or so.

  (Here it means "rain very heavily".)

- "I *brought my pigs to the wrong market*, for I had sold those big durians for only one dollar each", Supaphon said.

  (Here it means "fail in an undertaking to sell something")

- I'm sorry I *have other fish to fry* and I will not be able to attend the ceremony.

  (Here it means "have more important business to attend to".)

- He ordered a taxi to take him to the station, booked a seat on the train, and arranged for a friend to drive him to the airport, but then there was a train strike—*the best laid schemes of mice and men*.

  (Here it means "anybody's careful plans may fail".)

- She had only a little money and she had a long way to travel, yet she *took the bull by the horns* and walked a long distance along the mountain. She got to the destination at last.

  (Here it means "take bold action to overcome difficulties".)

10.2.5　From Military or Sailor's Life

Many English idioms have a close relation with military or nautical life, e.g. *stick to one's guns* (maintain one's position against attack or argument) and *to take the wind out of one's sails* (take away one's advantage or confidence).

- The two scholars began to *give a battle of words*.

  (Here it means "attack each other".)

- It was *war to the knife* between the two women who both fell in love with him.

  (Here it means "a bitter and ruthless antagonism".)

- We'd like to travel to Zhangjiajie for the holiday, but we *haven't the sinews of war*.

  (Here it means "short of money".)

- We shouldn't *throw our sword into the scale* to solve the problem.

  (Here it means "exercise military force".)

- Why shouldn't you have *stuck to your guns*?

  (Here it means "hold one's ground".)

- The old man *fights his battles* over again.

  (Here it means "talk something about the battles he used to fight".)

- If he stepped forward, there was a gorge; if he walked back, there was a wolf with its mouth open wide; it was a case of being *between the devil and the deep sea*.

  (Here it means "between two dangers".)

- I spent a whole year in Thailand and I never felt at home and got homesick. I *was just like a fish out of water*.

  (Here it means "a person in an uncomfortable situation and surroundings".)

- Famine followed *in the wake of* the disastrous flood.

  (Here it means "after".)

- None of us could do the maths exam, so we *are all in the same boat*.

  (Here it means "suffer bitterness together".)

10.2.6　From Literary Works

According to *A Brief History of the English Language*, the Bible was translated into English from Latin by a university professor named John Wycliffe. He held that people should use English when praying in church. Yet the English version showed the characteristics of the English people and this created a great influence on English and English literary works. Many idioms came from the Bible, such as *to raise Cain* (to make trouble), *at the last gasp* (at the point at which one must finish), *to smite hip and thigh* (to strike or beat ruthlessly), *like an apple of one's eye* (favorite), *to cast pearls before swine* (to offer something valuable or beautiful to those who cannot appreciate it), *to kick against the pricks* (to hurt oneself by useless resistance).

There are also many idiomatic expressions from some literary works written by some early English writers, especially Shakespeare. These idioms sound vivid and beautiful, e.g., *There is the rub* from *Hamlet*, *to meet somebody in the mouth* from *Henry V* and *King Lear*, *the milk of human kindness* from *Macbeth*, *a pound of flesh* from *The Merchant of Venice*.

Many idioms have originated from some mythological stories or allusions. For example, *sword of Damocles* came from an old Greek story. It was said that the tyrant Dionysius of Syracuse didn't like his minister Damocles, for he often said something that made the emperor unhappy. So Dionysius decided to invite Damocles to a rich banquet by hanging a sword with a thread right over his head. He was told to sit under the sword. He became very apprehensive. The idiom *sword of Damocles* means "threatened danger in the midst of prosperity". *Penelope's web* means "the work will never be finished". The story goes like this: Odysseus was fighting abroad. His beautiful wife Penelope was very faithful to him. During his absence, many young men came to woo Penelope. She promised to marry one of them, but she said that she should finish weaving a web. She wove it in the daytime and unwove it at night. Thus no one ever saw her finish her work. She did like this till her husband's return. *Sisyphean labor* also means "the work that can never be finished". In ancient Greece, king Sisyphus was greedy and evil-minded. He fell to hell after his death. His penalty was to push stones up the mountains and then let them roll down the slopes. He did the work without ending and suffered a great deal.

10.2.7　From Other Languages

The English language experienced a great change since the Normans conquered England in 1066. After that, many French words and Greek words entered the English language; and Latin words began to pour into the language due to the introduction of Christianity. So a great number of idiomatic expressions found their way into English.

1. Idioms from French

- *to break the ice*—to begin to speak (*rompre la glace*)
- *to make believe*—to pretend to oneself (*faire croire*)
- *to make both ends meet*—to have enough money to live on (*joindre les deux bouts*)
- *to be on the point of doing something*—to be about to do something (*être sure le point de*)
- *a tempest in a teacup*—disproportionately large fuss about something trivial (*une tempête dans un verre d'eau*)

2. Idioms from Latin

- *to take something with a grain of salt*—to be disinclined to believe something (*cum grano salis*)
- *on the Greek Calendars*—the day will never come (*ad kalendas Graecas*)

10.2.8   From Other Sources

Some idioms come from other sources, such as religious activities, games, etc. For example:

- *to be as poor as a church mouse*—very poor (from religious activities)
- *to go to the devil*—to become bad, ruined, or useless (from religious activities)
- *God helps those who help themselves.*—(proverb) you cannot depend solely on divine help, but must work yourself to get what you want. (from Benjamin Franklin)
- *to turn up trump*—to complete an activity successfully or to produce a good result, especially when you are not expected to. (from card games)

10.3   Classification of English Idioms

Of the various aspects of the English language, idioms show perhaps the greatest variety and are also the hardest to classify. Studies on English idioms to this day and various dictionaries of idioms have provided a variety of criteria for classifying idioms. In this chapter, we prefer the criterion of grammatical functions, that is, to classify the English idioms according to their grammatical functions, because such classification will be more helpful in the actual use of idioms. The difficulty in using idioms appropriately lies first in the difficulty of grasping the elusive and figurative meaning and then in the difficulty of determining the syntactic functions of idioms. Thus, knowledge of the grammatical functions of idioms will undoubtedly be beneficial to learners.

10.3.1 Nominal Phrases

Many noun phrases are composed of: (1) noun + noun; (2) noun + and + noun; (3) adjective + noun; (4) noun + 's/of + noun; and (5) noun + preposition + noun.

1. Noun + noun

- *a moot point*—a matter that was uncertain or undecided, so open to debate
- *apple-pie order*—neat and tidy
- *April fool*—somebody on whom a joke is played on the first of April
- *birthday suit*—nude, i.e., the way we are born
- *blood money*—favor made to somebody who betrays somebody else
- *brain drain*—the loss of the leading intellectuals and researchers of a country due to excessive emigration to other countries where conditions are better
- *brain trust*—a group of people with special knowledge who answer questions or give advice
- *conversation piece*—an unusual object that stimulates discussion
- *dogfight*—a fight in which two or more aircrafts are involved
- *John Bull*—the typical Englishman
- *skeleton staff*—minimum number of people to do a project or perform work
- *sheet anchor*—a source of aid in times of emergency or danger
- *Uncle Sam*—the US
- *Yankee trick*—mean trick
- *Yap head*—fool, knothead

2. Noun + and + noun

When reading we may come across an idiomatic expression composed of two nouns connected by "and". It is part of the "Siamese twins" as a British scholar, H. W. Fowler, termed it. Here are some examples:

- *Alpha and Omega*—from beginning to the end, the whole
- *bag and baggage*—with all one's possessions
- *bread and butter*—living, basic daily work
- *hammer and tongs*—(informal) do something, especially argue and fight, with a lot of energy and noise
- *heart and soul*—with a lot of energy and enthusiasm
- *hip and thigh*—without mercy, ruthlessly
- *life and soul*—with total commitment

- *staff and nonsense*—utter nonsense
- *tooth and nail*—with great violence and determination
- *town and gown*—the inhabitants of a college town and the students and teachers of the college
- *use and wont*—a habit
- *waifs and strays*—homeless children, odd things
- *ways and means*—various means or methods
- *weal and woe*—good and bad fortune
- *whims and fancies*—sudden desire or idea, often something unusual and unreasoning

3. Adjective + noun

Sometimes a modifier such as an adjective is used before a noun, which serves as the head. For example:

- *a born sailor*—one who seems naturally gifted for the work
- *a quixotic project*—a project as foolish and extravagantly romantic as these ascribed to Don Quixote
- *a red letter day*—a festival, a holiday
- *a shortcut*—a direct, cross path which shortens the way
- *a white-haired boy*—he who gets special treatment
- *an Indian summer*—a period of hot, dry weather in late autumn after a time of frost and even snow
- *fond dream*—good dream
- *French leave*—absence without permission
- *a Mickey Mouse job*—a job not of high quality; too easy
- *the Black Death*—in the 14th century the outbreak of bubonic plague in different parts of Europe which killed a very great number of people
- *white elephant*—something useless and unwanted but big and costly

4. Noun + 's/of + noun

Many expressive idioms are made up of two nouns in the genitive case ("'s" and "of" construction). Some examples are:

- *an apple of discord*—a subject of envy and strife
- *an apple of Sodom*—a kind of golden colored fruit found in the valley of the Dead Sea, but the taste is like ashes; it also has the meaning of disappointed expectation, results which belie hopes, pleasures which have a sting.

- *a diamond of the first water*—a reliable thing which is perfect of its kind
- *a Jack of all trades*—a person who can turn his hand to any kind of business
- *a man of spirit*—a courageous man
- *a mare's nest*—a discovery that seems interesting but is found to have no value
- *a son of Mars*—a sailor
- *cat's paw*—a person used by another as a dupe or tool
- *Hobson's choice*—no choice at all
- *King's weather*—fine weather; weather fit for a king
- *Penelope's web*—a job that cannot be finished
- *the crack of doom*—the end of the world

5. Noun + preposition + noun

Some idioms nominal in nature are combined with a preposition between two nouns.

- *a snake in the grass*—a secret foe, an enemy concealed from view, a sneaking, cunning person who openly pretends to be your friend and yet is in his heart a foe
- *castles in the air / castles in Spain*—something having so slight a basis that it is never likely to be realized
- *a friend at court*—a person who will be disposed towards you; who can exert influence on those who have it in their power to benefit you
- *a card in one's sleeve*—something unexpected in reserve
- *a fly in the ointment*—a person or thing that stops a situation, activity, plan, etc. from being successful as good as it could be
- *a bed of thorns*—a situation of great anxiety and apprehension
- *drug in the market*—a commodity whose supply greatly exceeds the demand for it
- *rule of thumb*—a quick, practical but not exact, way of measuring or calculating something
- *the sinews of war*—money, which buys the sinews, and makes them act vigorously

10.3.2　Verbal Phrases

Verbs collocated with different particles, prepositions, and other parts of speech can form different idioms. Usually, verbal phrases can be classified into the following kinds.

1. Transitive verb + noun

- *to bite one's tongue off*—to regret what one has said
- *to cut one's throat*—to do something that is likely to harm you, especially when you are angry and trying to harm somebody else

- *to dodge the column*—to avoid getting yourself in a position to fulfill something
- *to down tools*—to go on strike
- *to face the music*—to accept the difficulties, criticism, and unpleasant results that your words or action may cause
- *to follow one's nose*—to go in the same direction
- *to gild the lily*—to ornament something that is already good or pleasing and so spoil it
- *to hang fire*—to postpone
- *to have one's say*—to give one's opinion about something
- *to jump the queue*—to go to the front of a line of people without waiting for your turn
- *to make the grade*—to make a high enough standard in an exam, a job, etc.
- *to miss the boat*—to miss an opportunity
- *to stand Sam*—to foot the bill
- *to take one's last breath*—(euphemism) to die
- *to upset the apple cart*—to ruin carefully laid plans

2. Transitive verb + noun + preposition

- *to have a head on one's shoulders*—to be a sensible person
- *to keep an eye on*—to make sure that somebody or something is safe
- *to keep one's head above water*—to succeed in staying out of debt
- *to make a name for oneself*—to become successful and well known because of your skill in doing something very well
- *to put a premium on*—to consider something very important or valuable
- *to put a spoke in one's wheels*—to make it difficult for somebody to do something or to carry out their plans
- *to put the blame on*—to blame somebody for doing something
- *to shed light on*—to make a problem, etc easier to understand
- *to turn the laugh against somebody*—to put the laugh on somebody
- *to wash one's hands of something*—to refuse to go on with or take responsibility for

3. Intransitive verb + prepositional phrase

- *to bark up the wrong tree*—(figurative) to make the wrong choice; to ask the wrong person; to follow the wrong course
- *to beat about the bush*—to take too long before saying what you want to say; to avoid saying something directly
- *to breathe down one's neck*—(informal) to watch somebody too closely, and so

make him or her feel uncomfortable

- *to come into existence*—to begin existence, to begin to be
- *to dip into one's savings*—(figurative) to take out part of the money one has been saving
- *to fall by the way*—to leave a march or precession in exhaustion to recover beside the pathway
- *to jump down one's throat*—(figurative) to scold somebody severely
- *to jump to a conclusion*—(figurative) to judge or decide something without all the facts, to reach unwarranted conclusions
- *to leave a bad taste in one's mouth*—to leave a bad feeling or memory with somebody
- *to look for a needle in a bottle/haystack*—to look for one thing among many others, without the hope of finding it
- *to play to the gallery*—to perform in a manner that will get the strong approval of the audience; to perform in a manner that will get the approval of the lower elements in the audience
- *to seize upon a chance*—(literary) to grasp a chance tightly
- *to swim against the current of a river*—to swim in a direction opposite to the flow of the water
- *to tread on the neck of*—to oppress
- *to zip up your lip*—(informal) to be quiet

4. Intransitive verb + particle

- *to back down*—to yield to a person or a thing; to fail to carry through a threat
- *to chew out*—to scold
- *to come round*—finally to agree or consent to something; to return to consciously; to wake up
- *to die down*—to fade to almost nothing; to decrease gradually
- *to lay about*—to lie around
- *to pass away*—(euphemism) to die
- *to rattle off*—to recite something quickly and accurately
- *to run off*—to drive or travel off something, such as rails, tracks, a road, etc.
- *to throw up*—to vomit

5. Intransitive verb + particle + preposition

- *to creep up on*—to sneak up on somebody or something
- *to fall back on*—(literary) to fall backward onto somebody or something

- *to get on with*—to continue doing something
- *to give up on*—to give up trying to do something
- *to keep up with*—(literary) to advance at the same rate as somebody or something
- *to move in on*—(literary) to move closer to somebody or something; to make advances or aggressive movements toward somebody or something
- *to sit down on*—to be seated on something
- *to stand up for*—to take the side of somebody or something; to defend somebody or something
- *to stand up with*—to attend somebody who is being married
- *to wait up for*—(figurative) to stay up late waiting for somebody to arrive or something to happen

6. Verb + and + verb

- *to chop and change*—to change your plans, opinions, or methods too often
- *to cut and run*—(slang) to run away quickly
- *to forgive and forget*—to forgive someone and (attempt to) forget that the wrong they committed ever happened
- *to give and take*—to be willing to listen to other people's wishes and points of view and to change your demands, if this is necessary
- *to grin and bear it*—(informal) to accept something unpleasant without complaining
- *to kick and scream*—to complain
- *to live and let live*—to be open-minded toward or tolerant of others
- *to toss and turn*—to be unable to sleep because of worrying

7. Transitive verb + it (idiomatic *it*)

- *to catch it*—to be scolded, punished
- *to hotel it*—to make somebody live in a hotel
- *to make it*—to succeed in doing something
- *to pig it*—to live in a dingy environment
- *to rough it*—to live in a simple and not very comfortable way

"*It*" in each idiom has no practical meaning, and it serves as an object and does not refer to anything in particular.

8. Other patterns

Sometimes we may see the following patterns:

(1) Verb + adjective: *to make good* (to succeed at something); *to come clean* (to be honest

with somebody about something); *to make sure* (to check something and to be certain about it)

(2) Verb + noun + preposition + noun: *to see eye to eye* (to agree about somebody or something with somebody else)

(3) Verb + adjective + and + adjective + preposition: *to play fast and loose with* (to disregard one's promises or engagements)

(4) There are idiomatic verbal phrases composed of the link verb "to be". A lot of prepositional and other phrases are used together with "to be". Mainly we have four forms:

- to be + prepositional phrase: *to be on the wrong side of sixty* (more than 60 years old); *to be on good terms with oneself* (have a good, friendly, etc. relationship with somebody); *to be in one's bad/good books* (have/not have somebody's favor or approval); *to be in the doldrums* (to be quiet or depressed)

- to be + noun + prepositional phrase/preposition: *to be an excellent hand* (to be very good at something.); *to be double Dutch to one* (something impossible to understand to somebody); *to be an authority on* (to be an expert on something); *to be a slave to the bottle* (to drink excessively)

- to be + adjective + prepositional phrase: *to be born on the wrong side of the blanket* ([of a child] illegitimate); *to be born out of wedlock* (born to an unmarried mother); *to be easy on the eye* (to be pleasant to look at)

- to be + particle: *to be up* (to get up); *to be off* (closed); *to be out* (not at home); *to be on* (to be in operation); *to be down* (to be short of)

It is clear that examples in the fourth form have more than one meaning, but here only one of them is given for the sake of space. Moreover, their meanings are largely dependent on the context.

10.3.3 Adjectival Idiomatic Expressions

When an adjective or a particle is used with an appropriate preposition or particle, we call it an adjective phrase. We have the following types.

1. Adjective + preposition

- *abounding with*—having something in great numbers or quantities
- *conversant with*—(formal) familiar with something
- *exempt from*—free from an obligation, duty or payment

- *indispensable to*—absolutely essential
- *subsequent to*—(formal) following something; after
- *studded with*—decorated with many studs, precious stones
- *superior to*—better, stronger than somebody or something else
- *vexed with*—(formal) angry especially with trivial matters
- *void of*—without something; lacking something
- *zealous for*—enthusiastic about

2. Adjective + and + adjective

- *black and blue*—(figurative) bruised, physically or emotionally
- *bright and early*—very early in the morning or the workday
- *fair and square*—completely fair(ly); justly; within the rules
- *fast and furious*—very rapidly and with unrestrained energy
- *free and easy*—causal
- *high and dry*—(figurative) safe, unbothered by difficulties; unscathed
- *hot and heavy*—(figurative) referring to serious passion or emotions
- *null and void*—without legal force; having no legal effect
- *pure and simple*—absolutely; without further complication or elaboration
- *rough and ready*—strong, active, and ready for anything
- *slow and steady*—slow and constantly
- *sick and tired*—tired of somebody or something
- *thick and fast*—in large numbers or amounts and at a rapid rate

3. Adjective + prepositional phrase

- *loaded for bear*—(infovrmal) angry
- *near at hand*—close or handy to somebody
- *next to impossible*—almost impossible
- *up in the air*—(figurative) undecided about somebody or something
- *up to the minute*—(figurative) current
- *wet behind the ears*—(figurative) young and inexperienced
- *wide of the mark*—(literary) far from the target
- *young at heart*—(of an old person) still feels young and behaves like a young man

4. As + adjective + as + noun

This pattern is usually used to show striking comparisons. The phrases may be found in stories, magazines, newspapers, and books of travel. They are expressed in short pithy phrases such as *as black as midnight, as black as coal, as cold as ice, as smooth as velvet, as silent as the grave, as slippery as an eel, as meek as a lamb, as timid as a hare, as watchful as a hawk, as proud as a peacock, as brave as a lion, as ugly as a toad, as innocent as a dove, as tricky as a monkey, as stupid as a donkey, as stiff as a poker, as cool as a cucumber, as grave as a judge, as poor as a church mouse, as greedy as a wolf, as cunning as a fox.*

10.3.4　Adverbial and Prepositional Idiomatic Expressions

1. Adverbial idiomatic expressions

- *again and again*—repeatedly; again and even more times
- *far and wide*—everywhere and in many places; over a large area
- *here and now*—present, as opposed to the past and future
- *here, there, and everywhere*—from place to place
- *now and then*—sometimes; occasionally
- *off and on*—occasionally; erratically; now and again
- *out and about*—outside the house; outdoors
- *to and fro*—(of movement) toward and away from something

2. Prepositional idiomatic expressions

1) Preposition + noun

- *at random*—without method or conscious choice
- *at any cost*—(figurative) regardless of the difficulty or cost; no matter what
- *behind the scenes*—without receiving credit or fame; out of public view
- *by the way*—used to indicate that the speaker is adding information
- *for your life*—because you are in danger
- *in a sense*—in a way; in one way of looking at it
- *on the spot*—(literary) at exactly the right place; at exactly the right time
- *to a hair*—just the same
- *to one's heart's content*—(figurative) as much as one wants
- *under no circumstances*—(figurative) absolutely never
- *with flying colors*—easily and excellently
- *without a hitch*—smoothly and without difficulty

2) Preposition + noun + preposition

- *at the height of*—(figurative) at the most intense or forceful aspect of something
- *at the mercy of*—in the power of
- *at the rear of*—located at the back part of something

- *in accordance with*—according to
- *in consequence of*—as a result of
- *in consideration of*—in return of something; as a result of something
- *in control of*—in charge of
- *on the brink of*—to be very close to
- *with an eye to*—intending to do something

3) Preposition + noun + prepositional phrase

- *at the tip of one's tongue*—almost spoken at the point of being said
- *at the top of one's lungs*—as loud as you can, very loudly
- *in the pink of condition*—strong and well; in fine shape
- *on the knees of gods*—beyond human control; not to be decided by anyone
- *within an inch of one's life*—near to dying
- *with one's tail between one's legs*—a state of feeling beaten, ashamed

4) Preposition + adjective + noun

- *in a little bit*—(figurative) in a small amount of time
- *in full swing*—(figurative) at the peak of activity; moving fast or efficiently
- *in many respects*—with regard to some details
- *in the second place*—secondly; in addition
- *in short order*—very quickly
- *on good terms*—friendly with somebody; able to interact well and be friends with somebody
- *with a bold hand*—boldly arrogantly
- *with a heavy heart*—sadly
- *with a whole skin*—safe and sound
- *without further ado*—without further talk

5) Preposition + noun + preposition + noun

out of the frying pan into the fire—out of one trouble into worse trouble; from something back to something worse

6) Preposition + numeral + and + numeral

at sixes and sevens—in a state of confusion, of persons unable to come to an agreement

7) Verb + noun + adverb + preposition + noun

throw the baby out with the bathwater—when getting rid of something undesirable or unpleasant also reject something of real value

10.3.5 Proverbs

The place of proverbs, and sayings with respect to idioms is a controversial issue. A proverb is a short familiar epigrammatic saying expressing popular wisdom, a truth, or a moral lesson in a concise and imaginative way. Unlike the constructions of the idiomatic expressions mentioned before, proverbs are usually fixed sentences with a full meaning. We even consider *Out of sight, out of mind; Such carpenters, such chips* as sentences. Despite the absence of their subjects and predicate verbs, they still express a complete meaning. We may say English proverbs are a precious treasure of the language; they are an essential part of any language. They have come from ordinary people from all walks of life since a very early time. They have a very long history. *Union is strength* and *Keep the golden mean* may be traced back to more than 600 BCE; *Liars need good memories* may be traced back to more than 400 BCE. They have come down by word of mouth since then and are used by people even today. So we can say that proverbs have close relation with the history, customs, religion, culture, habits, and social styles of a country.

Proverbs are the product of the wisdom of the people. They are pithy, terse colloquialisms and easy to understand. Truth resides in them. They tell people how to think, how to live in this society, how to fight against the false, the evil, and the ugly, and maintain the true, the good, and the beautiful.

Proverbs can be used to express the following aspects.

1. Work

- *Actions speak louder than words.*—What you do is more significant than what you say.
- *All roads lead to Rome.*—There are many different routes to the same goal.
- *Man proposes, God disposes.*—People may make plans, but they cannot control the outcome of their plans.
- *No man can serve two masters.*—You cannot work for two different people, organizations, or purposes in good faith, because you will end up favoring one over the other.
- *No pains, no gains.*—If you want to improve, you must work so hard that it hurts.
- *Nothing ventured, nothing gained.*—If you do not take risks, you will never

accomplish anything.

- *Strike while the iron is hot.*—When you have an opportunity to do something, do it before you lose your chance.
- *Where there is a will, there is a way.*—If you truly want to do something, you will find a way to do it, in spite of obstacles.

2. Animal

- *The leopard cannot change its spots.*—A person's character does not change.
- *Every horse thinks his sack heaviest.*—Everyone thinks he or she has the hardest work to do or the most difficult problems to overcome.
- *Every dog has its day.*—Everyone gets a chance eventually.
- *Birds of a feather flock together.*—Similar people tend to associate with each other.
- *A bird in the hand is worth two in the bush.*—Having something for certain is better than the possibility of getting something better.
- *The last straw breaks the camel's back.*—The last little burden or problem causes everything to collapse.

3. Time

- *Time and tide wait for no man.*—Things will not wait for you when you are late.
- *Time hangs heavy on someone's hands.*—Time seems to go slowly when one has nothing to do.
- *Time is a great healer.*—Emotional pain will grow less as time passes.
- *The time is ripe.*—It is the most favorable time to do something.
- *Time works wonders.*—The passing of time can resolve many problems.

4. Virtue

- *Virtue is its own reward.*—You should not be virtuous in hopes of getting a reward, but because it makes you feel good to be virtuous.
- *The spirit is willing but the flesh is weak.*—People are not always physically capable of doing what they are willing to do.

5. Education

- *The best horse needs breaking, and the aptest child needs teaching.*—People all need to be educated.
- *Soon learnt, soon forgotten.*—Something that is easy to learn is easy to forget.

6. Behavior

- *Do not let the sun go down on your wrath.*—Do not stay angry with anybody; calm your anger by the end of the day.

- *Let every man skin his own skunk.*—Everyone should do his own job and not interfere with others; each person should do his own dirty work.

10.4 Syntactic, Structural, and Stylistic Features

The sections above deal with the source and classification of English idioms. In this section, a syntactic, structural, and stylistic analysis will be made so that the non-native student can learn to use them appropriately.

10.4.1 Syntactic Function

Using English idioms appropriately is hard for non-native speakers when learning the language. They can hardly determine their syntactic functions. Some have to judge the syntactic functions of idioms from their components on the surface.

The syntactic function of a phrase idiom usually corresponds with its central word and/or components. For example, a noun phrase is usually used as a subject, a complement, and an object, as illustrated in the first three examples. But on some occasions, a noun phrase operates as an adjunct as in each of the last three examples.

- A subject: "*Flesh and blood* can bear it no longer."
  (Here it means "living human body, especially with reference to its natural limitations".)

- A complement: "The bodies of men, munition, and money, may justly be called *sinews of war*."
  (Here it means "money, which buys the sinews, and makes them act vigorously".)

- An object: "We had *a bird's-eye view* of Oxford from the hill."
  (Here it means "a view seen from high above".)

- An adjunct: They *fight like cat and dog*.
  (Here it means "be continuously quarreling".)

- An adjunct: I'd *move between heaven and earth* to get a date with Andrew.
  (Here it means "try one's best".)

- An adjunct: He swallowed the bread *by leaps and bounds*.
  (Here it means "very quickly".)

A verbal phrase is usually used as a predicate in a sentence. E.g., "The joke about the elephant *brought the house down*." One can easily see that *to bring the house down* in the above sentence functions as a predicate.

Verbal phrases can be classified into two groups: intransitive verbal phrases and transitive verbal phrases. Some transitive phrases can be used passively, i.e. transitive use, while others can't be changed into the passive voice, i.e., intransitive use. The phrase *pitch into somebody* can be changed into its passive form as shown in the sentence "He hardly expected to be *pitched into* that way". The following phrase can also be used both actively and passively. For example:

- Though the schoolmistress was not in any sense of the word a scholarly woman, she had rare human qualities; all her pupils *looked up to her*. (Active)
- The kind of person that is needed as a youth club leader is one who can *be looked up to* by those with whom he has to deal. (Passive)

Let's see another example, "*Hold your tongue* since you know much about it." The phrase *hold one's tongue* (to refrain from speaking) can only be used in the active form though it is a transitive verbal phrase. Passivization is also inappropriate for the following verbal phrases: *split one's sides* (laugh heartily), *kick the bucket* (to die), *hit it off* (to get on well together), *mind one's own business* (to attend only to the things that concern one), etc.

Quite a few phrases are used mainly in their active forms, not often seen in the passive voice. Yet the following phrases used passively are acceptable, e.g., *steal the limelight* (to attract the most attention); *eat (one) out of house and home* (to eat so much that it is difficult to provide for). It doesn't seem impossible to say "*The limelight was stolen* by ninety-year-old Mr. Smith." or "During the three weeks we entertained John's school friends, we were *eaten out of house and home*."

As for prepositional phrases, they have different functions when used in sentences. Many expressions which are prepositional in the form are adverbial in meaning. For example, "At the last minute, Johnny came *out of the blue* to catch the pass and score a touchdown." (No one expected him to catch the pass.)

A prepositional phrase can also function as a complement in the following example: "Her friends thought she was *out of her mind* to marry the man." (Her friends thought she was crazy to marry him because he was not a good match.)

On the other hand, two idioms may be similar in structure, yet their functions may not be the same. Take *off one's hands* and *on one's hands* for example, their patterns are the same "preposition + noun" functioning as predicative as seen in the following sentence "Both my children start at boarding school next week. So they'll be *off my hands* and I'll have much more free time.", while the latter means "in one's possession" used as an adjunct as shown in the sentence "Business is poor at present and I've got a lot of stock *on my hands* which I can't sell."

Similarly, both *on the mend* (healing, becoming better) and *on the nose* (just right) are prepositional phrase idioms, yet the former functions as a complement, while the latter as an adjunct:

- Tom's broken leg is *on the mend*.
- He hit the ball *on the nose*.

Therefore, idioms may be identical in structure, yet different in syntactic function. So a non-native speaker sometimes can hardly tell what function an idiom has. He had better consult dictionaries frequently so as not to make mistakes in using idiomatic expressions. Hence, in learning an idiomatical expression, one should first find out what grammatical category it belongs to, and then see how it functions in a sentence.

10.4.2　Structural Features

1. Structural stability

As a rule, an idiom is rigid and one cannot substitute another synonymous word for any individual word in it, and the arrangement of each word is fixed. Generally speaking, one may not amplify, delete or change any element of an idiom. For instance, you cannot add "the" to the idiom out *of question* which means "possible" and delete "the" from *out of the question* which means "impossible". It would be ridiculous to say, "He was born with a pearl in his mouth." instead of "He was *born with a silver spoon* in his mouth."; or "Oxen might fly" instead of "*Pigs might fly*".

Idioms have many forms or structures. Some are short, like *in tears* (crying), *on duty* (at work); some are long, such as *to put a thin down in black and white* (to put it in writing), *to cut one's coat according to one's cloth* (to plan one's aims and activities in line with one's resources and circumstances). On the other hand, an idiom can take a regular structure, or an irregular and even a grammatically incorrect structure. A native speaker will have little trouble saying *Diamond cut diamond*. The noun "diamond" takes its singular form, yet no "s" is added to the verb "cut"; usually when the subject singular in number is followed by a predicate verb with an "s" attached to it. This proverb is not incorrect, yet it's grammatically incorrect.

Structural stability also means grammatical inseparability. It implies that the grammatical meaning or, to be more exact, the part-of-speech meaning of an idiom is felt as belonging to the word group as a whole irrespective of the part-of-speech meaning of the component words. In comparing the free word group, e.g., *long time*, and the idiom, e.g., *in the long run*, we observe that in the free word group the noun *time* and the adjective *long* preserve the part-of-speech meaning proper to these words taken in isolation. The whole group is viewed as composed of two independent units (adjective and noun). In the idiom *in the long run*, the part-of-speech meaning belongs to the group as a single whole. *In the long run* is an adverbial expression grammatically equivalent to single adverbs, e.g., *finally*, *ultimately*, *firstly*, etc. It is observed that in the case of the idiom under discussion, there is no connection between the part-of-speech meaning of the member words (*in*—preposition, *long*—adjective, *run*—noun) and that of the whole word-group. The grammatical inseparability of idioms viewed as one of the aspects of idiomaticity enables us to regard them as grammatically equivalent to single words.

2. Structural variability

Although idiomatic expressions are structurally fixed, it does not mean that we can never make a change. Structural variability does happen when people are to achieve rhetorical effect in a particular situation. When idioms are used in actual context, they do experience grammatical changes such as different forms of verbs, and agreement of personal pronouns and numbers. One can easily find where "*to separate the silk purse from the sow's ears*" comes from. It arises from the proverb "*One can't make a silk purse out of a sow's ear.*"

It is not unusual for writers to give a new twist to an old saying by making slight changes for rhetorical effect. For example:

- *A horse of the same color.*—Shakespeare (from *a horse of another color*)
- He is *every other inch a gentleman.*—Rebecca West (from *every inch a gentleman*)
- *If a thing is worth doing, it is worth doing badly.*—G. K. Chesterton (from *If a thing is worth doing, it is worth doing well.*)

While changes in idiom structure should be made with the utmost caution, a certain amount of alteration is possible in the following ways:

1) Replacement

(1) By changing verbs

- *to call over the coals / to haul over the coals*
- *to repeat by heart / to know/say/learn by heart*
- *to get one's hand in / to have/keep one's hand in*

- *to keep an eye on / to have an eye on*
- *to make a figure / to cut a figure*
- *to catch hold of / to get/seize/take hold of*
- *to keep one's word / to break one's word*
- *to take heart / to lose heart*

(2) By changing nouns

- *to beat the air / to beat the wind*
- *on the second Sunday of next week / on the second Monday of next week*
- *down in the bushes / down in the mouth*
- *a drop in the ocean / a drop in the bucket*
- *on the increase / on the decrease*
- *in the know / in the dark*
- *die in harness / die in one's boots*

(3) By changing adjectives

- *to cut a poor figure / to cut a sorry figure*
- *in good feather / in high/fine/full feather*
- *on a large scale / on a big/vast scale*
- *by all means / by no means*
- *take long views / take short views*

(4) By changing adverbs or prepositions

- *drop in / drop over / drop by*
- *give a handle for / give a handle to*
- *turn on / turn off*
- *go with the stream / go against the stream*
- *by the lump / in the lump*
- *have two strikes on one / have two strikes against one*
- *to sit on / to sit upon*

2) Insertion

- *to pull a face / to pull a long face*
- *to haul over the coals / to haul over red-hot coals*
- *to take pains / to take great pains*
- *to take one's stars / to take one's lucky stars*
- *to flow with milk and honey / to flow with intellectual*

- *from one's heart / from the bottom of one's heart*
- *as broad as long / as broad as it is long*

3) Shortening or a slight change

- *birds of a feather* from *Birds of a feather flock together*.
- *to teach your grandmother* from *Teach your grandmother to suck eggs*.
- *a black sheep* from *There's a black sheep in every flock*.
- *the last straw* from *It is the last straw that breaks the camel's back*.
- *velvet paws* from *Velvet paws hide sharp claws*.
- *Jack of all trades* from *Jack of all trades and master of none*.
- *Man proposes and disposes* from the proverb *Man proposes, God disposes*.
- *Like son, like father* from *Like father, like son*.

4) Using synonyms

- *pad in the straw / snake in the grass*
- *stick to one's guns / hold one's ground*
- *a horse of another color / another pair of shoes*

5) Position-shifting

The positions of certain constituents in some idioms can be shifted without any change in meaning. For example:

- *day and night / night and day*
- *young and old / old and young*
- *pin back one's ears / pin one's ears back*
- *turn the radio up / turn up the radio*
- *do somebody a favor / do a favor for somebody*
- *play somebody a trick / play a trick on somebody*
- *fortune's wheel / wheel of fortune*
- *lie near somebody's heart / lie near the heart of somebody*

10.4.3 Stylistic Features

The stylistic features of idioms are not always the same. They are constantly changing and shifting with the development of language and the progress of society. They maybe formal now on some occasions and maybe informal then on other occasions. It's somewhat difficult for non-native speakers to tell their characteristics in different situations. Yet quite a number of idioms are used colloquially and slangily. For example:

- The teacher had a thorough knowledge of his subject, but he could not *put it across*.
- I should refuse even to consider the house at that price. He is trying to *put it across you*.

In the first sentence, *to put it across* means "to communicate something to an audience", so it is colloquial. But in the second sentence, *put it across somebody* is slangy and means "to trick somebody into paying too high a price for something".

1. Idioms used in both formal spoken and written English

- The kind of person who will *spill hairs* is usually the kind who likes arguing for arguing sake. (to make very fine and pointless distinctions in arguing)
- "Substitute *spinning yarns* for doing sums and you have exactly my story", I said. (to tell stories)

Other phrases: *to accord with* (to agree with or match up with something), *to address oneself to* (to turn one's complete attention to something), t*o make up one's mind* (to decide), *on trial* (in a legal case before a judge), *behind the times* (old-fashioned), *fine feathers make fine birds* (If you dress elegantly, people will think you are elegant), *partake of* (to have a portion of something).

2. English idioms used in an informal way

- Mary was usually very quiet, but at the farewell party, she *kicked up her heels* and had a wonderful time. (to celebrate freely)
- He *doubles in brass* as a porter and doorman. (to do two different things)

Other phrases are: *hand it to* (to admit the excellence of), *nothing doing* (will not do), *fuss and feather* (unnecessary bother and excitement), *full of oneself* (interested only in oneself), *as comfortable as an old shoe* (pleasant and relaxed), *month of Sundays* (a very long time), *as the salt of the earth* (as the most important one).

3. Colloquialisms

- He can argue *until hell freezes over*, nobody will be convinced. (forever)
- He's fed up with army discipline; every time I see him, he tells me how *cheesed off* he is. (tired and sick)
- Every night during the summer, we *kip out* on the beaches. (sleep in the open air)
- Uncle Tom is a *big wheel* in Washington; maybe he can help you with your problem. (an influential or important person)
- Joe Green is the wrong man for the job; he is always trying to *make waves*. (create a disturbance, a sensation)

- Let's not get into big city politics, that's a different *can of worms*. (a complex problem, or complicated situation)

4. Slang

- Throw away that *cancer stick*! Smoking is bad for you! (cigarette or something which is harmful)
- I'm sleepy; let's *hit the sack*. (go to bed)
- Stop *dishing the dirt*, Sally, it's really unbecoming! (gossip or spread rumors about others)
- After a few drinks, the man *felt no pain* and began to act foolishly. (be drunk)
- When his wife overdrew their bank account without telling him, Mr. Wood suddenly found himself really *in the soup*. (in serious trouble; in confusion)

5. Literary expressions

- Strange things *come to pass* in troubled times. (take place; happen)
- And *be it that* indeed that I have erred, my error remains with myself. (even though)
- Famine followed *in the wake of* the war. (right after; following)
- The police *gave the lie to* the man who said that he had been at home during the robbery. (call somebody a liar)
- Sally is a novelist *of note* in India. (notable; well-known)
- That was where I *crossed swords* with Brown in the discussion of financing the new project. (have an argument with; fight)

Stylistic features of idioms, however, are constantly shifting, and what is slang today may be informal tomorrow. Idioms used too frequently or indiscriminately may become clichés and trite sayings. In addition, slangy expressions are often peculiar to social or regional varieties. Some may be used only in British settings, others may be appropriate only in the American contexts, and still, others may be suitable for certain groups of people. All this needs care on the part of the user in the course of production.

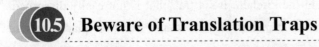 **Beware of Translation Traps**

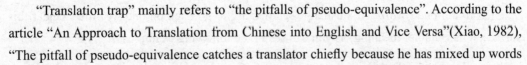

"Translation trap" mainly refers to "the pitfalls of pseudo-equivalence". According to the article "An Approach to Translation from Chinese into English and Vice Versa"(Xiao, 1982), "The pitfall of pseudo-equivalence catches a translator chiefly because he has mixed up words which appear to have a similar significance but in reality call up different ideas."

You cannot guess the real meaning of some idioms from their surface. If you judge the meaning of every individual word from their appearance, you will probably make an error. Just like an unfaithful friend of yours, he may betray you. So Martin H. Manser described in his *A Dictionary of Everyday Idioms* (Manser, 1983) that any idiom, whatever type it is, is deceptive. You may wonder why the idiom *move heaven and earth* does not mean "make an earth-shaking change" but "make every possible effort".

In translating idioms, there are many pitfalls that are quite easy to cause you to fall into them without any notice. Another example that may present you with a pitfall is *white-headed*. If you think *white-headed* is used to refer to an old person with white hair covering his head, you have fallen into the pitfall you have made for yourself. If you are not aware of its real meaning, you will not understand this idiom in the following example: "The *white-headed* youths are playing an important role in our socialist construction." It means "highly favored", but "aged people" is a trap. You can hardly guess what *take the bull by the horns* really means; you may probably explain it like this: "take the animal away by holding its horns".

As we all know, not all idioms are equivalent to Chinese. Only a few are completely equivalent to some extent, e.g., *to break the record* (打破纪录); *to pull the chestnut out of the fire* (火中取栗); *armed to the teeth* (武装到牙齿); *white terror* (白色恐怖); *at one's wit's end* (智穷计尽); *Talk of the devil and he is sure to appear* (说曹操，曹操到). Some correspond to each other on the surface; in fact, they are not of the same meaning. They can't be rendered into another language word for word. So we have to beware of the translation trap in rendering them. They are as closely knit as they themselves appear to be. Their construction may be nearly the same, yet they are not equivalents at all or just the opposite. Here are some more examples.

(1) *To have one's tail up*. It can't be translated as "be proud" or "to take pride in". In fact, this idiom means "be carefree/happy". E.g., Jenny really *had her tail up* after she won the competition.

(2) *If you don't like the heat, get out of the kitchen*. One may think that the idiom must have something to do with cooking in the kitchen. It's a trap that is not easily discerned. Regardless of its meaning of appearance, it means "If you cannot stand the place/pressure required to do something, you should stop doing it".

(3) *To eat one's words*. It's usually regarded as "to go back on one's words". Under this surface, it has another meaning, as you can see in the following examples:

- John had called Harry a coward, but the boys made him *eat his words* after Harry bravely fought a big bully.

- I want to *eat my words* when I found out that she had painted the picture which I criticized so caustically.

- He refused to withdraw the accusation, saying that not all the arguments in the world make him *eat his words*.

In the first sentence, *to eat one's words* means "to take back something one has said, to admit something is not true." In the second sentence, it means "deeply regret what one has said", while in the third sentence, the phrase means "to take back one's words; to unsay what one has said". From the above examples we can see that *to eat one's words* means "to retract and to recant".

(4) *One-horse race.* It can easily be mistranslated into "a race in which only one horse takes part". According to *Word Wise: A Dictionary of English Idioms* (Clark, 1989), this idiom means "a contest whose winner is known, even before it takes place". For example:

- The speed contest has turned into *a one-horse race* because she will be sure to be the winner.

- The champion has no real competition and the contest has turned into *a one-horse race*.

(5) *A piece of cake.* This idiom may be understood as "a kind of food which can be eaten". In fact, it means "very easy undertaking" and "easy task" in the following sentence: "My job is *a piece of cake*, one of the easiest I've ever had". So the meaning has nothing to do with "cake" itself.

(6) *To give a dog a bad name and hang him.* According to *The Advanced Learner's Dictionary* of *Current English*, under the entry of "dog", the idiom means "to give a person a bad reputation, slander him, and the bad reputation will remain". In *A New English-Chinese Dictionary* published in 1979, this idiom is explained nearly the same as the meaning mentioned above. It is translated as "一旦给人加个坏名声,他就永远洗刷不掉"; e.g., "*Give a dog a bad name and hang him* is true in George's case, for no one ever has a good word to say for him now." But in the second edition of *A New English-Chinese Dictionary*, the idiom is rendered as "谗言可畏" and "欲加之罪,何患无辞". Actually, "欲加之罪,何患无辞" in *Brewer's Dictionary of Phrases and Fables* published in 1975 is explained as "He who has a mind to beat his dog will easily find a stick." and in *A Dictionary of English Phrases* published in 1980 by some teachers from Xiamen University, it is explained as "If you want a pretense to whip a dog, say that he ate the frying pan".

(7) *Touch and go.* Non-native learners are easy to translate the idiom as "explode at a

touch; full of risk, flare up at the slightest provocation" and neglect its real meaning. Let's see how the idiom is used in the following examples:

- At one time while they were climbing the cliff, it was *touch and go* whether they could do it.

  (Here it means "they were in a dangerous place and might have fallen".)
- The doctors are now hopeful that he will make a recovery, but for several days it was *touch and go*.

  (Here it means "the precariousness of a situation".)
- It was *touch and go*. For the remainder of the night, young duke hovered between life and death in the old wainscoted bedroom to which we carried him.

  (Here it means "a narrow escape".)

According to *Brewer's Dictionary of Phrase and Fable*, the idiom *touch and go* came from such a story: Once two carts passed through a small and narrow lane from opposite directions at almost the same time. Their wheels touched one another. Finally, the owners of the carts solved the problem with great effort and the carts went away in their respective directions. The idiom thus means "be in a dangerous situation; a narrow escape or extremely doubtful or precarious".

(8) *Song and dance.* The idiomatic expression may be understood as "the performance of song and dance", yet its idiomatic meaning has nothing to do with "song and dance" itself. It has other meanings if not translated literally. The following are some examples:

- I met Nancy today and she gave me a long *song and dance* about her family.

  (Here it means "foolish or uninteresting talk; dull nonsense". The whole sentence means "She talked for a long time foolishly about her family and it was very uninteresting".)
- Billy gave the teacher a *song and dance* about his mother being sick as an excuse for being late.

  (Here it means "a long lie or excuse". The whole sentence means "Billy told the teacher a long lie".)
- It is only a small cut and there is no need to make such a *song and dance* about it.

  (Here it means "make a fuss about something". The whole sentence means "It is only a small cut and there is no need to make a fuss about it.")

Without consulting dictionaries, especially widely used ones, we will translate idioms without understanding their real meaning. So we have to avoid such pitfalls in learning English.

Exercises

I. State whether the following statements are true or false. In case a statement is false, briefly explain why.

1. An idiom contains at least two words.

2. Idioms are fixed in structure and so can never be changed.

3. Idioms are usually difficult to understand because the meanings of idioms are not in many cases the total of individual words.

4. Stylistically speaking, most idioms are neither formal nor informal.

5. Some idioms deny analysis in terms of grammar.

6. All idioms are used in their figurative senses.

7. A variation of an idiom is the same idiom used in a different sense.

8. Since each idiom is a semantic whole, each can be replaced by a single word.

9. Idioms are characterized by terseness, expressiveness, and vividness.

10. Semantic unity and structural stability are general features of idioms, but there are many exceptions.

II. Replace the underlined word or phrase in each of the following sentences with an idiomatic expression, for which the prompt word is given in the brackets.

1. That fabric is made of a material that <u>burns easily</u>. (catches _____)

2. <u>Suddenly</u> there was a loud scream from that dark room. (all _____)

3. The nurse <u>watched and cared for</u> the baby while we went to the party. (took _____)

4. Mr. Carl soon <u>became accustomed to</u> life in China. (got _____)

5. Children <u>pretended</u> that they were grown-ups. (made _____)

6. Everything in the refrigerator <u>has the flavor of</u> rotten eggs. (tastes _____)

7. They <u>believed too easily</u> that they had lost their property. (swallowed _____)

8. How did the shipwreck <u>happen</u>? (come _____)

III. Write the corresponding proverbs according to the meaning given in the following and then translate them into Chinese.

1. The early bird catches the worm.

2. Don't cry over spilled milk.

3. Out of sight, out of mind.

4. Man proposes, God disposes.

5. Put the cart before the horse.

IV. Match the phrases in Column A with their appropriate explanations in Column B.

A	B
a white elephant	fail at last
turn out crabs	a very costly possession that is worthless to its owner and only a cause of trouble
to bite one's tongue off	to be concerned in some way with a large number of different plans, arrangements, etc.
a chip of the old block	a disabled person, an incompetent, useless person
to snap one's fingers at	to keep secret, to shut one's mouth
to have a finger in the pie	to take a threatening tongue, to show by threatening word or action one's desire or intention to injure
a lame duck	feel sorry for what one has just said
to button up one's lips	a son who looks or acts like his father
to show one's teeth	to show contempt for; to disregard

V. The following text was written in highly figurative and idiomatic language. Read the passage, pick out the idioms and explain their meanings. Then rewrite the passage in standard straight-forward idiom-free language, keeping the original meaning.

Sam is a real cool cat. He never blows his stack and hardly ever flies off the handle. What's more, he knows how to get away with things... Well, of course, he is getting on, too. His hair is pepper and salt, but he knows how to make up for lost time by taking it easy. He gets up early, works out, and turns in early. He takes care of the hot dog stand like a breeze until he gets time off. Sam's got it made; this is it for him.

Chapter *11*

Differences Between American English and British English

The large-scale colonization of America by British settlers began in the 17th century. These immigrants brought with them their mother tongue, the English language, but they soon found that in their new homeland, many aspects of the physical and cultural environment had no equivalents in their mother country. They had to create names for the strange people, animals, and plants they encountered, and find new expressions for their new experiences to bridge the lexical gap. All these new terms they added to their word stock. As time went on, and as the life and culture of these settlers developed in comparative isolation from what was going on in England, the difference was reflected in the language as well. Gradually, a new variety of English—American English, emerged and evolved into a national American standard, parallel to the simultaneous growth and development of the national standard in English itself.

American English has grown steadily in international significance, parallel to the growth of American political, economic, technological, and cultural influences worldwide. By the late 19th and early 20th century, the United States had emerged out of its splendid isolation as an economic and, ultimately, political superpower. Since World War Ⅱ, the United States has been dominant in many areas of science and technology, such as computers, airlines, etc. Moreover, the United States has 70% of all the native speakers of English in the world. All these factors make American English the most important variety of English and a more and more important medium for communication all over the world.

This chapter will begin with a brief account of the growth of American English—a variety or national standard of English used in the United States. Then some pages will be devoted to the discussion of the characteristics of American English. Finally, a comparison will be made between American English and British English with regard to pronunciation, spelling, grammar, usage, and vocabulary.

11.1 Growth of American English

The development of English goes along with the settlement of colonization and expansion of the nation. The earliest settlers came to North America with Early Modern English and the language is largely the English of South-East English. Its subsequent development was affected by a number of factors: the source of the original British dialect, maintenance of contact with the "home" country, patterns of settlement, influences of languages other than English, and social and geographical mobility. In the course of development, three periods are to be distinguished.

11.1.1 Before Independence (1607 CE–1789 CE)

This period is also called the colonial period and begins with the settlement at Jamestown (Virginia) and ends with the ratification of the Constitution in 1789. At the beginning of the 17th century, America was a continent thinly populated by tribal Native Americans (American Indians), whose territory was plundered by colonists from several European countries, mainly Britain, Spain, Holland, and France. The earliest British settlement was established in 1607 in Jamestown, Virginia. Later in 1620, about 102 British immigrants, many of whom were Puritans, sailed across the Atlantic on the ship "Mayflower" and established Plymouth Colony in Massachusetts successfully. Afterward, more immigrants arrived from Britain and settled in areas along the Atlantic coast. By 1733, the original thirteen English colonies had been set up.

The early immigrants had learned as children to speak and write English in the last quarter of the 16th century. Hence, the language they brought with them was Elizabethan English, the language spoken by Shakespeare and Milton, and Bunyan, which belonged to the early stage of Modern English. In certain respects, American English is closer to the English of Shakespeare than modern British English is. It is in the main similar to present-day English but had some differences in spelling, pronunciation, grammar, and vocabulary. Below is a brief account of these differences in terms of spelling, pronunciation, grammar, and vocabulary.

1. Spelling

In the 17th century, many English words were spelled differently from their modern forms. In a pamphlet written by some Puritan pioneers in 1603, we may find such words as *cleare* (clear), *dutei* (duty), *goodnes* (goodness) (*Webster's Ninth New Collegiate Dictionary*, 1991: 26).

2. Pronunciation

The previous changes in sounds had made the English pronunciation during the early stage of Modern English basically the same as that of today. Yet a study of the rhymes of the verses written at that stage would show changes in pronunciation since then. For example, in the following couplet, the pronunciation of *tea* at that time was evidently /te:/, not /ti:/.

- Here thou, great Anna! When three realms *obey*,
  Dost sometimes consel take—and sometimes *tea*.

3. Grammar

The second person pronoun *thou* (also *thee, they, thine*) and the accompanying verb ending *-(e)st* still remained in use. They were freely employed both in verse and prose, but in contemporary English, they are only used in prayers and sometimes in poetry.

4. Vocabulary

The greatest difference lies in vocabulary. Since the Elizabethan period, thousands of words and idioms have been formed and borrowed on both sides of the Atlantic, while some expressions have become obsolete.

The early settlers must have begun to make Americanisms as soon as they arrived on American shores, for they found themselves in a new environment with new landscape features, plants, and animals that were different from anything they had seen in their homeland. And they found they were in a very diverse linguistic culture. They had to find words to name all the strange objects and cope with the new conditions. New words and expressions were coined or borrowed from the indigenous tribes, or new meanings were given to words brought from home. They borrowed some of these words from the Native Americans, such as *hickory, opossum, persimmon, raccoon,* and *squash*, but they also took existing English words and applied them in a new way, such as *bullfrog, catfish, copperhead, eggplant,* and *live oak*. Meanwhile, the English colonists' contact with the immigrants from other European countries brought about borrowings from them too: *boss, cookie, sleigh* from Dutch; *prairie, rapids, shanty* from French; *canyon, ranch, scow* from Spanish.

The colonists won their independence in 1783. Before then, American English was looked down upon as a colonists' branch of the language of the mother country, which was regarded as the norm by both the British and American speakers. The flow of expressions across the Atlantic was then generally westward; only the American words designating native objects and landscape features were noticed and sometimes used by the British.

11.1.2   From Independence to the Early 19th Century (1789 CE–1860 CE)

At the time of the American Revolution, especially in the years immediately following it, Americans were beginning to be conscious of their language. The common strife of braving the hardships of life, fighting against British tariffs, and ultimately political control led to the emergence of a sense of nationality. In the field of language, this patriotic fervor was manifested by the argument for the consideration and recognition of the American variety or standard of English. Americans went on forming words and phrases with their own linguistic materials and adopting words from indigenous inhabitants and from immigrants from other European countries. Moreover, Thomas Jefferson thought that the Americans were more tolerant of innovations and that these innovations might eventually justify calling the language of America by a name other than English.

Moreover, Sir William Craigie, the eminent editor of *A Dictionary of American English on Historical Principles*, pointed out that "...for some two centuries... the passage of new words or senses across the Atlantic was regularly westwards... with the 19th century... the contrary current begins to set in, bearing with it many a piece of drift-wood to the shores of British, there to be picked up and incorporated in the structure of the language." (Pyles & Alego, 2004: 218)

In 1816, *A Vocabulary, or Collection of Words and Phrases*, which has been supposed to be peculiar to the United States of America, was published. The compiler, John Pickering, claimed that American English has a much stronger propensity than British to add new words to the vocabulary.

Noah Webster, a lawyer who turned to teaching, was instrumental in the development of many characteristically American spellings as counterparts of British spellings. He wrote three books on English and was out to prove that English in America was distinctively American and his spelling handbooks which advocated spelling reform sold about 80 million copies in his own day and were highly influential in the development of a standard form of American English, making a major contribution to the uniformity of English throughout the United States. His spelling reform received support from other prominent Americans, including Benjamin Franklin. Besides, other changes that naturally grew out of political differences were reflected in vocabulary, such as *congress(ional)*, *governor*, *sheriff*, and *presidential*. Although many of these words are also used in Britain, they differ in their meaning and frequency of use.

Thus it might be near the truth to say that American English had taken root and begun to influence British English by the early 19th century.

11.1.3   From the Early 19th Century to the Present Time (1860 CE–Present)

The United States continued to develop into a superpower in the 20th century. It played an important part in World War Ⅰ and a decisive role in World War Ⅱ.

During these years, thousands of inventions came about; and the American way of living, symbolized by motor cars, movies (especially talkies), pop songs, radio programs, etc., began increasingly sophisticated.

Scientific and technical inventions, improved means of production and transportation, new institutions, and new life all needed new expressions. American English grew at an accelerating speed. Below are some American words and phrases which appeared before World War Ⅱ: *air-conditioned, immunology, pain-killer, powerhouse, filling station, freight train, station wagon*, *brain trust*, *straw vote*, *chain store*, *jukebox*, *milkshake*, *newsreel*, etc.

After these two world wars, the United States has become literally the leader of the western world. Meanwhile, it has undergone tremendous growth in the economy. Consequently, the growth of American power has promoted the spread of Americanism. Foster (1981: 13) remarks, "Languages do not exist in a vacuum but are powerfully affected by social, political, economic, religious and technical change… The tremendous increase in the political, military, and economic strength of the United States, coupled with the relative decline of Great Britain and the Commonwealth, has inevitably led to heightened prestige for the American way of doing things… This vigorous stream of Americanisms must inevitably make some impression on the language of Britain…" Political and economic exchanges and such mass media as American movies, radio and TV programs, popular songs, advertisements, newspapers, journals, and novels all serve as channels for the passage of Americanism into British English.

We have seen throughout the above discussion that from the very beginning of the settlement, American English began to diverge from British English. This divergence came about for a number of reasons, including the physical separation of America from Britain, the different physical conditions encountered by the settlers, contact with non-native speakers of English, developing political differences, and the growing American sense of national identity (Fennel, 2005).

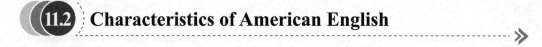

11.2 Characteristics of American English

11.2.1 Conservatism and Innovation

It is a surprising but unquestionable fact that numerous expressions in current use in the United States have become archaic in England. American English has also preserved a number of old features in pronunciation and grammar that have gone out of use in the standard speech of English. Thus archaism or conservatism is often regarded as a characteristic of American English.

Earlier in the 17th century, the language used by the first settlers in America was Elizabethan English, the language spoken by Ben Jonson and Shakespeare, which belonged to the early stage of Modern English. As the language gradually changed in England on the other side of the Atlantic, American English has not come to share the changes undergone in the mother country in many aspects.

To illustrate, changes that occurred in standard British English during the 18th century, such as the loss of preconsonantal and final /r/ and the shift from "flat" /æ/ to "broad" /ɑ:/ are not reflected in American English away from the Atlantic coast. Except for eastern New England and the coastal South, which seem to have followed the British practice, the /r/ sound is regularly retained before consonants and in the final position in American English as in *barn*, *car*, *march*, and *quarter*. The British pronunciation /ɑ:/, as in *ask*, *can't*, *class*, *dance*, *fast*, *half*, and *path*, has likewise had no effect upon the natural speech of Americans outside eastern New England, eastern Virginia, and the Charleston area. Americans pronounce *either* and *neither* with the vowel of *teeth* or *beneath*, while in England these words have changed their pronunciation since the American colonies were established and are now pronounced with an initial diphthong /ai/. British English long ago lost its secondary stress in words like *dictionary*, *millinery*, and *obligatory*. This secondary stress is regularly retained in American English.

In grammar and usage, American retention of *gotten* is a typical example of conservatism. This form, the usual past participle of *get* in older British English, survives in present standard British English mainly in the phrase "ill-gotten gains", but it is very much alive in American English, being the usual past participial form of the verb in the sense of "obtain, acquire". Another familiar instance is *aim to*, a former British usage widely current in the 18th century. The word *loan*, for another instance, when used as a transitive verb, is labeled an Americanism in most dictionaries. Current British usage prefers *lend*. But the verbal use of *loan* originated in England, perhaps as early as 1200. *Loan* occurred in a verbal function in American writings as early as in 1729. Thereafter, dictionary citations are mostly quoted from American writings.

Other words which have been obsolete in Britain but in current use in the United States include *druggist*, *railroad*, *jeans*, *molasses*, *chinch*, *homespun*, *greenhorn*, *loophole*, *offal*, *adze*, *to whittle*, *to wilt*, *to loan*, *burly*, *deft*, *ornate*, *bay-window*, *catty-cornered*, etc.

Conservatism forms one aspect of American English. In fact, the Elizabethan tradition and the frontier spirit combined to form an essential characteristic of American English— creativeness or innovation. Americanisms have enriched every facet of the vocabulary, and many of them have spread to use in English worldwide. When the first settlers were confronted by flora and fauna that were largely unfamiliar to them, they had to find words to designate the various species. Some of these words they borrowed from the Native Americans, such as *moose*, *opossum*, *chipmunk*, *porgy*, *terrapin*, *skunk*, *squash*, *raccoon*, and *woodchuck*, but in most cases, they formed great numbers of expressive compounds out of the existing English word stock such as *jimson-weed* (Jamestown weed), *June bug*, *live oak*, *bullfrog*, and *catfish*. Similarly, they needed terms to designate topographical features different from any known in the Old World, such as *backwoods*, *underbrush*, and *watergap*. American social life has created words like *greenback*, *groceteria*, *hotdog*, *junior college*, and *soap opera*, most of which have already entered British English. The individual character of the American political and administrative system required the introduction of words such as *congressional*, *presidential*, *gubernatorial*, *congressman*, *caucus*, *mass meeting*, *selectman*, *statehouse*, and *land office*. The creative spirit of American English is also reflected in the process of adding new meanings to existing words. For instance, the word *mainstream*, when used as a verb, means "draw (handicapped children) into the mainstream of life". The verb *buy* acquires a new meaning "accept" as in "He would not *buy* that idea"; *sell* can mean "make somebody accept" as in "He is trying to *sell* us on linguistics". The two slang terms *trip* and *key* mean respectively "the hallucinatory experience produced by taking drugs" and "a kilo of a drug, especially hashish".

In terms of word formation, the enrichment of American English can be concluded briefly as follows:

(1) Many new compounds are formed and the practice has been carried on up to this day, such as *backdrop*, *badlands*, *foothill*, *flatlands*, *landslide*, *moonwalk*, *space shuttle*, *overview*, *rock star*; many of these are phrases used as adverbs or (often) hyphenated attributive adjectives: *non-profit*, *for-profit*, *free-for-all*, *ready-to-wear*; many compound nouns and adjectives are open: *happy hour*, *fall guy*, *outer space*.

(2) Another way to form words is conversion, especially from noun to verb, e.g., *to access* (to have an access to), *to tomahawk* (to fight with a tomahawk), *to holiday* (to spend holidays), *to model* (to act as a model), *service* (as a car), *to interface*, *corner*, *torch*, *exit* (as in exit the lobby), *factor* (in mathematics), *gun* (shoot), etc.

(3) Some affixes are preferred by Americans and used rather freely and productively, e.g.,

- *super-*: *super-films*, *super-star*
- *-nik*: *protestnik*, *popnik*, *no-good-nik*
- *-ize*: *fetishize*, *prioritize*, *burglarize*, *accessorize*, *itemize*, *editorialize*, *hospitalize*, *generalize*, *prioritize*

(4) American readiness for making neologisms also finds expression in blends and back-formation, e.g.,

- Blends: *Amerindian* (American + Indian), *Medicaid* (medical + aid), *motel* (motor + hotel)*, guesstimate* (guess + estimate)
- Back-formation: *locate*, *fine-tune*, *evolute*, *curate*, *donate*, *emote*, *upholster*, *peeve*, *enthuse*

(5) Many words come from the word-formation processes of clippings and acronyms, e.g.,

- clippings: *co-ed* (coeducational), *deli* (delicatessen), *math* (mathematics)
- acronyms: *NASA* (National Aeronautics and Space Administration)

(6) New meanings for existing words, e.g., *sucker* (dupe), *squeeze* (a boyfriend or girlfriend), to *fire* (dismiss)

(7) Phrases originating in America: Early American phrases are the products of the frontier life; those coined in later days still keep the vivid, sometimes humorous flavor. The following examples may illustrate the point: *to have an ax to grind, to bark up the wrong tree, in the doghouse, couch potato, lame duck,* etc.

In the above ways, America makes her contribution to the English language and alongside comes the differentiation between the American and the British vocabulary. From the above features, people often maintain that a considerable number of American expressions are pungent and forceful. It is also claimed that Americans like to use short words such as clippings and acronyms. Furthermore, it is often mentioned that compared with their British counterparts, American words are more self-explanatory, such as *get the hang of, long-distance call, typesetter, sidewalk against trunk call, compositor, pavement, under the weather,* etc.

11.2.2 Heterogeneity

The United States is known as a "melting pot", and it is true with regard to language. American English has in the course of its development supplemented its word stock by adoptions from many other languages and has become heterogeneous in nature. The following is a brief account of the main foreign elements which have enriched the vocabulary of American English. And the words reflect the experience of early English settlers.

1. Native Americans

Influences from Native American (Amerindian) languages on American English vocabulary were extensive. The early English colonists were confronted with a land whose topography, meteorological phenomena, trees, plants, birds, and animals were frequently quite different from what they had known in England. It was natural for those colonists to borrow from the various Amerindian language words denoting the unfamiliar features of the continent. The native people of America spoke approximately one thousand different languages or dialects.

Early Amerindian loan words naming creatures include *caribou, opossum, moose, skunk, menhaden*, *terrapin*, and *woodchuck*. A good many native plants, vegetables, trees, and shrubs bear names of Amerindian origin: *hickory*, *pecan*, *squash*, *persimmon*, and *catalpa*. Other borrowings from the Amerindian include words denoting foods and customs: *chocolate*, *hominy*, *johnnycake*, *succotash*, *tomahawk*, *totem*, and *powwow*. Many borrowings formed derivatives, e.g., *caucus* gave rise to *caucusable*, *caucusdom*, *caucuser*, and *caucusified*. Some early Americanisms were translations of Amerindian words or phrases such as *firewater*, *pipe of peace*, *to bury the hatchet*, *to play opossum*. There are quite a few loan translations from Amerindian compounds, such as *Great White Father* (George Washington), *Father of Waters* (the Mississippi River), *happy hunting ground* (grave), etc. Quite a few compounds contain the word *Indian* as in *Indian summer* (a period of calm dry sunny weather in late autumn), *Indian corn* (maize).

2. French

Contacts with the French colonists in Louisiana and along the Canadian border brought in many words pertaining to frontier life in America, such as *armoire*, *bateau*, *bayou*, *beignet*, *bureau*, *butte*, *cache*, *chowder*, *caribou*, *jambalaya*, *levee*, *portage*, *praline*, *prairie*, *rapids*, *shanty*. The French term *prairie* forms the following compounds: *prairie hen*, *prairie squirrel*, *prairie fire*, and *Prairie State* (Illinois). Some of the words were themselves borrowed from Native Americans, e.g., *bayou*, *caribou*. Later, loan words were added as American English and English in general have been incorporating French elements up to this day.

3. Spanish

American English words borrowed from the Spanish immigrants are numerous, because the English immigrants contacted the Spanish colonists from the earliest days of their adventure, and as great numbers of Spanish speakers remained in and around the United States after the Mexican War (1846–1848), numerous Spanish terms entered American English. The majority of words refer to food and drink, such as *taco*, *tortilla*, *salsa*, *tequila*, *margarita*, *fajita*, *burrito*, and *nachos*. However, there are others that refer to more abstract concepts such as *fiesta*, *siesta*, *macho*, *machismo*, and *mestizo*. The Spanish suffix *-eria* helps to form words like *cafeteria*, *groceteria*, *bookateria*, *snacketeria*, and *smoketeria*.

4. Dutch

The Dutch were another group of early colonists, and the Dutch presence, with New York as the center, was sufficiently long and extensive to make contributions to American English. The latter incorporated a number of geographical terms used in the region of the Hudson: *kill* (creek, stream, river), and *clove* (valley), which also appear in place names. The Dutch *Sante*

Klaas became the English *Santa Claus*. A prominent feature of Dutch loan words is their popularity among people, such as *boss, coleslaw, cookie, cruller, Santa Claus, scow, sleigh,* and *stoop*.

5. German

Despite the large number of Germans in this country long before the outbreak of the Revolution, few German words entered the American vocabulary until about the middle of the 19th century, when many new German immigrants arrived. Unlike the above elements of the American vocabulary, the German loan words consist mostly of food and drink terms, such as *hamburger* (hence *cheeseburger, eggburger,* etc.), *frankfuter, noodle, pretzel, sauerkraut, sots, smearcase*; and words reflecting everyday social contacts, with no flavor of pioneer life, such as the word *fresh* (not old), *loafer, pinochle, poker, semester, seminar,* because the Germans came to the new continent not as colonists under their national flag, but as incoming citizens.

6. African elements

Considering the unequal social and economic relationship between black slaves and white masters, the African contribution is rather meager. Some words of African origin are *banjo, blues, chimpanzee, juba, jazz, goober, gumbo, hoodoo, tote, voodoo,* and *zebra*. However, Black English, a dialect spoken by thousands of black Americans, should be considered more important.

7. Italian

The loan terms from Italian are mostly food items such as *pizza, pizzeria, tutti frutti, minestrone, spaghetti, macaroni, zucchini, mozzarella,* and *pastrami*.

In addition, American English has borrowed words and phrases from many other foreign languages, such as *nosh* from Yiddish, *smorgasbord* from Swedish, *sukiyaki* from Japanese, and *chow mein* from Chinese. Many of the words from other languages are also familiar to speakers of British English, either through later contact with speakers of the original languages or via American English.

11.2.3 Uniformity in Speech

Although local and regional variations are noticeable on the Atlantic seaboard, yet there can be little doubt that from a geographical point of view, American English is characterized by relative uniformity in comparison with British English and other European languages since the high degree of physical, geographical and social mobility has been a feature of the United States almost throughout its history. As a nation on wheels, Americans like to be *on the go* instead of *staying put*. They are unsettled and keep moving frequently from place to place. This mobility causes a ceaseless mingling of people from different regions and walks of life. As a result, the local speech of any part of the country is almost intelligible to a visitor from any other part. Besides, school education and mass entertainment such as motion pictures, radio, and TV, have exerted a uniformizing influence. "Artists" in all these media have striven to achieve a type of American speech unmarked by local, regional, or class peculiarities.

Nevertheless, regional dialects do exist. There are three major dialectal areas (Northern, Midland, and Southern) and a smaller one (eastern New England). Each dialect has its own distinctive features in word choice and pronunciation (accent). But the dialect picture is never a neat one, because of widespread north-south movements within the country, and the continuing inflow of immigrants from different parts of the world. As a result, the sharp divisions between regional dialects gradually began to blur and their differences are almost wholly intelligible so that they seldom interfere with communication. So the dialects in America are generally much more homogeneous than they are in Britain. Distinctions in grammar are scarce. A few familiar instances of dialectal differences in word choice are eastern New England *sour milk cheese*, Inland Northern *Dutch cheese*, and New York City *pot cheese*. What is *tonic*, for another instance, to the New Englander is *soda*, to the New Yorker and *pop* to the Southerner. In pronunciation, the letters *wh-* is generally pronounced /w/ in most parts of the United States except in the southern area along the eastern coast and the remote regions of the northern territory where *wh-* is read /hw/. The study of these dialectal differences should not, however, obscure the picture of an essentially homogeneous nature of American English, whose regional and social variations are far less than British English. The language of the country, instead of becoming more divided into provincial dialects, is becoming more assimilated to itself as a whole and to a national standard.

11.2.4 Verbose and Plain Style in Writing

A grave defect as seen in American legal and bureaucratic documents is a tendency to convey an idea in as complicated a way as possible. The style is long-winded and circumlocutory, adorned with archaic, multisyllabic words and majestic turns of phrases that even educated readers cannot understand. Compare the following two pairs of sentences, in which the first sentence of each pair, long and difficult to understand, can be expressed clearly with the second sentence respectively.

- The buyer further promises to pay the holder hereof a delinquency and collection charge for default in the payment of any, installments above recited, where such default has continued for a period of ten days, such charge not to exceed 5% of the installments in default or the sum of five dollars, whichever is the lesser.

- You also promise to pay a late fee if your payment is more than 10 days overdue. This late fee will be 5% of the amount overdue or five dollars whichever is less.

- Do not become involved in a colloquy with the bench, but proceed without delay or discharge your obligation for violation of the ordinance in question.

- Don't argue with the judge, pay the fine.

The verbosity of American bureaucratic writing is further illustrated by such circumlocutory expressions as *act in subservience to the dictates of reason* (be guided by reason), *call into requisition the services of the family physician* (send for the doctor), and *offer some brief observations* (say a few words).

Nevertheless, we observe "the Plain English Movement" which developed in the United States in the 1970s and was progressing in the 1990s. For the past two decades, the American government and private businesses have been trying to reduce the paperwork burden on themselves and their clients with the effort to simplify the language in legal, government, business, technical and academic documents. In fact, a very widespread notion among Americans is that anything really worth saying can be said in "plain English". Since the mid-1970s, a handful of government documents and many insurance and banking documents have been rewritten into plain English. There are new handbooks and training programs to help writers, designers, and teachers. Plain English has even been mandated in a few federal and state laws and regulations concerning government documents. *The Magnusorn-Moss Act* sets requirements for readable warranties. *The Electronic Funds Transfer Act* demands clear writing in automatic banking rules. *The Employment Retirement Income Security Act* requires readable pension plan summaries. In California, beginning January 1st, 1983, all state agencies must write their documents in "plain, straightforward language". In Michigan, all state forms that are reviewed under the new state *Paperwork Reduction Act* have to be in plain language (Redish, 1985). All these changes illustrate "the Plain English Movement" in the United States, which also reflects the general trends toward simplicity in contemporary English.

11.2.5　Popularity of Slang

American English is known for its copious slang expressions and the popularity of slang is regarded as one of its marked traits. It is true that American English abounds in slang expressions. Why are Americans so fond of using slang expressions? Linguists suggest that creativeness in speech might be one of the essential factors. Further, as Americans have gone through hard struggles, rapid progress, and quick changes, including moving frequently from place to place and hopping from job to job, they need expressions like slang to carry out quick and effective communication.

Here are some popular slang expressions: *Howdy?* (How do you do? / How are you?); *Long time no see.* (I haven't seen you for a long time.); *I'm a basket case.* (I'm very much exhausted.); *full of hot air* (full of empty talk).

11.3 Differences Between American English and British English

American and British English are both variants of World English. As such, they are more similar than different, especially with "educated" or "scientific" English. They differ at the levels of phonetics, phonology, vocabulary, and to a lesser extent, grammar and orthography. Despite the fact the disparity between the two varieties is showing a tendency to diminish in recent years as British English is heavily influenced by American English, the differences between the two are still noticeable. Americans often use different words for the same common objects; they make frequent use of words and phrases that are seldom or never heard in Britain; they have different repertoires of everyday intensives and cuss words; they pronounce many words differently and their talk is based upon different speech tunes. The same thing, of course, runs the other way. In short, British and American English differ from each other in certain ways as shown below.

11.3.1 Differences in Pronunciation

Since the early colonists arrived in America, divergence in pronunciation has begun gradually to develop. On the one hand, changes occurred in the United States. On the other hand, the pronunciation of England has undergone further changes and a variety of southern English has come to be recognized as the English received standard, i.e., the RP (Received Pronunciation). Today, the variant of pronunciation or accent would readily identify a speaker as belonging to one country or the other. In this section, by British pronunciation or American pronunciation, we mean the variety in its country which is most associated with national broadcasting and least restricted to its geographical distribution. And the chief differences lie in the vowel sounds.

1. Differences in vowels

	AmE /æ/	BrE /ɑ:/
after	/ˈæftər/	/ˈɑːftə(r)/
class	/klæs/	/klɑːs/

	AmE /ɑ/	BrE /ɒ/
master	/ˈmæstər/	/ˈmɑːstə(r)/
fast	/fæst/	/fɑːst/
advance	/ədˈvæns/	/ədˈvɑːns/

	AmE /ɑ/	**BrE /ɒ/**
hot	/hɑːt/	/hɒt/
shop	/ʃɑːp/	/ʃɒp/
stop	/stɑːp/	/stɒp/

	AmE /ɔː/	**BrE /ɒ/**
dog	/dɔːg/	/dɒg/
fog	/fɔːg/	/fɒg/
moth	/mɔːθ/	/mɒθ/

	AmE /iː/	**BrE /e/**
leisure	/ˈliːʒər/	/ˈleʒə(r)/
premier	/prɪˈmɪr/	/ˈpremɪə(r)/

	AmE /:r/	**BrE /ʌr/**
hurry	/ˈhɜːri/	/ˈhʌri/
worry	/ˈwɜːri/	/ˈwʌri/

	AmE /uː/	**BrE /juː/**
assume	/əˈsuːm/	/əˈsjuːm/
constitute	/ˈkɑːnstɪtuːt/	/ˈkɒnstɪtjuːt/
issue	/ˈɪʃuː/	/ˈɪʃjuː/
nuclear	/ˈnuːkliər/	/ˈnjuːkliə(r)/

Finally, American speech is characterized by its "drawl" or relatively slow tempo and prolongation of stressed vowels; it shows less variation in the level of the voice than British English, that is, Americans speak slower and flatter than Englishmen.

2. Differences in consonants

With consonants the most remarkable difference is that in British English the letter *r* is silent except in expressions like *far away* where a linking *r* is used, whereas in American English, *r* is pronounced in all positions: car /kɑːr/, hard /hɑːrd/. The digraph *wh* is pronounced /w/ in British English, but /hw/ in American English: *where*, BrE /weə(r)/, AmE /hwe/; *what*, BrE /wɒt/, AmE /hwɔt/.

What is more interesting is that the words *letter* and *ladder* in American English sound nearly the same, because in American English there is a parallel change of intervallic consonant *t* to a kind of *d*, in words such as *letter*, *bitter*, *shutter*, *waiter*, *writer*, *petal*, etc. When Americans pronounce such words, they sound like *ladder*, *bidder*, *shudder*, *wader*, *rider*, *pedal*, etc.

3. Differences in the pronunciation of individual words

	AmE	BrE
ate	/eɪt/	/et/
depot	/ˈdiːpəʊ/	/ˈdepəʊ/
ego	/ˈiːgəʊ/	/ˈegəʊ/
epoch	/ˈepək/	/ˈiːpɒk/
lieutenant	/luːˈtenənt/	/lefˈtenənt/
mamma	/ˈmæmə/	/məˈmɑː/
progress	/ˈprɑːgres/	/ˈprəʊgres/
schedule	/ˈskedʒuːl/	/ˈʃedjuːl/
tomato	/təˈmeɪtəʊ/	/təˈmɑːtəʊ/
vase	/veɪs/	/vɑːz/
zenith	/ˈziːnɪθ/	/ˈzenɪθ/

4. Differences in word stress

AmE	BrE
ˈaddress	adˈdress
ˌadverˈtisement	adˈvertisement
ˈcigarette	ˌcigaˈrette
ˈdetail	deˈtail
ˈdonate	doˈnate
ˈlaboˌratory	laˈboraˌtory
ˈmigrate	miˈgrate
ˈrecess	reˈcess
ˈvibrate	viˈbrate

The differences between British and American pronunciation are not so dramatic as to make them unintelligible to each other. Only some of the differences are striking and many others often escape the notice of the layperson.

11.3.2 Differences in Spelling

There are sets of regular spelling differences that exist between American English and British English. Some are due to American innovations or overt attempts at spelling regularization and simplification, especially by Noah Webster in his 1806 dictionary. The most characteristic differences between British and American practice today are owed to him. Some of his innovations have been adopted in Britain. Others simply reflect the fact that English spelling was variable in earlier times and the two varieties adopted different variants as standard. Generally speaking, the American and British systems are essentially the same, except that, as the following divergences show, the American spellings are shorter and simpler than their English counterparts.

Divergences	American spelling	British spelling
or–our	color	colour
	favor	favour
	honor	honour
	labor	labour
	odor	odour
	vapor	vapour
er–re	center	centre
	fiber	fibre
	liter	litre
	meter	metre
	theater	theatre

But the following compounds are spelled alike in both varieties of English: *gas-meter*, *water-meter*, and *thermometer*.

Divergences	American spelling	British spelling
l–ll	councilor	councillor
	counselor	counsellor
	jeweler	jeweller
	marvelous	marvellous
	traveler	traveller

But exceptions occur with *enrolment* (BrE), *enrollment* (AmE); *distil* (BrE), *distill* (AmE); *fulfil* (BrE), *fulfill* (AmE); *skilful* (BrE), *skillful* (AmE).

Divergences	American spelling	British spelling
se–ce	defense	defence
	license	licence
	offense	offence
	pretense	pretence
et–ette	cigaret	cigarette
	epaulet	epaulette
	omelet	omelette
gram–gramme	centigram	centigramme
	kilogram	kilogramme
	program	programme
g–gue	catalog	catalogue
	dialog	dialogue
	epilog	epilogue
	monolog	monologue
ction–xion	connection	connexion
	deflection	deflexion
	inflection	inflexion
	reflection	reflexion
ize–ise	analyze	analyse
	civilize	civilise
	dramatize	dramatise
	naturalize	naturalise
	utilize	utilise

Spelling variation also occurs with such words as:

American spelling	British spelling
acknowledgment	acknowledgement
annex	annexe
check	cheque
draft	draught
jail	gaol
goodby	good-bye

gray	grey
judgment	judgement
curb	kerb
plow	plough
pajamas	pyjamas
skeptic	sceptic
story	storey
tire	tyre
wagon	waggon
whiskey	whisky

The differences illustrated above often pass unnoticed, and partly because a number of British spellings are still current in the United States, partly because some of the American innovations are now common in Britain. Generally speaking, some alternatives are permissible in both countries.

11.3.3　Differences in Grammar and Usage

On the whole, American English and British English use the same grammar system. Differences in grammar are relatively minor, and normally do not affect mutual intelligibility. The following are some main divergences.

1. The use of modal verbs

1) *shall* and *will*

British English uses *shall* with the first-person subject, singular or plural, and uses *will* with the second- or third-person subject, singular or plural. American English, however, employs *will*, no matter which person the subject is in.

American English can even use *will I/we* to make an inquiry: *Will I be able to go out tomorrow? Will we finish working at 3:30?*

2) *ought to* and *should*

American English rarely adopts the negative form of *oughtn't to*, but prefers *shouldn't*:

- You *oughtn't* to waste your money on drinking. (BrE)
  You *shouldn't* waste your money on drinking. (AmE)
- The child *ought to* be punished, *oughtn't* he? (BrE)
  The child *ought to* be punished, *shouldn't* he? (AmE)

American English occasionally uses *oughtn't* without *to*: *You oughtn't have said that.*

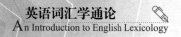

3) *used to* and *did use to*

- He *used to* live in London, usedn't he? (BrE)

  He *didn't use to* live in London, didn't he? (AmE)

- *Usedn't* she *to* go to school by bike? (BrE)

  Didn't she *use to* go to school by bike? (AmE)

4) *can't* and *must not*

British English usually uses *can't* to express an epistemic meaning whereas American English sometimes uses *must not*:

- He *can't* be in his car. (BrE)

  He *must not* be in his car. (AmE)

- He *can't* have been to your home. He doesn't know your address. (BrE)

  He *must not* have been to your home. He doesn't know your address. (AmE)

The contracted form *mustn't* is occasionally seen in American English:

- "I never took a picture of you," he said. "Why is that?"

  "I *mustn't* be pretty," she said.

5) *Do you have* and *have you (got)*

P. Christopherson remarks in *An Advanced English Grammar* that "in British English, the auxiliary *do* is not normally used with *have* (in negative and interrogative sentences), except to indicate something habitual". Thus we distinguish between "I haven't got a cold at the moment." and "I don't often have colds.". However, such a distinction does not exist in American English, which usually uses the construction with *do*:

- *Have you (got)* any children? (BrE)

  Do you have any children? (AmE)

But due to the influence of American English, since the early 1970s, many speakers of British English, especially the younger generation, have begun to use "*Do you have…*" as Americans do, and "*Have you got…*" has become much less frequent even in Britain.

Moreover, the construction "*Did you have…*" is used in both British and American English to refer to a past action: "*Did you have any* money at that time?" One may hear "*Had you* any money at that time?" in British English, but the construction is considered archaic.

2. The use of subjunctive mood

American English generally preserves the traditional subjunctive form, whereas British

English adds *should* to the subordinate clause except in legal or formal writings. For example:

- I insist that you *should* attend the meeting. (BrE)

  I insist that you attend the meeting. (AmE)

On the other hand, subjunctive forms such as "*Were this true…*" and "*If we are in danger…*" seem more common in England than in America, but less so in both countries than they once were (Hook, 1975: 269).

3. The mood used after *as if*

In British English, the subjunctive is required in the subordinate clause after *as if* or *as though*, whereas in American English the indicative mood, even the present participle will be right. For example:

- I feel *as if* we've never parted. (BrE)

  He stared at the girl *as if* seeing her for the first time. (AmE)

4. The position of adverbs

American English sometimes moves an adverb immediately after the subject instead of its normal position after the first auxiliary. The following are examples:

- I would *never* have thought that you were wrong. (BrE)

  I *never* would have thought that you were wrong. (AmE)

- She will *probably* go home tomorrow. (BrE)

  She *probably* will go home tomorrow. (AmE)

5. The agreement of subject and predicate

With regard to collective nouns, the British are much more likely than Americans to use a plural verb form, like "the public *are*…" (Algeo & Pyles, 2004). For example:

- The audience *were* enjoying every minute of the show. (BrE)

  The audience *was* enjoying every minute of the show. (AmE)

6. The use of noun attributes

British English uses plural noun attributes much more often than American English. The following are examples:

- There is a serious *drugs* problem in the country. (BrE)

  There is a serious *drug* problem in the country. (AmE)

- The workers decided to form a new *trades* union. (BrE)

  The workers decided to form a new *trade* union. (AmE)

7. The treatment of a repeated subject after the indefinite pronoun *one*

One is repeated, as in *One* cannot succeed unless *one* tries hard. (BrE)

He is used, as in *One* cannot succeed unless *he* tries hard. (AmE)

8. The use of the article

With words like *school*, *hospital*, and *church*, when the idea expressed concerns the use made of the building, the definite article is not used in British English but used in American English. For example:

- He has gone to school. (BrE)

  He has gone to *the* school. (AmE)

9. The relative positions of direct and indirect objects

When the direct and indirect objects after an intransitive verb are both pronouns, there arises the problem of their sequence. Standard on both sides is a sentence like "Give it to me.", but British usage sometimes (though infrequently) omits the marker *to*: "Give it me." Here are more examples:

- I won't tell it you.
- Are you quite sure you could not give it me yourself?
- My books, let me show them you.

10. Tense difference

British English speakers say "Have you had your supper?" and "I've already eaten." while American English speakers say "Did you have your supper?" and "I already ate."

11. The way of expressing dates

In British English, the usual order of expressing dates is "day-month-year", while in American English the sequence is "month-day-year". Fox example:

- 15th September, 1990 (or "15.09.1990" or "15/09/1990") (BrE)

  September 15th, 1990 (or "09.15.1990" or "09/15/1990") (AmE)

12. The treatment of *come* and *go*

In American English, *come* and *go* can be followed directly by a bare infinitive, but in British English, the connecter "and" should be used in between. For example:

- *Come* and look at it. (BrE)

  Come look at it. (AmE)

- *Go* and tell her about it. (BrE)

  Go tell her about it. (AmE)

In usage, British and American English contain such variants as:

AmE	BrE
aim to do	aim at doing
on/at the weekend	at the weekend
differ than	differ from
in ten years	for ten years
from June through September	from June to September
give up on	give up
on/in the playground	in the playground
on the list	in the list
on the train	in the train
miss out on	miss
nine before eleven	nine to eleven

Often, these differences are a matter of relative preferences rather than absolute rules; and most are not stable, since the two varieties are constantly influencing each other.

11.3.4　Differences in Vocabulary

There are thousands of words that either differ in total meaning, or in one particular sense or usage. But it is necessary to point out that the bulk of the vocabulary (in both British English and American English) belongs to general English and that Americanisms and Briticisms are found chiefly in colloquial English, while rarely used in the written language, especially in scientific writings. In the written language, the difference between the British and the American use of words is often so slight that it is difficult to tell in the case of a serious book, on which side of the Atlantic it is written.

Vocabulary differences between the two varieties are due to several factors. The most obvious one is that new objects and experiences were encountered in North America which needed naming, either by adapting British English vocabulary or by creating new words, e.g., *corn* is the general British English term for *grain* and denotes the common grain crop, which is *wheat* in England but *maize* in North America, which is originally named "Indian corn".

Technological and cultural developments which have occurred since the divergence of the two varieties have also been a cause of differences in vocabulary, such as *trunk* (AmE) vs. *boot* (BrE), *private school* (AmE) vs. *public school* (BrE).

A third reason for vocabulary differences is the influence of other languages. American English has borrowed many words from a variety of languages.

Finally, independent linguistic change within each variety may be the cause of some differences. One variety may preserve archaisms that the other has lost or may introduce new meanings for old words that the other had not introduced.

The differences between American and British vocabulary can be classified into three kinds: (1) words without counterparts or equivalents; (2) same words, different meanings; (3) same ideas, different words.

1. Words without counterparts or equivalents

When the early settlers came to North America, they encountered many phenomena that they had not known in the Old World; naturally, they needed expressions to denote animals, plants, foods, and features of landscape and life, which were either borrowed from the Native Americans and non-English immigrants or coined by the settlers themselves to bridge the lexical gap.

The early borrowings from Amerindian languages include *caribou*, *hickory*, *pecan*, *pemmican*, *sachem*, *tepee*, *terrapin*, *wetback*, *wigwam*, etc. Special mention should be made of place names from Amerindian tongues. Every state has some, and about half of the names of states themselves are of Native American origin. Many cities bear Native American names, as well as thousands of towns and hamlets, streams, and mountains, and all the Great Lakes except Superior.

Meanwhile, the early settlers made contact with non-English immigrants and borrowed from them such words as *canyon* and *tornado* (Spanish), *portage* and *prairie* (French), *frankfurter* and *hamburger* (German), *Santa Claus* and *sleigh* (Dutch), *banjo* and *voodoo* (African). Many other borrowings can be found in any English dictionary.

Sometimes, instead of borrowing a name for a previously unfamiliar phenomenon, the English settlers would simply apply in a new way words that they already knew. When the settlers heard a bird that meowed, it was natural to name it *catbird*, and a fish with "whiskers" suggesting those of a cat was of course named *catfish*. *Lightning bug* and *razorback* (hog) were named in similar ways. Foot was combined with other words to create a number of compounds: *foot box*, *foot cavalry*, *foot evil*, *foot gin*, *foothills*, *footlog*, *foot-muff*, *foot scraper*, *foot screw*, *foot trail*, *footwear*, *foot wheel*—none of which are recorded in the *The Oxford English Dictionary*.

2. Same words, different meanings

There are at least three factors that account for this linguistic phenomenon. First, some words remained popular in America but became obsolete in England. *Druggist* is often quoted as an American term to contrast with the British *chemist*, but *druggist* was originally used in England to replace *apothecary* in the early 17th century and was then itself replaced by *chemist* in the late 18th century, while in America *druggist* continued in use. Americans use *loan* as a verb, whereas it was displaced by *lend* as early as the 18th century in England. Second, some words were given different meanings from west of the Atlantic, often simply because of faulty identification. For instance, a *robin* in America is a thrush with a reddish breast, but in England, the name is that of a warbler with an orange breast. Mistaking the native grouse for a *partridge*, the early settlers called it a *partridge*, and a *partridge* it continues to be. Other examples are *beech* and *lark*, which are actually two different species of plants and birds on both sides of the Atlantic. Third, many words simply change their meaning in the United States without a clear reason.

All these combined to account for the fact that quite a number of the same words have different meanings on both sides of the Atlantic. The following examples may be used to illustrate the point: the word *lumber*, which originally meant "disused goods" in Britain, was given the new sense of "timber"; the numeral *billion* means "a million million" in British English, but Americans have changed it to mean "a thousand million" in the United States.

The following is a list of terms that mean different things or concepts in the US and the UK:

	AmE	BrE
barn	place to keep live-stock, hay, etc.	place for storing grain, etc.
clerk	salesperson	office worker
corn	maize	wheat, rye, oats
dry goods	textiles	barley grain or other non-liquids
faculty	teaching staff	university school or college
guy	fellow, any person	a ridiculous figure
homely	ugly (of people)	down to earth, domestic (= AmE *homey*)
nervy	bold, full verve, cheeky	nervous
pants	trousers	underpants
pavement	road surface	footpath, sidewalk
pressman	an operator of a printing house	a newspaperman
public school	a municipally run school	a private school
rock	a stone of any size	a large stone

| *to tick off* | to make angry | to scold |
| *veteran* | an ex-serviceman of any age | an old soldier of long service |

3. Same ideas, different words

In comparing American and British English, people commonly pay more attention to different words in the two variants for a common idea or object. This type has the majority of lexical differences between the two varieties. But owing to the interactions between the two varieties of English, especially the impact of American English on its British counterpart, the difference tends to diminish and become trivial; that is, an American or British word tends to be used by speakers on both sides of the Ocean. In consequence, part of the word list (which is shown in the following) easily goes out of date, and the problem of what to include constantly presents itself.

Randolph Quirk, a famous British linguist, remarks (Quirk et al., 1985):

> *The long and imposing lists of so-called distinctively British and American words and usages are 75 percent misleading; it turns out either that both the words so neatly separately are used in one or the other country, or that both are found in both countries but are used in slightly different contexts or in different proportions.*

For instance, *automobile*, considered the American equivalent of *car* or *motor car*, is practically a formal word in America, the ordinary term being the supposedly British *car*; one usually finds *baggage* as the American equivalent of British *luggage*, though *luggage* has come to be very commonly used in American English. In spite of the fact mentioned above, the long list of British and American terms suggested by linguists could at least show the main situation and indicate in which country a particular term is often used.

A list of AmE vs. BrE vocabulary (not exhaustive) is provided in the Appendix at the end of the book.

Note that some words, while identical in one semantic sphere or part of speech, can be different in another, e.g., both varieties of the words *hood* and *bonnet* refer to two distinct types of head covering, but when refereeing to the covering of a car engine, American English uses *hood* and British English uses *bonnet*. As for the use of the variants, most speakers seek to compromise linguistic differences and tolerate diversity. If one person says *pail* and the other *bucket*, they may get along fine without giving up their preferences.

The difference between the British and the American vocabulary today is lessened as many American words have made their way into British use, and their number seems to be on the increase rather than on the decrease.

11.4 A Brief Summary

Colonization by the British resulted in the settlement of large numbers of English people in America. They brought with them Elizabethan English and made modifications and additions to it as they adapted to the new environment. The divergence between American and British English has multiplied as the language develops simultaneously due to different national histories, demographics, and cultural development, and the way in which the national language has thus developed differently in parallel with the differing national needs. Since the independence and further growth of the United States, American English has evolved from a "colonial branch" to a variant or national standard of English.

The characteristics of American English are apparent: creativeness in enriching the language versus conservativeness in preserving a number of archaic features; the use of short and poignant expressions which include slang; verbose and plain style in writing; heterogeneity manifested by heavy borrowings from other tongues; and relative uniformity. These properties combine to make American English a distinctive variety of the English language.

Differences do exist and can be readily felt between American and British English in pronunciation, spelling, grammar, and vocabulary. But the concept of difference must not be taken too far, as the basic word stock, grammar, and phonetic system of both variants are essentially the same. Moreover, with the advent of globalization, the high degree of mutual intelligibility and shared development make the two varieties close cousins, despite all of the political, social, and cultural differences between the two countries.

As long as the environment, institutions, and other conditions of the United States and Britain remain different, it seems improbable that American and British English will become identical. Nevertheless, since the structures of the two varieties are basically the same, and communication and mass media are developing at an increasing rate, it is also impossible that they will eventually become mutually unintelligible languages.

To the outside world, compared with British English, American English is monolithic—representative of American culture. It has played a large part in the emergence of English as a world language. So for a non-native learner, it is best to be receptive to both varieties, know the differences, and be able to communicate with either Americans or the British.

Exercises

I. Briefly answer the following questions.

1. What are the historical factors that have caused American English to emerge and develop?

2. What are the main characteristics of American English? Give examples for illustration.

3. Can you give some examples to illustrate the differences between American English and British English in pronunciation, spelling, grammar, usage, and vocabulary?

4. Should American English be considered a variety of English or a separate language? What is your viewpoint?

II. Give the American and British pronunciations for each of the following words.

1. ate   **2.** clerk   **3.** dormitory   **4.** futile   **5.** grasp

6. knock   **7.** soar   **8.** tomato   **9.** vase   **10.** worth

III. Give the different meanings of the following words when they are used in American English and British English.

1. barn   **2.** billion   **3.** davenport   **4.** dumbwaiter   **5.** lumber

6. primary (*n.*)   **7.** sick   **8.** table (*v.*)

IV. Change the following British spellings into American ones.

1. draught   **2.** cosy   **3.** civilise   **4.** gaol   **5.** offence

6. inflexion   **7.** scepticism   **8.** ensure   **9.** harbour   **10.** waggon

Chapter 12

Vocabulary Learning

Vocabulary is of paramount importance for communication. Learning new vocabulary is considered an integral part of learning a new language. Therefore, both teachers and researchers delve into methods and approaches to ameliorate the vocabulary learning process for language learners learning a new language. According to Hedge (2000), vocabulary learning involves at least two aspects of meaning. The first aspect involves the understanding of its denotative and connotative meaning and the second one involves understanding the sense relations among words. We have learned these two aspects in Chapter 5. In this chapter, we will explore in great-depth aspects of vocabulary knowledge and approaches to learning vocabulary, and also introduce a wide spectrum of resources for vocabulary learning.

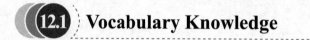 ## Vocabulary Knowledge

What does knowing a word involve? A simple answer to this question would be: knowing a word means knowing its pronunciation, stress, spelling, grammatical properties, and its meaning. Knowing a word also means knowing how and when to use it to express the intended meaning. This explanation may look quite simple and straightforward, but as we learn more about a word, we will find that complications arise as the form of a word as well as its meaning is far more complicated than we think it is. Moreover, we are often not able to find a one-to-one equivalent from the vocabulary of one language to another. Learning a word involves learning more than just the word itself. Lexical items can be phrases, clauses, or sentences.

12.1.1　Components of Vocabulary Knowledge

Laufer (1990) regards that knowing a word includes knowing its form (spoken and written), word structure (morphological), syntactic pattern in a phrase/sentence, meaning (referential, affective, and pragmatic), and lexical relations with other words (such as synonymy, antonymy, hyponymy, and paradigmatic and syntagmatic relations), and common collocations. Paradigmatic relation refers to the substitutional relation between a set of linguistic items, that is, linguistic forms (letters, words, and phrases) can be substituted for each other in the same position in a word or sentence. For example, *b*, *p*, *s*, and *f* are in paradigmatic relation in the words *bit*, *pit*, *sit*, and *fit*. So are *nature*, *love*, *beauty*, and *honesty* in the sentences: Nature purifies the mind. Love purifies the mind. Beauty purifies the mind. Honesty purifies the mind. Syntagmatic relation refers to the relationship between any linguistic elements which are simultaneously present in a structure. For example, in the word *bit*, *b*, *i*, and *t* are in syntagmatic relation. Similarly, *nature*, *purifies*, *the*, and *mind* in the sentence "Nature purifies the mind." are in syntagmatic relation.

According to Nation (2020), knowing a word means knowing its form (spoken, written, and word parts), meaning (form-meaning mapping, concept and referents, and associations), and use (grammatical functions, collocations, and contextual constraints on use), and function (frequency and appropriateness). Table 12-1 indicates that knowing a word involves knowing the form and the meaning of a word and the ability to use the word.

Table 12–1　What is involved in knowing a word[1] (Nation, 2020: 16)

Form	Spoken	R	What does the word sound like?
		P	How is the word pronounced?
	Written	R	What does the word look like?
		P	How is the word written and spelled?
	Word parts	R	What parts are recognizable in this word?
		P	What word parts are needed to express the meaning?
Meaning	Form and meaning	R	What meaning does this word form signal?
		P	What word form can be used to express this meaning?
	Concept and referents	R	What is included in the concept?
		P	What items can the concept refer to?
	Associations	R	What other words does this make us think of?
		P	What other words could we use instead of this one?
Use	Grammatical functions	R	In what patterns does the word occur?
		P	In what patterns must we use this word?
	Collocations	R	What words or types of words occur with this one?
		P	What words or types of words must we use with this one?
	Constraints on use (register, frequency...)	R	Where, when, and how often would we expect to meet this word?
		P	Where, when, and how often can we use this word?

1　R in the table stands for receptive, and P stands for productive.

It should be noted that the various aspects of word knowledge are not equally important. For initial learning, we would expect spoken word form and the form-meaning connection to be the first aspects that would be learned for most words. This knowledge allows the beginnings of comprehension. For a survival vocabulary intended for productive use, spoken word form, the form-meaning connection, and some very basic grammatical knowledge would be important. Other aspects of knowledge can become focuses of attention as proficiency develops.

12.1.2 Receptive and Productive Vocabulary Knowledge

From the above section, we know that word knowledge is multifaceted and includes the following essential variables: form, meaning, and use. In addition to form, meaning, and use, vocabulary knowledge can be seen as either receptive (passive) or productive (active) (Nation, 2001; Read, 2000). In other words, there exists in word knowledge a receptive and productive duality. For example, an English language learner may recognize the meaning of a recently learned word in a reading passage (receptive) but might not be able to spell the word accurately, pronounce it intelligibly in speech, or use it correctly in an essay or in a conversation (productive).

Receptive knowledge, also known as the *size*, or *breadth*, of a learner's vocabulary, represents the ability to recognize the form, meaning, and use of a vocabulary item and is related to listening and reading and indicates that learners are able to perceive the form of a word and retrieve its meaning or meanings, that is, people can just recognize the basic meaning or meanings of a word. Productive knowledge enables the learner to use the item in the right form, meaning, and use, and is associated with speaking and writing and indicates that learners are able to retrieve the proper spoken or written form or meaning that they intend to deliver. For example, as far as the form of a word is concerned, receptive vocabulary knowledge involves recognizing its spoken and written form when learners encounter it in listening and reading activities, while productive vocabulary knowledge includes being able to pronounce and spell the word correctly in writing and speaking. Similarly, the receptive knowledge of the structure of a word involves recognizing its basic free morpheme and bound morphemes, whereas being able to produce some derivations of the word may be part of the productive knowledge of the word.

In natural language acquisition situations, most words are learned receptively through extensive exposure. Only a small proportion of words become productive. The receptive vocabulary of any learner would be much larger than his or her productive vocabulary. The ratio for the sensitive scoring method was 93% and that for strict scoring was 77% (Laufer &

Paribakht, 1998). The gap between productive and receptive vocabulary is relatively small at high-frequency levels but becomes increasingly wider as the frequency level decreases.

Receptive vocabulary knowledge needs to be further developed into productive knowledge in order to be used in a communication context. The development from receptive to productive vocabulary can be seen on a continuum, starting from a superficial familiarity with the word and ending with an ability to use the word correctly in free production. The process of progressing on this continuum is the development of qualities or depth of one's lexical knowledge, also known as vocabulary depth (Qian, 2002, 2005; Read, 2000).

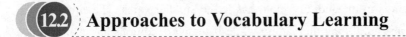

12.2 Approaches to Vocabulary Learning

Vocabulary learning is a cumulative process, both in increasing the number of words known and in increasing the depth of knowledge of words. Although vocabulary is vital for successful language learning and communication, researchers are not in general agreement about the best way to learn the vocabulary of a new language. Various language methods and techniques have been developed to assist learners with their vocabulary learning, among which a main distinction is usually made between incidental and intentional learning approaches (Schmitt, 2010). The major difference between these two complementary approaches is the intentionality (or lack of) to learn new lexical items and commit them to memory. In incidental learning, vocabulary gains accrue as a by-product; whereas in deliberate learning, learners have a specific goal, that is, to learn vocabulary.

12.2.1　Incidental Vocabulary Learning

Incidental vocabulary learning was first proposed by William E. Nagy, Patricia A. Herman, and Richard C. Anderson in 1985. Incidental learning refers to the process of learning something without the intention of doing so. In other words, it is learning one thing while intending to learn another. It is generally acknowledged that incidental learning, or the "picking up" of new words, is the major mode of vocabulary acquisition for children. Some researchers have reported children's vocabularies increase by more than 5,000 words a year (Nagy & Anderson, 1984). What is intriguing is that this massive vocabulary growth seems to occur without much help from teachers. How and where all this vocabulary learning occurs is still open to question. Some researchers (e.g., Nagy et al., 1985) claim that the only plausible explanation seems to be some type of incidental learning from context. Words learned incidentally from context are likely to constitute a substantial proportion of children's yearly vocabulary growth.

Investigations on the incidental acquisition of vocabulary are abundant and have mainly focused on learning from reading. Some findings indicate that extensive reading can benefit both L1 and L2 learners at all levels. According to Coady (1997), the role of graded (i.e., simplified) readers is to build up learners' vocabulary and structures until they can graduate with more authentic materials. Low-proficiency learners can benefit from graded readers because they will be repeatedly exposed to high-frequency vocabulary. Studies exploring extensive reading treatments have generally revealed larger gains than those examining the effect of shorter reading tasks.

Learning new words incidentally from listening is also possible, but the added difficulty in noticing unknown words in the auditory input has led to smaller gains. The simultaneous presentation of written and aural input in reading-while-listening conditions has also afforded the incidental acquisition of single words (Webb & Chang, 2015), with some evidence suggesting that this bimodal input condition might be superior to listening-only (Brown et al., 2008) and reading-only (Webb & Chang, 2012) conditions.

Multimodal exposure that combines both verbal and visual information has also been shown to create the conditions for incidental vocabulary learning to occur. Single words can be learned from watching television programs and captioned videos, and the benefits seem to be higher than reading-only conditions. By contrast, very few studies have investigated the incidental learning of multiword items and the focus has long been on the acquisition of collocations. The available studies have shown that collocations can be successfully learned from reading and reading-while-listening conditions.

The relative effectiveness of different input modes has recently been compared and results point to an advantage of the reading-while-listening mode over reading-only and listening-only. Some studies found that listening led to higher gains than reading, suggesting that listening might play a more prominent role in the acquisition of two-word combinations than of single words (e.g., Webb & Chang, 2022). Researchers hold that the presence of intonation contours and prosodic forms of multiword units may help learners identify them as chunks and might support their learning.

A direct comparison of the incidental learning of single words and multiword units has only been carried out by Laufer & Girsai (2008). The gains of the meaning-focused instruction group in their study, who completed only communicative tasks (i.e., reading comprehension and pair/group discussion), indicated that collocations were better learned from incidental exposure than single words, and this was the case both for the immediate and delayed posttests. However, the gains were in general quite low, leading them to conclude that the group that did not receive focused instruction showed very little learning. The combination of reading with focused activities led to better gains for both single words and collocations.

Overall, the same type of input modes that are beneficial for the incidental acquisition of single words seems to lead to the learning of multiword units (particularly collocations). Incidental learning gains for both types of items seem to be boosted when written and auditory input are combined in reading-while-listening conditions. Although listening has led to the smallest gains in single-word learning, initial evidence suggests that it may play a greater role in the learning of multiword units, pointing at a differential effect of input modes on the learning of collocations and single words.

While abundant investigations have been carried out, which show that learning of word meanings from context does occur, there are also some researchers who argue that incidental learning of vocabulary is a rather ineffective process. For example, Beck et al. (1983: 180–181) voiced a general skepticism of learning from written context as the source of vocabulary growth:

> *The reliance of basal reading programs on story context and independent use of the glossary as the central methods of vocabulary development is at best appropriate for the most motivated and competent readers. Children most in need of vocabulary development, less-skilled readers who are unlikely to add to their vocabulary from outside sources, will receive little benefit from such indirect opportunities.*

Researchers hold that the likely reasons include: (1) in truly natural texts, only some contexts, probably a small percentage, give much information about the meaning of a word; (2) at best, only one of the possibly many meanings of the word is supported by the context; and (3) the context will supply information about only some aspects of this one meaning of the word. Therefore, they conclude that vocabulary growth from context is a gradual matter.

Despite the uncertainties and debates over the efficacy of incidental vocabulary learning, the strength of incidental learning from context lies in its long-term, cumulative effects. Although a single encounter with a word would seldom lead to a full knowledge of its meaning, we believe that substantial, if incomplete, knowledge about a word can be gained on the basis of even a single encounter. Therefore, if coupled with a sufficiently large volume of exposure to written language, incidental learning from context should be able to account for a substantial amount of vocabulary growth.

In a nutshell, in the long run, most words in both first and second languages are probably learned incidentally, through extensive reading and listening, and more recently, viewing.

Nagy et al. (1985) concluded that (for native speakers of English) learning vocabulary from context is a gradual process, estimating that, given a single exposure to an unfamiliar word, there was about a 10% chance of learning its meaning from context. Likewise, L2 learners can be expected to require many exposures to a word in context before understanding its meaning.

12.2.2　Intentional Vocabulary Learning

Different from incidental vocabulary learning approaches which engage learners in a communicative activity without a particular focus on vocabulary, approaches that include an effort to attend to and learn words are viewed as being intentional vocabulary learning methods. Words such as *intentional*, *deliberate*, *instructed*, and *explicit* are often used synonymously in the literature. It should be noted that distinguishing between incidental and deliberate approaches is sometimes notoriously tricky because there can be deliberate or intentional learning in incidental approaches. For instance, we could easily imagine a situation where a learner is reading a text for comprehension, encounters an unknown word, and makes a deliberate and intentional effort to guess it from context and commit it to memory. We would then argue that there is intentionality and deliberate learning in this case, even though the condition was not intended to lead to deliberate learning. Therefore, incidental–intentional approaches should be viewed as a continuum rather than a dichotomy.

Intentional vocabulary-learning activities can be defined in several ways. The way to define intentional vocabulary learning as conscious learning and incidental vocabulary learning as subconscious learning is problematic because conscious word learning likely varies between words and between learners within individual tasks, as we argued just now. Intentional word learning can also be defined by whether participants know that they will be tested on their word learning. This definition is frequently used in research in psychology and allows differentiation between incidental learning, where participants are unaware of a subsequent vocabulary test, and intentional learning, where they know they will be tested. Perhaps the most common and inclusive definition of intentional vocabulary learning is completing activities that are designed to promote word learning. Such activities clearly focus attention on the words to be learned. For example, crossword puzzles, word searches, semantic mapping, word lists, word parts tables, and Pictionary all meet this definition. In this coursebook, we will adopt this final definition because it has ecological validity within the field of applied linguistics; inside and outside the language learning classroom, students complete tasks with the purpose of learning words.

The use of vocabulary activities that explicitly direct learners' attention to unknown lexical items creates the conditions for deliberate learning to occur. This happens for example, when learners memorize a set of words from word lists, translation pairs, or flash cards. Therefore, some researchers regard intentional learning activities as being the most effective and providing the greatest chance that words will be learned. For example, Schmitt (2008: 341) explicitly stated that "intentional vocabulary learning almost always leads to greater and faster gains, with a better chance of retention and of reaching productive levels of mastery than incidental vocabulary learning".

There are many ways to intentionally learn vocabulary. For example, Morgan & Rinvolucri (2004) described 118 inventive and varied activities designed to develop vocabulary knowledge, covering such areas as writing activities, pre-text activities, working with texts, bilingual texts, and activities, using corpora and concordances, words, and the senses, word sets, revision activities, word games and dictionary exercises, and word history. In a more recent publication, Webb & Nation (2017) profiled 23 approaches to learning words that they viewed as being most effective and offered concrete suggestions on how to maximize the effectiveness of using intentional vocabulary learning techniques.

With so many ways of learning words, it is important to understand the extent to which different approaches are effective. Investigations of the effect of explicit vocabulary activities on the acquisition of single words abound. Previous research has shown that a variety of explicit exercises and task types are effective for the acquisition of single words, with learning rates that go up to 70% in some studies. Some of the methods investigated include memorization and mnemonic techniques such as the keyword method; written vocabulary activities, such as fill-in-the-blanks and original sentence writing; and first language translation, just to name a few. Empirical evidence has also shown that new vocabulary can be learned from pushed-output activities that make learners produce language orally, and that these activities support learners in the challenging transition from receptive to productive knowledge. Deliberate learning of single words does not only lead to the acquisition of declarative knowledge of vocabulary (at the receptive and productive level), but also to the development of the automaticity and fluency with which newly learned words are processed, triggering the acquisition of both representational and functional aspects of vocabulary knowledge.

In addition to research on the explicit vocabulary activities of learning single words, there are also studies examining the effect of explicit activities on the learning of multiword units. Recent research has provided evidence that multiword items can be deliberately learned from a range of activities that present items both in context and in a decontextualized manner. Multiword sequences can be learned from receptive activities, such as presenting multiword units in sentences with translations, and from productive tasks that require learners to produce the multiword sequences in gapped sentences and in free sentence writing. There are also some activities that are especially (or even exclusively) relevant for the learning of multiword units, as they focus on exploiting a feature that is particularly salient in multiword sequences. Deliberate learning through activities that attempt to engage learners with salient features of multiword units, such as through building connections between idiomatic and literal meanings and through focusing on sound patterns has been shown to lead to gains in learners' knowledge of multiword units. These approaches are likely to be more effective for the teaching of multiword units than single words.

In this section, we introduced various activities that hold promise for improving both incidental and intentional vocabulary learning. However, deciding which activity or approach is best for vocabulary learning is problematic, because of the many methodological and contextual differences among the existing studies (Schmitt, 2008). Neither intentional nor incidental vocabulary learning seems to be effective *per se* and one does not have priority over the other (Nation, 2001; Read, 2004). A combination of both may make a perfect strategy although some researchers argue that there is no absolute way for learning vocabulary since it depends upon many factors. Schmitt (2008) concurs and believes that different approaches to vocabulary instruction must be applied in different stages. Although there is no best way to learn vocabulary, there is indeed a unanimous view that the effectiveness of a particular task depends on the degree of involvement and engagement with the unknown vocabulary. As proposed by Laufer & Hulstijn (2001), the task's involvement load, i.e., the amount of need, search, and evaluation that it leads learners to do, affects word learning and retention. Research has shown that explicit activities with differing levels of involvement lead to different learning rates. To learn vocabulary effectively and efficiently, learners need to have extensive exposure to various modes of input on the one hand and be intensively involved in vocabulary learning activities on the other hand.

12.3 Resources for Learning Vocabulary

Vocabulary learning is a daunting task, and there are many useful resources that language learners can resort to. Two types of resources will be dealt with in this section, which are dictionaries and online resources.

12.3.1 Dictionaries

Lexicology is closely related to dictionaries. On the one hand, lexicology is mainly concerned with the form, meaning, and usage of words and other lexical items and dictionaries list words and lexical units as entries, and provide illustrations for the above features. On the other hand, what is included under each entry in dictionaries is based on the findings of lexicology, while the illustrations provided in dictionaries are widely used by lexicologists in their research.

On a practical level, every language learner needs a dictionary, because it is impossible for a learner, even a native speaker, to know all the words and lexical items of a language. A dictionary is always an important reference.

There are different types of dictionaries as a result of different demands for dictionaries. Different criteria have been used to classify them.

(1) General and special dictionaries. According to the purposes that dictionaries serve, they can be divided into general and special dictionaries. General dictionaries, also called general-purpose dictionaries, are more commonly seen and used. They are compiled for everyone and everyday use. They usually contain far more word entries and are a lot thicker. For example, the well-known *Oxford Advanced Learner's English-Chinese Dictionary* (Hornby, 2018) carries 57,100 entries and is approximately 2,000 pages long. General dictionaries cover the vocabulary of all fields of knowledge and provide such information about words as forms, pronunciations, functions, meanings, and usages.

Special dictionaries, which are also called specific-purpose dictionaries or restricted dictionaries, are compiled for professionals and researchers in specific fields such as linguistics, literature, law, and medical science. They contain technical terms pertaining to specific fields or one sector of the vocabulary in a language, and usually provide the meanings and contents of the terms. A dictionary of synonyms and antonyms, for example, is also a special dictionary.

(2) Monolingual and bilingual dictionaries. Dictionaries can also be classified according to the number of languages in which they are compiled. In this case, they fall into monolingual, bilingual, and multilingual dictionaries, with the first two types being more popular. Monolingual dictionaries are made in one language, usually by native speakers, while bilingual dictionaries are compiled in two languages. In most cases, in bilingual dictionaries, the entries are defined and explained in the target language (the language to be learned) with translations in the second language (usually the user's mother tongue).

The question is: Which type of dictionary should be used by second/foreign language learners, or in our case, ESL/EFL learners? For intermediate learners of English, it is advisable to use bilingual dictionaries (in this case, English-Chinese dictionaries) because intermediate learners have not acquired a sufficient English vocabulary to understand the English definitions and illustrations. Some people think English-English dictionaries would fit only advanced English learners and scholars (Cai & Tian, 2014: 216), but even advanced learners and scholars may, once in a while, turn to a bilingual dictionary for an accurate understanding of a word, because bilingual definitions may complement each other. Just as Baxter (1980: 335) said, "students are not encouraged to totally exclude their bilingual dictionaries; undoubtedly, a judicious combination of the two would be the most productive."

(3) Printed and electronic dictionaries. Dictionaries, according to the media, can be classified into printed dictionaries and electronic dictionaries. Printed dictionaries, or paper dictionaries, are conventional ones, usually thoroughly proofread, accurate, and generally error-free. They are comparatively cheap and can be used, free of such requirements as electric power conditions and digital technological support. Printed dictionaries, however, have their own weaknesses. They tend to be outdated at the time of their publication. Dictionary compiling is time-consuming, and it takes years for an authoritative dictionary to come out. As a result, it is impossible to find neologisms even in a newly-published paper dictionary. That is why we have *6,000 Words*, *9,000 Words*, and *12,000 Words* as supplements to *Webster's Third New International Dictionary*. Printed dictionaries, except for pocket dictionaries, are too big and heavy for users to carry, so users may not have access to them when they want to consult them.

De Schryver (2003), according to the electronic medium, divided electronic into dictionaries on stand-alone computers (e.g., handheld dictionaries, such as pocket electronic dictionaries [PEDs] or reading pens) and robust-machine dictionaries (typically stored in CDs, DVDs, or hard disks) and dictionaries on networked computers (intranet and Internet dictionaries). Dictionaries on networked computers are also called online dictionaries and are further classified into institutional Internet reference works and collective multiple-language internet reference works, depending on who compiles such dictionaries for whom and whether they are available for free or not (Fuertes-Oliviera, 2009). Institutional Internet reference works are dictionaries created by an identifiable institution and may be free to use or not. Collective multiple-language reference works, such as Wiktionary, are usually free and result from collaborative effort taken by a community of users.

Electronic dictionaries also have their advantages and disadvantages. They usually provide the pronunciation of the word, which is valuable for learners. Handheld dictionaries, such as pocket electronic dictionaries or reading pens, are characterized by their handiness and easy access. Users can consult them whenever and wherever they want to so long as the batteries are not flat. However, they are generally more expensive than printed dictionaries. And due to their limited screen size, only a small portion of all the definitions and illustrations under the same entry can be displayed at one time.

Robust-machine dictionaries in CDs, DVDs, and hard disks require hardware support for operation and must be installed on a computer before they can be used, so they cost much more. However, once installed, they save users the time and trouble of flipping through the pages of printed dictionaries. With a laptop computer, users can use them everywhere. Moreover, robust-machine dictionaries have larger display screens so that users can compare the definitions and illustrations under the same entry. "A number of monolingual English dictionaries are available in the CD format. These include the 20-volume OED (The Oxford English Dictionary, 2nd edition), as well as single-volume desk and concise dictionaries, such as *Collins English Dictionary* and *Concise Oxford English Dictionary... The Oxford Advanced Learner's Dictionary*, *Longman Dictionary of Contemporary English* and *Cambridge Advanced learner's Dictionary* are also available in electronic form. In many cases, the CD-ROM is sold together with the printed dictionary." (Jackson & Amvela, 2007: 171).

Online dictionaries are updated, with new words and usages added much more frequently. They offer immediate, direct access to a word's spelling and meanings, sometimes plus a host of ancillary information, including its variant spellings, pronunciation, inflected forms, origin, and derived forms, as well as supplementary notes on matters of interest or concern about how the word is used. Again, users need to have easy access to a computer and the computer must be connected to the Internet.

A large number and a great variety of dictionaries are available, which may be difficult for us to make a choice. The following factors can be taken into consideration when choosing a dictionary.

(1) The user's English level. Dictionaries are compiled for users of different English levels. Some are designed for college students, others are for high-school students, and still, others are for children. Therefore, users are advised to choose a dictionary that suits their English level instead of one that everybody else uses. Dictionaries usually have prefaces or special sections explaining their purposes, targeted users, and presentation of entries, etc., so it is easy to find whether a dictionary is proper to the user's English level.

(2) The user's needs. Dictionaries are compiled for different purposes. There are dictionaries made for specialists, for general users, and for a particular field, etc., so users should choose dictionaries according to their specific needs. For example, if a person is

engaged in writing and translating documents of a particular field such as chemistry, a dictionary of chemistry will be his/her best choice because a general dictionary may not contain valid and adequate definitions for the specific terms in chemistry. If the same person, however, wants to find out the nuances between synonyms, a dictionary of synonyms will benefit him/her most.

(3) The contents of a dictionary. For EFL/ESL learners of intermediate and advanced levels, the following contents are necessary for a general dictionary.

- The current meaning or meanings of words, phrases, and expressions;
- The current spelling (American and British) of words;
- The exact pronunciation (American and British) of words, and their breakdown into syllables;
- The proper usage of words, preferably demonstrated by illustrative sentences or phrases;
- Entries for prefixes, suffixes, and combining forms;
- Slang and colloquial expressions in common use;
- Foreign terms and phrases frequently encountered in the English language;
- Common idioms involving the headwords. (From Zhang, 1992:381)

(4) The date of publication. Language is always changing. On the lexical level, old words are getting obsolete, live words pick up new meanings or have their meanings changed, and new words are created. As mentioned above, dictionary-making is time-consuming, and "a dictionary begins to go out-of-date the moment it is published" (*9,000 Words*, 1983, preface). Therefore, when choosing a dictionary, users should choose the latest edition and always take notice of the date of publication.

12.3.2　Online Resources for Vocabulary Learning

Digital technologies have been developed to cater to vocabulary learning. The impressive range of online resources available for vocabulary learning includes online dictionaries, corpora, and online tools, to name a few.

1. Online dictionaries

In the previous section, we have introduced different types of dictionaries and the selection of dictionaries. Owing to technological advancement, we now have another choice in the use of dictionaries, i.e., online dictionaries. An online dictionary is a dictionary that is accessible via the Internet through a web browser. Many dictionaries have been digitized from their print versions. They can be made available in a number of ways: free, free with a paid subscription for extended or more professional content, or a paid-only service. Some online dictionaries are organized as lists of words, similar to a glossary, while others offer search features, reverse lookups, and additional language tools and content such as verb conjugations, grammar references, and discussion forums. The following is a list of five widely-used online dictionaries.

Longman Dictionary of Contemporary English Online (LDOCE). The site offers over a million corpus examples (exceeding the paper version's) and includes sound files for every word, 88,000 example sentences, and various tools for study, teaching, examinations, and grammar.

Collins Online Dictionary and Reference Resources. It draws on a wealth of reliable and authoritative information from vast databases of language both in English and in other languages.

Oxford English Dictionary (OED). It documents 600,000 words through 3.5 million illustrative quotations from over 1,000 years of history across the English-speaking world. Different from dictionaries of current English, in which the focus is on present-day meanings, the OED is a historical dictionary, offering both present-day meanings and the history of individual words, and of the language—traced through 3 million quotations, from classic literature and specialist periodicals to film scripts and cookery books.

Cambridge Dictionary Online. It is made up of four dictionaries: *Cambridge Dictionary of American English*, *Cambridge Learner's Dictionary*, *Cambridge International Dictionary of Phrasal Verbs*, and *Cambridge International Dictionary of Idioms*.

The Louvain English for Academic Purposes Dictionary (LEAD), is designed as an integrated dictionary and corpus tool to help non-native speakers write academic texts in English. Corpus data in LEAD is meant to be customized to its users' needs in terms of discipline and mother tongue background. LEAD is both a dictionary and a writing-aid tool that when used successfully should contribute to learning. LEAD offers options to search for English academic words and expressions. It can be used to access:

- Definitions and examples of word use in context (preferred position in the sentence, typical collocations, and recurrent phrases);
- Charts to help users remember salient features (e.g., frequency differences across genres);
- Warnings against frequent errors, and usage notes that compare learner and expert writing;

- Context-sensitive lexicographical treatment of phraseology, as corpora of expert and learner writing, has been used in the compilation of the tool;
- Numerous exercises on various EAP language functions.

2. Corpora

Corpora are principled collections of naturally occurring spoken, written, or multimodal data which are stored in electronic format for quantitative and qualitative analysis.

CLARIN, the short form of Common Language Resources and Technology Infrastructure, provides easy and sustainable access to digital language data (in written, spoken, or multimodal form) for scholars in the social sciences and humanities, and beyond. It also offers advanced tools to discover, explore, exploit, annotate, analyze or combine such datasets. Currently, overviews are available for 12 corpora families, 5 families of lexical resources, and 4 tool families at its site. The corpora families and lexical resources are presented as follows.

Corpora families:
- Computer-mediated communication corpora
- Corpora of academic texts
- Historical corpora
- L2 learner corpora
- Literary corpora
- Manually annotated corpora
- Multimodal corpora
- Newspaper corpora
- Parallel corpora
- Parliamentary corpora
- Reference corpora
- Spoken corpora

Families of lexical resources:
- Lexica
- Dictionaries
- Conceptual Resources
- Glossaries
- Wordlists

The following corpora are available for searching (most also for downloading): the Brown family (Brown, LOB, FLOB, Frown, BLOB, and BE06) prepared at Lancaster (BLOB and BE06 not for downloading), FLOB and Frown, ACE (Australian Corpus of English), COLT (Corpus of London Teenage Language), Helsinki Corpus of English Texts, Helsinki Corpus of Older Scotts, Helsinki CEECS (Corpus of Early English Correspondence Sampler), and London-Lund Corpus.

BNC, the British National Corpus, is a 100,000,000-word collection of samples of written and spoken language from a wide range of sources, designed to represent a wide cross-section of British English, both spoken and written, from the later part of the 20th century.

The Corpus of Contemporary American English, or COCA, is a large, genre-balanced corpus of American English. It has more than one billion words of text from eight genres (spoken, fiction, popular magazines, newspapers, academic texts, TV and Movies subtitles, blogs, and other web pages).

Both BNC and COCA are created by Mark Davies, Professor of Linguistics at Brigham Young University. The website offers links to 17 corpora, known as the BYU Corpora, which are News on the Web (NOW), iWeb: The Intelligent Web-based Corpus, Global Web-Based English (GloWbE), Wikipedia Corpus, Coronavirus Corpus, COCA, Corpus of Historical American English (COHA), the TV Corpus, the Movie Corpus, Corpus of American Soap Operas, Hansard Corpus, Early English Books Online, Corpus of US Supreme Court Opinions, TIME Magazine Corpus, BNC, Strathy Corpus (Canada), and CORE Corpus.

At the website there are also many corpus-based resources that allow readers to (1) see detailed entries for the top 60,000 words in English (definitions, genre variation, collocates, concordance lines, synonyms)—all on one page; (2) enter and analyze your own text, find keywords from your text, compare phrases to COCA, and see detailed information (see above) for each word; (3) get detailed information from the Academic Vocabulary List (including detailed information on each word, and analyzing your own academic texts); and (4) download large amounts of corpus-based data, including word frequency, collocates, and n-grams.

3. Online tools

Besides online dictionaries and corpora, some online tools provide learners with information on single words and multiword expressions. Some of these resources are simply lists of collocations, as is the case of the academic collocation list, which contains over 2,400 academic collocations.

The WordNet site at Princeton University is a large lexical database of English. Nouns, verbs, adjectives, and adverbs are grouped into sets of cognitive synonyms (synsets), each expressing a distinct concept. WordNet is also freely and publicly available for download.

WordNet's structure makes it a useful tool for computational linguistics and natural language processing.

Different from the above tools which present static lists of words, there are also online resources that can offer a more flexible approach. One example is SkELL (Sketch Engine for Language Learning). It is a tool for students and teachers of English that can be used to easily check how a particular phrase or a word is used by real speakers of English. If the user clicks on Wordsketch, a list of words which occur frequently together with the searched word appears, and those words are sorted into various categories, such as "verbs with a noun as object" and "adjectives that can modify a noun". If the user wants more context, clicking on the desired word combination (e.g., food allergies) generates example sentences of the multiword expressions found in corpora.

Another example of an online tool that allows users to highlight multiword expressions in a text is IDIOM Search. The online interface allows users to test a new algorithm for extracting the most set phrases from a text ranging from simple collocations and proper nouns to idioms and proverbs.

One more example is the Word and Phrase Info tool, which allows users to enter any text and see useful information about words and phrases in the text. The information accessed is based on data from COCA. In addition to information at the single-word level (e.g., highlighting of all of the medium and lower-frequency words in the text, or of academic words), clicking on any word in the text gives access to a detailed word sketch with resortable concordance lines, and frequency of the word (overall, and by genre). The Word and Phrase Info tool allows for searches on selected phrases in the text (and provides related phrases in COCA).

Aijmer, K. 2014. *Conversational Routines in English: Convention and Creativity*. New York: Routledge.

Albee, E. 1962. *The Zoo Story*. New York: Samuel French.

Algeo, J. & Pyles, T. 2004. *The Origins and Development of the English Language* (5th ed.). Chicago: Thomson Learning.

Allen, W. 1975. *Death Knocks*. New York: Samuel French.

Anderson, L. & Stageberg, C. 1975. *Introductory Readings on Language*. New York: Holt, Rinehart & Winston.

Atwan, R. & McQuade, D. 1988. *Popular Writing in America*. Oxford: Oxford University Press.

Bahns, J. & Eldaw, M. 1993. Should we teach EFL students collocations? *System*, *21*(1): 101–114.

Bahns, J., Burmeister, H. & Vogel, T. 1986. The pragmatics of formulas in L2 learner speech: Use and development. *Journal of Pragmatics*, *10*(6): 693–723.

Bardovi-Harlig, K. & Stringer, D. 2017. Unconventional expressions: Productive syntax in the L2 acquisition of formulaic language. *Second Language Research, 33*(1), 61–90.

Bauer, L. 1983. *English Word-Formation*. Cambridge: Cambridge University Press.

Baxter, J. 1980. The dictionary and vocabulary behaviour: A single word or a handful?. *TESOL Quarterly*, *14*(3): 325–336.

Beck, I. L., Mckeown, M. G. & McCaslin, E. S. 1983. Vocabulary development: All contexts are not created equal. *The Elementary School Journal*, *83*(3): 177–181.

Bell, N. 2012. Formulaic language, creativity, and language play in a second language. *Annual*

Review of Applied Linguistics, *32*: 189–205.

Biber, D., Conrad, S. & Cortes, V. 2004. If you look at…: Lexical bundles in university teaching and textbooks. *Applied Linguistics*, *25*(3): 371–405.

Biber, D., Johansson, S., Leech, G., Conrad, S., Finegan, E. & Quirk, R. 1999. *Longman Grammar of Spoken And Written Englis*h. Harlow: Longman.

Bloomfield, L. 1933. *Language*. London: George Allen & Unwin.

Brown, R., Waring, R. & Donkaewbua, S. 2008. Incidental vocabulary acquisition from reading, reading-while-listening, and listening. *Reading in a Foreign Language*, *20*: 136–163.

Bygate, M. 1988. Units of oral expression and language learning in small group interaction. *Applied Linguistics*, *9*(1): 59–82.

Cai, L. & Tian, G. 2014. *English Lexicology: A New Coursebook*. Beijing: Foreign Language Teaching and Research Press.

Carroll, L. 1871. *Through the Looking-Glass*. London: Macmillan.

Cheng, W., Greaves, C. & Warren, M. 2006. From n-gram to skipgram to concgram. *International Journal of Corpus Linguistics*, *11*(4): 411–433.

Chomsky, N. 1965. *Aspects of the Theory of Syntax*. Cambridge: MIT Press.

Clark, J. O. E. 1989. *Word Wise: A Dictionary of English Idioms*. London: Harrap's Reference.

Coady, J. 1997. L2 vocabulary acquisition through extensive reading. In J. Coady & T. Huckin (Eds.), *Second Language Vocabulary Acquisition*. Cambridge: Cambridge University Press, 225–237.

Conklin, K. & Schmitt, N. 2012. The processing of formulaic language. *Annual Review of Applied Linguistics*, *34:* 45–61.

Cortes, V. 2015. Situating lexical bundles in the formulaic language spectrum: Origins and functional analysis developments. In V. Cortes & E. Csomay (Eds.), *Corpus-Based Research in Applied Linguistics*. Amsterdam: John Benjamins, 197–216.

Coulmas, F. 1979. On the sociolinguistic relevance of routine formulae. *Journal of Pragmatics*, *3*: 239–266.

Davies, M. 2004. *British National Corpus (from Oxford University Press)*: *100 million words, 1980s–1990s*. Available online at the BNC website.

Davies, M. 2008. *The Corpus of Contemporary American English (COCA): 520 million words, 1990–present*. Available online at the COCA website.

De Schryver, G. 2003. Lexicographers' dreams in the electronic-dictionary age. *International Journal of Lexicography*,*16*(2): 143–199.

Du, L., Elgort, I. & Siyanova-Chanturia, A. 2021. Cross-language influences in the processing of multiword expressions: From a first language to second and back. *Frontiers in Psychology*, *12*: 1–18.

Durrant, P. 2017. Lexical bundles and disciplinary variation in university students' writing: Mapping the territories. *Applied Linguistics*, *38*(2): 165–193.

Eliot, G. 1861. *Silas Marner*. Ware: Wordsworth Editions.

Ellis, N. C. 2002. Frequency effects in language processing: A review with implications for theories of implicit and explicit language acquisition. *Studies in Second Language Acquisition*, *24*(2): 143–188.

Erman, B. & Warren, B. 2000. The idiom principle and the open choice principle. *Text*, *20*(1): 29–62.

Foster, B. 1981. *The Changing English Language*. Basingstoke / Hong Kong: Macmillan.

Foster, P. 2001. Rules and routines: A consideration of their role in the task-based language production of native and non-native speakers. In M. Bygate, P. Skehan & M. Swain (Eds.), *Researching Pedagogic Tasks: Second Language Learning, Teaching, and Testing*. Harlow: Longman, 75–94.

Fowler, H. W., Fowler, F. G. & Crystal, D. 1982. *The Concise Oxford Dictionary*. Oxford: Oxford University Press.

Fowler, H. W. 1965. *A Dictionary of Modern English Usage*. Oxford: Oxford University Press.

Freeman, D. C. 1970. *Linguistics and Literary Style*. New York: Holt, Rinehart & Winston.

Fuertes-Olivera, P. A. 2009. The function theory of lexicography and electronic dictionaries: Wiktionary as a prototype of collective free multiple-language internet dictionary. In H. Bergenholtz, S. Nielsen & S. Tarp (Eds.), *Lexicography at a Crossroads: Dictionaries and Encyclopedias Today, Lexicographical Tools Tomorrow*. Bern: Peter Lang, 99–134.

Gardner, D. & Davies, M. 2007. Pointing out frequent phrasal verbs: A corpus-based analysis. *TESOL Quarterly*, *41*(2): 339–359.

Garnier, M. & Schmitt, N. 2015. The PHaVE List: A pedagogical list of phrasal verbs and their most frequent meaning senses. *Language Teaching Research*, *19*(6): 645–666.

Gomez, R. L. 2002. Variability and detection of invariant structure. *Psychological Science*, *13*(5): 431–436.

Gove, P. B. 1961. *Webster's Third New International Dictionary of the English Language*. Springfield: Merriam-Webster.

Hallin, A. E. & Van Lancker-Sidtis, D. 2017. A closer look at formulaic language: Prosodic characteristics of Swedish proverbs. *Applied Linguistics*, *38*(1): 68–89.

Harrison, J. 1994. *Legends of the Fall*. New York: Delta.

Haspelmath, M. 2011. The indeterminacy of word segmentation and the nature of morphology and syntax. *Folia Linguistica*, *45*(1): 31–80.

Hayakawa, S. I. 1982. *Use the Right Word: A Modern Guide to Synonyms*. New York: *Reader's Digest* Association.

Hedge, T. 2000. *Teaching and Learning in the Language Classroom*. Oxford: Oxford University Press.

Hook, J. N. 1975. *History of the English Language*. New York: The Ronald Press.

Hornby, A. S. 2018. *Oxford Advanced Learner's English-Chinese Dictionary* (9th ed.). Beijing: The Commercial Press.

Jackson, H. & Amvela, E. Z. 2007. *Words, Meaning and Vocabulary: An Introduction to Modern English Lexicology*. London: Athenceum Press.

Jespersen, O. 1904. *How to Teach a Foreign Language*. London: Swan Sonnenschein & Co.

Jiang, N. A. & Nekrasova, T. M. 2007. The processing of formulaic sequences by second language speakers. *The Modern Language Journal*, *91*(3): 433–445.

Kipfer, B. A. (Ed.). 2010. *Roget's International Thesaurus* (7th ed.). Glasgow: Collins Reference.

Laufer, B. 1998. The development of passive and active vocabulary in a second language: Same or different? *Applied Linguistics*, *19*(2): 255–271.

Laufer, B. 1990. Ease and difficulty in vocabulary learning: Some teaching implications. *Foreign Language Annals*, *2*: 147–155.

Laufer, B. & Girsai, N. 2008. Form-focused instruction in second language vocabulary learning: A case for contrastive analysis and translation. *Applied Linguistics*, *29*: 694–716.

Laufer, B. & Hulstijn, J. 2001. Incidental vocabulary acquisition in a second language: The construct of task-induced involvement. *Applied Linguistics*, *22*(1): 1–26.

Laufer, B. & Paribakht, T. 1998. The relationship between passive and active vocabularies: Effects of language learning context. *Language Learning*, *48*(3): 365–391.

Laufer, B. & Waldman, T. 2011. Verb-noun collocations in second language writing: A corpus analysis of learners' English. *Language Learning*, *61*(2): 647–672.

Leech, G. 1981. *Semantics* (2nd ed.). Harmondsworth: Penguin Books.

Lin, P. M. S. 2012. Sound evidence: The missing piece of the jigsaw in formulaic language research. *Applied Linguistics*, *33*(3): 342–347.

Lin, P. 2018. *The Prosody of Formulaic Sequences: A Corpus and Discourse Approach*. New York: Bloomsbury.

Lin, P. M. S. & Siyanova-Chanturia, A. 2015. Internet television for L2 vocabulary learning. In D. Nunan & J. C. Richards (Eds.), *Language Learning Beyond the Classroom*. New York: Routledge, 165–174.

Lo, D. H. 1980. *10,000: A Dictionary of New English*. Beijing: The Commercial Press.

Macis, M. & Schmitt, N. 2017. Not just "small potatoes": Knowledge of the idiomatic meanings of collocations. *Language Teaching Research*, *21*(3): 321–340.

Majuddin, E., Siyanova-Chanturia, A. & Boers, F. 2021. Incidental acquisition of multiword expressions through audiovisual materials: The role of repetition and typographic enhancement. *Studies in Second Language Acquisition*, *43*(5): 985–1008.

Manser, M. H. 1983. *A Dictionary of Everyday Idioms*. London: Macmillan.

Maugham, W. S. 1951. *The Summing Up*. New York: The New American Library of World Literature.

Maugham, W. S. 1992. *The Summing Up*. London: Penguin Classics.

McArthur, T. 1981. *Longman Lexicon of Contemporary English*. Harlow and London: Longman.

McCarthy, M. 1990. *Vocabulary*. Oxford: Oxford University Press.

McDonald, S. A., & Shillcock, R. C. 2003. Low-level predictive inference in reading: The influence of transitional probabilities on eye movements. *Vision Research*, *43*(16): 1735–1751.

Meillet, A. 1921/1982. *Linguistique Historique et Linguistique Générale*. Paris: Champion.

Morgan, J. & Rinvolucri, M. 2004. *Vocabulary*. Oxford: Oxford University Press.

Murphy. M. 2003. *Semantic Relations and the Lexicon: Antonymy, Synonymy and Other Paradigms*. Cambridge. Cambridge University Press.

Murphy, M. L. 2003. *Semantic Relations and the Lexicon*. Cambridge: Cambridge University Press.

Murphy, M. L. 2003. *Semantic Relations and the Lexicon: Antonymy, Synonymy and Other Paradigms*. Cambridge: Cambridge University Press.

Nagi, W., Herman, P. & Anderson, R. 1985. Learning words from context. *Reading Research Quarterly*, *20*: 233–253.

Nagy, W. E. & Anderson, R. C. 1984. How many words are there in printed school English? *Reading Research Quarterly*, *19*(3): 304–330.

Nagy, W. E. Herman, P. & Anderson, R. C. 1985. Learning words from context. *Reading Research Quarterly*, *20*(2): 233–253.

Nation, I. S. P. 1990. *Teaching and Learning Vocabulary*. Boston: Heinle and Heinle.

Nation, I. S. P. 2001. *Learning Vocabulary in Another Language*. Cambridge: Cambridge University Press.

Nation, I. S. P. 2020. The different aspects of vocabulary knowledge. In S. Webb (Ed.), *The Routledge Handbook of Vocabulary Studies*. London: Routledge, 15–29.

Nesselhauf, N. 2005. *Collocations in a Learner Corpus*. Amsterdam: John Benjamins.

Newport, E. & Aslin, R. N. 2004. Learning at a distance I: Statistical learning of non-adjacent dependencies. *Cognitive Psychology*, *48*(2): 127–162.

Ogden, C. K. & Richards, I. A. 1946. *The Meaning of Meaning*. New York: Harcourt Brace.

Omidian, T. & Siyanova-Chanturia, A. 2020. Semantic prosody revisited: Implications for language learning. *TESOL Quarterly*, *54*(2): 512–524.

Omidian, T. & Siyanova-Chanturia, A. 2021. Parameters of variation in the use of words in empirical research writing. *English for Specific Purposes*, *62*: 15–29.

Omidian, T., Akbary, M. & Shahriari, H. 2019. Exploring factors contributing to the receptive and productive knowledge of phrasal verbs in the EFL contexts. *Word*, *65*(1): 1–24.

Omidian, T., Ballance, O. J. & Siyanova-Chanturia, A. 2021. Replicating corpus-based research in English for Academic Purposes: Replication of Cortes (2013) and Biber and Gray (2010). *Language Teaching*, *56*(1): 1–9.

Omidian, T., Beliaeva, N., Todd, L. & Siyanova-Chanturia, A. 2017. The use of academic words and formulae in L1 and L2 secondary school writing. *New Zealand Studies in Applied Linguistics*, *23*(2): 39–59.

Omidian, T., Shahriari, H. & Siyanova-Chanturia, A. 2018. A cross-disciplinary investigation of multi-word expressions in the moves of research article abstracts. *Journal of English for Academic Purposes*, *36*: 1–14.

Omidian, T., Siyanova-Chanturia, A. & Biber, D. 2021. A new multidimensional model of writing for research publication: An analysis of disciplinarity, intra-textual variation, and L1 versus LX expert writing. *Journal of English for Academic Purposes*, *53*, 101020.

Omidian, T., Siyanova-Chanturia, A. & Durrant, P. 2021. Predicting parameters of variation in the use of academic formulas in university student writing. In P. Szudarski & S. Barclay (Eds.), *Vocabulary Theory, Patterning and Teaching*. Bristol: Multilingual Matters, 160–184.

Omidian, T., Siyanova-Chanturia, A. & Spina, S. 2021. Development of formulaic knowledge in learner writing: A longitudinal perspective. In S. Granger (Ed.), *Perspectives on the Second Language Phrasicon: The View from Learner Corpora*. Bristol: Multilingual Matters, 178–206.

Otto, J. 1951. *The Philosophy of Grammar*. London: Routledge.

Pawley, A. & Syder, F. H. 1983. Two puzzles for linguistic theory: Nativelike selection and nativelike fluency. In J. C Richards & R. W. Schmidt (Eds.), *Language and Communication*. London: Longman, 191–226.

Pope, A. 1941. *The Rape of the Lock*. London: Methuen & Co.

Qian, D. D. 2002. Investigating the relationship between vocabulary knowledge and academic reading performance: An assessment perspective. *Language Learning*, *52*(3): 513–536.

Qian, D. D. 2005. Demystifying lexical inferencing: The role of aspects of vocabulary knowledge. *TESL Canada Journal*, *22*(2): 34–54.

Qian, D. D. 2008. Investigating the relationship between vocabulary knowledge and academic reading performance: An assessment perspective. *Language Learning*, *52*(3): 513–536.

Quirk, R. 1963. *The Use of English*. London: Longman.

Quirk, R., Greenbaum, S., Leech, G. & Svartvik, J. 1985. *A Comprehensive Grammar of the English Language*. London: Longman.

Read, J. 2000. *Assessing Vocabulary*. Cambridge: Cambridge University Press.

Read, J. 2004. Research in teaching vocabulary. *Annual Review of Applied Linguistics*, *24*: 146–161.

Reuterskiöld, C. & Van Lancker-Sidtis, D. 2013. Retention of idioms following one-time exposure. *Child Language Teaching and Therapy*, *29*(2): 219–231.

Ritchie, G. 2003. *The Linguistic Analysis of Jokes*. London: Routledge.

Schmitt, N. 1998. Tracking the incremental acquisition of second language vocabulary: A longitudinal study. *Language Learning*, *48*(2): 281–317.

Schmitt, N. (Ed.). 2004. *Formulaic Sequences*. Amsterdam: John Benjamins.

Schmitt, N. 2008. Instructed second language vocabulary learning. *Language Teaching Research*, *12*(3): 329–363.

Schmitt, N. 2010. *Researching Vocabulary: A Vocabulary Research Manual*. Basingstoke: Palgrave Macmillan.

Schmitt, N. 2014. Size and depth of vocabulary knowledge: What the research shows. *Language Learning*, *64*(4): 913–951.

Seidle, J. & McMondie, W. 1978. *English Idioms and How to Use Them*. London: Oxford University Press.

Seidle, J. & McMondie, W. 1988. *English Idioms and How to Use Them* (5th ed.). Oxford: Oxford University Press.

Shakespeare, W. 2010. *The Winter's Tale*. London: Arden Shakespeare.

Sinclair, J. 1987. *Collins COBUILD English Language Dictionary*. London: Harper Collins Publishers.

Siyanova, A. & Schmitt. N. 2007. Native and nonnative use of multi-word versus one-word verbs. *International Review of Applied Linguistics*, *45*: 119–139.

Siyanova, A. & Schmitt, N. 2008. L2 learner production and processing of collocation: A multistudy perspective. *Canadian Modern Language Review*, *64*(3): 429–458.

Siyanova-Chanturia, A. & Omidian, T. 2019. Key issues in researching multi-word expressions. In S. Webb (Ed.), *The Routledge Handbook of Vocabulary Studies*. London: Routledge, 529–544.

Siyanova-Chanturia, A. & Lin, P. M. 2018. Production of ambiguous idioms in English: A reading aloud study. *International Journal of Applied Linguistics*, *28*(1): 58–70.

Siyanova-Chanturia, A. & Nation, P 2017. Teaching communicative vocabulary. In H. P. Widodo, A. Wood & D. Gupta (Eds.), *Asian English Language Classrooms: Where Theory and Practice Meet*. London: Routledge, 98–112.

Siyanova-Chanturia, A. & Pellicer-Sanchez, A. (Eds.). 2019. *Understanding Formulaic Language: A Second Language Acquisition Perspective*. New York: Routledge.

Siyanova-Chanturia, A. & Spina, S. 2020. Multi-word expressions in second language writing: A large-scale longitudinal learner corpus study. *Language Learning*, *70*(2): 420–463.

Siyanova-Chanturia, A., Conklin, K. & Van Heuven, W. J. 2011. Seeing a phrase "time and again" matters: The role of phrasal frequency in the processing of multiword sequences. *Journal of Experimental Psychology: Learning, Memory, and Cognition*, *37*(3): 776–784.

Siyanova-Chanturia, A., Conklin, K., Caffarra, S., Kaan, E. & van Heuven, W. J. 2017. Representation and processing of multi-word expressions in the brain. *Brain and Language*, *175*: 111–122.

Smith, A. H. 1980. *The Encyclopedia Americana* (International Edition). Danbury: American Corporation.

Taguchi, N. (Ed.). 2009. *Pragmatic Competence*. Berlin: Mouton de Gruyter.

Ullmann, S. 1977. *Semantics: An Introduction to the Science of Meaning*. Oxford: Basil Blackwell.

Underwood, G., Schmitt, N. & Galpin, A. 2004. The eyes have it: An eye-movement study into the processing of formulaic sequences. In N. Schmitt (Ed.), *Formulaic Sequences*. Amsterdam: John Benjamins, 153–172.

Vespignani, F., Canal, P., Molinaro, N., Fonda, S. & Cacciari, C. 2010. Predictive mechanisms in idiom comprehension. *Journal of Cognitive Neuroscience*, *22*(8): 1682–1700.

Vilkaitė, L. & Schmitt, N. 2019. Reading collocations in an L2: Do collocation processing benefits extend to non-adjacent collocations?. *Applied Linguistics*, *40*(2): 1–27.

Vitello, S. & Rodd, J. M. 2015. Resolving semantic ambiguities in sentences: Cognitive processes and brain mechanisms. *Language and Linguistics Compass*, *9*(10), 391–405.

Waldren, R. A. 1967. *Sense and Sense Development* (2nd ed.). London: Andre Dertsch.

Webb, S. & Chang, A. 2012. Vocabulary learning through assisted and unassisted repeated reading. *Canadian Modern Language Review*, *68*(3), 267–290.

Webb, S. & Chang, A. 2015. How does prior word knowledge affect vocabulary learning progress in an extensive reading program?. *Studies in Second Language Acquisition*, *37*: 651–675.

Webb, S. & Chang, A. C. S. 2022. How does mode of input affect the incidental learning of collocations?. *Studies in Second Language Acquisition*. *44*(1), 35–56.

Webb, S. & Nation, I. S. P. 2017. *How Vocabulary Is Learned*. Oxford: Oxford University Press.

Winston, M., Chaffin, R. & Herrmann, D. 1987. A taxonomy of part-whole relations. *Cognitive Science*, *11*: 417–444.

Wood, D. 2002. Formulaic language in acquisition and production: Implications for teaching. *TESL Canada Journal, 20*(1): 1–15.

Wray, A. 2002. *Formulaic Language and the Lexicon*. Cambridge: Cambridge University Press.

奥托·叶斯柏森 . 2014. 现代英语语法 . 北京：世界图书出版公司 .

杰弗里·N. 利奇 . 1987. 语义学 . 李瑞华等，译 . 上海：上海外语教育出版社 .

伍谦光 . 1988. 语义学导论 . 长沙：湖南教育出版社 .

肖军石 . 1982. 英汉、汉英翻译初探 . 北京：商务印书馆 .

杨连瑞 . 2010. 新编英语词汇学 . 青岛：中国海洋大学出版社 .

张韵斐 . 1992. 现代英语词汇学概论 . 北京：北京师范大学出版社 .

Appendix:

Difference Between American English and British English

American English	British English
absorbent cotton	cotton wool
account	bill/account
adhesive tape	sellotape
aisle	gangway
allowance	pocket money (child's)
alumnus	graduate (of a school or university)
antenna	aerial (radio/TV)
anyplace/anywhere	anywhere
apartment	flat
apartment house	block of flats
appetizer	starter
apron	pinny/apron
attic	loft
attorney/lawyer	barrister, solicitor
automobile	motorcar
baby carriage / baby buggy	pram (perambulator)
baby stroller	push-chair
bachelor party	stag night
back up lights	reversing lights
baggage	luggage
baggage room	left luggage office
balcony	gallery (theatre)
ballpoint	biro
ballyhoo	exaggerated publicity
bandaid	plaster/elastoplast

bar	public house
barber	gentlemen's hairdresser
barrette	hairslide
baseboard	skirting board
bathe	bath
bathrobe	dressing-gown
bathroom/restroom/washroom	public convenience
bathtub	bath
beauty parlour	ladies' hairdresser
bill	bank note
billboard	hoarding
billion = thousand million	billion = million million
biscuit	scone
blank	form
bobbie pin / bobby pin	hair grip / kirby grip
body shop	panel beater
bomb (disaster)	bomb (success)
bought/charged	put down / entered (goods)
bowl (e.g., for pudding)	basin
broil	grill
buck	quid
buffet	sideboard
bulletin board	notice board
busy (phone)	engaged
cafeteria	canteen
call collect	reverse charges
call/phone	ring up
can	tin
candy	sweets/chocolate
candy store	sweet shop / confectioner
caravan	convoy
carnival	fair (fun)
celluar phone	mobile phone
CEO (chief executive officer)	managing director
change purse	purse
checkroom	cloakroom

check (restaurant)	bill
checkers	draughts
cheese cloth	butter muslin / cheese cloth
chips / potato chips	crisps
city government / municipal government	corporation / local authority
closet	cupboard
clothes pin	clothes peg
college	university
comforter	eiderdown
commuter ticket	season-ticket
concert master	leader (1st violin in orchestra)
conductor	guard (railway)
confectioner's sugar	icing sugar
connect	put through (telephone)
cookie	biscuit (sweet)
corn	maize/grain
corn starch	corn flour
cotton batting	cotton wool
cotton candy	candyfloss
cracker	biscuit (savoury)
crazy bone	funny bone
cream of wheat	semolina
crepe	pancake
crib	cot/crib
crossing guard	lollipop lady
cuff (pants)	turn-up (trousers)
currency exchange	bureau de change
custard	egg custard
custom made	made to measure
davenport/couch	sofa
dead end	cul-de-sac
deck	pack (of cards)
denatured alcohol	methylated spirits
derby	bowler/hard hat
desk clerk	receptionist
dessert	pudding

detour	diversion
diaper	napkin/nappy
directory assistance	directory enquiries
divided highway	dual carriageway
dizzy	giddy
downtown	centre (city/business)
draft	conscription
drapes	curtains
dresser/bureau	chest of drawers
drug store / pharmacy	chemist's shop
druggist	chemist
drygoods store	draper
dump	tip
dungarees/jeans	blue jeans
duplex	semi-detached
editorial	leader
eggplant	aubergine
electric cord / wire	flex
elementary school / grade school	primary school
elevator	lift
engineer	driver
enlisted man	private soldier
eraser	rubber
exhausted	shattered
faculty (of university)	staff (academic)
fall	autumn
faucet	tap
first floor	second floor
fish sticks	fish fingers
flashlight	torch
flatcar	truck (railway)
floor lamp	standard lamp
football	soccer
freeway/throughway	motorway
freight train / car	goods train / waggon
freight truck	goods truck (railway)

french fries	chips
friend	friend/mate
front desk	reception (hotel)
galoshes	wellington boots / wellies
garbage can / trash can	dustbin/bin
garbage/trash	rubbish
garden	vegetable / flower garden
garter	suspender
garter belt	suspender belt
garters	suspenders
gas station	filling station / petrol station
gas/gasoline	petrol
gear shift	gear lever
general manager	managing director/MD
generator	dynamo
give a buzz	give a bell (to phone)
globe	bulb
goose bumps	goose pimples
grade	class/form (school)
grade crossing	level crossing (railway)
grade school	elementary school
grading scheme	marking scheme
graduate student	post graduate
green thumb	green fingers
gym shoes	plimsolls
hamburger	beefburger
hamburger bun	bap
hamburger meat	mince
hardware	ironware
hardware store	ironmonger
hat check girl	cloakroom attendant
high school	grammar school
highway/expressway	motorway
holds up stockings	suspenders
homely (= ugly)	homely (= pleasant)
hood	bonnet (car)

hophead/acid-head	drug-addict
hot lunch	school dinner
housewares	hardware
incorporated	limited (company)
information assistance	directory enquiries
installment plan	hire purchase
instructor	lecturer
intermission	interval
intern	work placement / work experience
intersection	junction/crossroads
interstate	motorway
jail	gaol
janitor	caretaker/porter
jello	jelly
jelly	jam
jelly roll	swiss roll
john/bathroom/washroom	lavatory/toilet/w.c./loo
jump rope	skipping rope
jumper	pinafore dress
kerosene	paraffin
kindergarten	reception
knickers	knickerbockers
labor union	trade union
last name	surname
lawyer	solicitor or barrister
lease/rent	let
legal holiday / national holiday	bank holiday
license plate	number plate
lima bean	broad bean
line	queue
line-up	identification parade
liquor	spirits (drink)
liquor store	off-licence store
living room	sitting room / lounge / drawing room
lobby/foyer	foyer
long distance call	trunk call / long distance

lost and found	lost property
luggage car	van
lumber	timber
mail	post
mail box	pillar box / letter box
mail/mailbox/mailman	post / pillar box / postman
make reservation	book
man/guy	bloke/chap/lad/man
manager	director (company)
math	maths
median strip / divider	central reservation
molasses	black treacle
monkey wrench	spanner
moron/idiot	berk/pillock/pratt/plonker
mortician	undertaker
movie	film
movie house / theater	cinema
muffler	silencer (car)
muffler	silencer (on a car)
mutual fund	unit trust
news dealer / news stand	newsagent
night stick	truncheon (police)
nipple	teat (baby's bottle)
odometer	mileometer
off ramp	slip road
office	surgery (doctor's/dentist's)
one way ticket	single ticket
one-storey house	bungalow
open house	open day / open evening
orchestra seats	stalls (theatre)
outlet/socket	point / power point / socket
overalls	dungarees
overpass	flyover
overseas	abroad
pacifier	dummy
package	parcel

paddle	bat (ping pong)
pantry	larder
pants/slacks	trousers
pantyhose	tights
parka	anorak
parking lot	car park
pass	overtake (vehicle)
pay station or public	public call box
pedestrian underpass	subway
pee	wee
penitentiary	prison
period	full stop (punctuation)
person-to-person call	personal call
pharmacy/drugstore	chemist's shop
phone booth	phone-box/call-box
phonograph / record player	gramophone / record player
pit	stone (fruit)
pitcher	jug
pollywog	tadpole
popsicle	iced lolly
pot holder / oven mitt	oven cloth / gloves
potato chips	crisps
powdered sugar	icing sugar
precinct	district
president	chairman (business)
principal	headmaster
private school	public school
public school	council school
pullman car (railway)	sleeping car
pull-off	lay-by
pump	court shoe
purse / pocket book	handbag
pushpins or thumbtacks	drawing pins
push-up	press-up
railroad	railway
raincheck	postponement

raincoat	mackintosh
raisin	sultana
rare	underdone
realtor	estate agent
recess	play time / break time
rent	hire
reservation	advanced booking
roast	joint (meat)
robe	dressing gown
roller coaster	big dipper
roomer	lodger
round trip ticket	return ticket
rubber	contraceptive/condom
rubbing alcohol	surgical spirit
run	stand (for public office)
run (in stocking)	ladder
sack lunch / bag lunch	packed lunch
sales clerk / sales girl	shop assistant
sales/revenue	turnover
scab	blackleg/scab
scallion / green onion	spring onion
schedule	time-table
school principal	headmaster/headmistress
scotch tape	sellotape
scratch pad	scribbling pad/block
second floor	first floor
sedan	saloon car
semester (2 in a year)	term academic (3 in a year)
sewer pipe	drain (indoors)
shade	blind (window)
sheers/under drapes	net curtains
sherbet	ice/sorbet
shoestring	bootlace/shoelace
shopping bag	carrier bag
shopping cart	shopping trolley
shorts / jockey shorts	briefs/underpants

shorts/underwear	pants (boy's underwear)
shot	jab (injection)
shredded	desiccated (coconut)
sideburns	sideboards (hair)
sidewalk	pavement/footpath
silent partner	sleeping partner
sled	sledge/toboggan
slice	rasher (bacon)
slingshot	catapult
smock	overall
smoked herring	kipper
sneakers	trainers
sneakers / tennis shoes	gym shoes / plimsolls
soccer	football/soccer
soda cracker	cream cracker
spatula / egg lifter	fish slice
spool	cotton reel
squash	marrow
stairway	staircase
stand in line / line up	queue
station wagon	estate car
stop lights / top signals	traffic lights
stove	cooker
straight	neat (drink)
street car	tram car
strings	laces
stroller	pushchair
sub-division	housing estate
subway	tube/underground
superhighway/speedway	motorway
suspenders	braces
sweater/pullover	jumper/sweater/pullover
tag	label
takeout restaurant	takeaway
tea cart	tea trolley
teachers lounge	staff room

telephone booth	kiosk/box (telephone)
texas gate	cattle grid
thread	cotton
thumbtack	drawing pin
ticket office	booking office
tic-tac-toe	noughts and crosses
top	roof/hood (car)
trade	custom
trade in	exchange
traffic circle	roundabout (road)
traffic signals	traffic lights
trailer truck / semi trailer	articulated lorry
trailer / camper / mobile home	caravan
trashcan	dustbin
traveling salesman	commercial traveller
truck	lorry
trunk	boot (car)
turnip/rutabaga	swede
turtle neck	polo neck
tuxedo	dinner jacket
two weeks	fortnight
typesetter	compositor
underpants	knickers (women's)
underpass	subway
undershirt	vest
underwear	smalls (washing)
underwear/panties	pants/underwear/knickers
vacation	holiday
vacuum	hoover
vacuum cleaner	hoover
vest	waistcoat
waiting line	queue
wall to wall carpet	fitted carpet
wash cloth	flannel
water heater	immersion heater (electric)
weather bureau	meteorological office

weather stripping	draught excluder
windshield	windscreen
wire	telegram
with or without?	black or white? (coffee)
witness-stand	witness-box
yard	garden
zero	nought
zip code	postal code
zipper	zip-fastner
zucchini	courgette